NEW WORKS IN ACCOUNTING HISTORY

T0303968

edited by

RICHARD P. BRIEF
Leonard N. Stern School of Business
New York University

THE BIRTH OF INDUSTRIAL ACCOUNTING IN FRANCE AND BRITAIN

TREVOR BOYNS
JOHN RICHARD EDWARDS
MARC NIKITIN

Routledge
Taylor & Francis Group

LONDON AND NEW YORK

First published 1997 by Garland Publishing Inc.

Published 2013 by Routledge
711 Third Avenue, New York, NY 10017
2 Park Square, Milton Park, Abingdon, Oxfordshire OX14 4RN

First issued in paperback 2014

Routledge is an imprint of the Taylor and Francis Group, an informa business

Library of Congress Cataloging-in-Publication Data

Boyns, Trevor.
  The birth of industrial accounting in France and Britain / Trevor
Boyns, John Richard Edwards, Marc Nikitin.
      p.   cm. — (New works in accounting history)
  Includes bibliographical references and index.
  ISBN 0-8153-3038-3 (alk. paper)
  1. Accounting—France—History. 2. Accounting—Great Britain—
History. I. Edwards, J.R. II. Nikitin, Marc III. Title. IV. Series.
HF5616.F7B69 1997
657'.0941—dc21   97-25939

ISBN 13: 978-1-138-87933-1 (pbk)
ISBN 13: 978-0-8153-3038-7 (hbk)

The Institute of Chartered Accountants
in England & Wales

Contents

Introduction

In the modern world, where the links between national economies are becoming ever closer through the growth and development of trading blocs, such as the European Union, the growing economic power of multinational enterprises and the growing significance of global financial markets, it is not altogether surprising that the issue of harmonisation of accounting practices has been an item for serious discussion within the accounting profession and amongst accounting academics for a number of years.[1] In relation to global financial markets, the major concern is with the harmonisation of financial reporting methods but, in the context of economic unions such as the European Union, with its Single European Market, harmonisation of methods of cost accounting (e.g. through the adoption of uniform costing) are also of concern since this may affect competition. Whilst the concern with harmonisation is very much a contemporary one, the need for it reflects the fact that, over the centuries, accounting practices have developed differently in different countries. It seems clear that if the process of harmonisation is to proceed with any degree of success, it will be necessary to understand the processes by which current practices have evolved, and to identify the factors that have influenced those processes. It is within this framework that the Research Board of the ICAEW in London and *le Centre de Recherche de l'Ordre des experts comptables et de la Compagnie des commissaires aux comptes* in Paris, decided to jointly fund a series of annual research projects in a number of fields in order that "a better understanding of the differences between the UK and France" in these areas could be gained.

The area examined in this book falls loosely under the category of 'accounting integration' where, according to the 'Call for Anglo-French research projects' issued jointly by the two research bodies, research should "explain how the accounting systems in both countries are designed so as to integrate cost and financial accounting". The basis for such studies obviously stems from the late twentieth century distinction between financial accounting on the one hand and cost or management accounting on the other.[2] The authors of this book had previously been working independently on the early development of accounting for industrial enterprises within their own countries. Their combined proposal to the two research boards argued that a comparison of the birth and early development of industrial accounting within Britain and France would be a useful exercise in gaining an insight into the similarities and differences in respect of accounting integration. The research, therefore, is premised on the view that in order to understand modern day similarities and differences, it is necessary to understand how the current practices and systems have come into being; an inquiry which is, of course, the natural province of accounting and business historians such as ourselves. This book is thus a slightly amended version of the English language project report originally presented to the ICAEW in August 1996.

Comparative research, especially on an international basis, however, is not an easy thing. In particular, one important factor that has affected the preparation of this work has been cultural differences. Whilst contemporary cultural differences in the eighteenth and nineteenth century may possibly have played a role in determining the different accounting systems used, it is clear that modern cultural differences also create problems for projects involving comparative research. Perhaps somewhat naively, we embarked upon this project without fully appreciating the difficulties that might arise from different perceptions of what were important issues. Thus issues which did not appear to be of great importance to the British members of the team, were considered more important by the French member, and vice versa. Questions raised by one party were sometimes difficult for the other party to comprehend and/or provide meaningful answers, since such questions were either considered of little relevance or were not matters which they had ever thought of addressing, let alone into which they had carried out any detailed research. In addition to posing different sorts of questions, cultural differences also generate divergent approaches to the way in which answers are compiled. Thus it is important to recognise that this text, in the English language, has been compiled by one British member of the team from materials supplied by all of the members. Possibly it therefore reflects a more Anglo-centric view than had it been compiled by the French member of the team. It is hoped, however, that whilst the nuances of particular points and arguments may have been lost in the process of translating French items for inclusion in the book, or by their 'anglicization', the main arguments presented in this book provide a 'true and fair' representation of the consensus views of all members involved in the research project.

Notes

1   The interest in harmonisation within Europe, for example, seems to have been one of the main factors behind the launch of the journal *The European Accounting Review* in 1992.

2   The term management accounting tended to come into common usage in the middle of the twentieth century. In Britain, for example, its use developed in the 1950s following the visit to America of the Management Accounting Team, led by Ian Morrow, under the auspices of the Anglo-American Council on Productivity.

Acknowledgment

We would like to thank the Research Board of the Institute of Chartered Accountants in England and Wales and *le Centre de Recherche de l'Ordre des Experts Comptables et de la Compagnie des Commissaires aux Comptes* for their joint funding which made possible the collaborative research project which has resulted in the publication of this book. Dr. Boyns and Professor Edwards would also like to thank the Economic and Social Research Council (grant reference R000233749) for financial assistance which made possible the carrying out of detailed research into the archives of firms in the British coal, iron and steel industries, some of which is summarised in chapter 4.

The authors would also like to thank both Rosemary Boyns and David Williams for their help in translating material from French to English. We alone remain responsible, however, for the views expressed.

The Birth of Industrial Accounting
in France and Britain

Chapter 1 - Setting the scene

In this chapter we seek to provide a justification for our research, and to present an indication of the scope and structure of the book. We first outline the usefulness of accounting history, then provide a brief review of alternative approaches to accounting history and indicate the methodology used to undertake the research which forms the basis for this book. Having discussed the usefulness of comparative history, we present our reasons for believing that a comparative study of France and Britain may provide particular insights into the development of accounting. We then indicate the scope of the book and conclude with a brief summary of the structure of the remainder of the book and present an indication of our main findings.

The usefulness of accounting history

Whilst there has undoubtedly been an increasing interest in the historical development of accounting, on both sides of the Channel, during the last fifteen years or so, one may legitimately ask the question, 'What use is research into accounting history?' It would be difficult to sustain the argument that the solution to problems facing accountants today are to be found in business archives spanning several centuries. Nevertheless the usefulness of historical research in accounting has formed the basis of a comprehensive debate and any reader wishing to weigh up all the relevant arguments for and against should consult the recent paper by Bernard Colasse (1995) published in the *Revue Française de Comptabilité*. The question of the usefulness of history, however, is by no means new. One French historian, Fustel de Coulanges (1830-1889), remarked that "*L'histoire ne résoud pas les problèmes: elle nous apprend à les examiner*" (history does not solve problems; it teaches us how to examine them) (quoted in Marrou (1954, p.153)). At the beginning of the twentieth century, C.W. Haskins (1904, p.141), first dean of the School of Commerce, Accounting and Finance at the University of New York, argued that the knowledge of accounting history permitted us to "better . . . understand the present and to foretell or control the future". J.H. Vlaemminck (1956, p.9) preferred to express it in a less peremptory manner, but was also optimistic: "historical research can be justified more readily if it buttresses our present accounting methods and imposes a more rational approach to the future direction of accounting." More recently, J.R. Edwards (1989a, pp.3-6) has indicated four possible reasons for studying accounting history: recreational; explanatory; problem solving; and prediction. On the first count, it is legitimate to study accounting history for purposes of pure enjoyment; on the second count, it helps us to understand our past and provide us with an appreciation of how our current practices and problems came about; and on the third and fourth counts, it may provide insights for the solution of present-day accounting problems and/or help to predict future likely developments. Accounting history, therefore, can be important for providing perspective.

It is in the light of these arguments in favour of historical research into accounting that we find justification for our study. However, as Baxter (1981) has pointed out, caution should be exercised over expecting too much of historical research. A knowledge of history, for example, will not help investors make good choices since it can never be a substitute for personal judgement. However, it can indirectly aid the provision of solutions to problems, by helping us understand the nature and origins of the problems. Thus the aim of researchers in the field of accounting, as in other social sciences, is somewhat different from that of natural scientists such as biologists and physicists. While members of all such groups may consider that they carry out research in order to discover solutions to problems facing society, it would be difficult to maintain the argument that accounting research, or that of other social sciences, is as fundamental to human existence as that of natural scientists. None amongst us can pretend to be attempting to isolate the gene of unemployment or to discover a vaccine against bankruptcy. Indeed, the role of accounting research is more in the Maieutic fashion, that is, the Socratic process of helping a person to bring into full consciousness conceptions previously latent in his mind. Or, to put it another way, accounting research is a matter, through an effort of clarification and theoretisation of practice, of throwing light on problems, of making things visible, and thereby enabling solutions to emerge from within the bosom of an enterprise. It is moreover one of the experiences of the history of management science to have shown on numerous occasions that innovations born in the practices of several advanced enterprises, are nourished by the doctrinal efforts of several 'researchers', before they become general and benefit a large number.

The point of departure for our reflections is to be found in the many questions that have been raised in recent years about the efficacy of, and difficulties associated with, the application of systems of costing based upon full costs. Since the publication of Johnson and Kaplan's *Relevance Lost* (1987), accounting researchers have followed two distinct lines of study: some have preferred to study the implementation of new systems of management control, in the belief that tomorrow's theories develop out of the innovatory practices of some of today's enterprises; others have preferred to look to the past to determine the methods actually used to calculate costs and to attempt to identify the conditions which gave rise to the development of those methods. These two approaches are not necessarily contradictory. They can, and have, existed side by side and mutually enrich one another to develop a better understanding of the ideas behind cost calculation.

The knowledge of accounting history therefore has an essential objective of helping us to understand and give answers to several questions: 'How have we arrived where we are? What are the errors to avoid? What are the circumstances which have brought such and such about? Our approach can be summed up in the poetic words of Henri-Irénée Marrou (1954, p.241), for whom "Historical knowledge expands, in almost limitless proportions, my knowledge of man, his many realities, and his infinite virtualities - far beyond the narrow limits of my own experience of real life."

Different approaches to accounting history

Whilst the reasons for studying history put forward by Edwards (1989b) may be accepted by historians, there has been much debate in recent years over the method by which accounting historians should carry out their studies and what should be the key focus of their work. In recent years, accounting history has seen the development of what has come to be termed the 'new' accounting history, based on attempts to utilise particular perceptions of the ideas of the French philosopher, Michel Foucault. Thus, Miller, together with certain collaborators (Miller and O'Leary, 1987; Miller and Napier, 1993), and others such as Hoskin and

Macve (1986, 1988a,b, 1992, 1993, 1994) and Loft (1986, 1990), have attempted to utilise Foucauldian ideas, especially the concept of power-knowledge relationships, to understand aspects of the historical development of accounting. Foucauldian accounting historians believe that their methodological approach is broader than that followed by other accounting historians, and are particularly critical of what they call 'traditional' accounting history. While they may be right to argue that some past accounting historians have suggested that accounting was relative and progressive (Littleton, 1933, p.361), this is clearly not true of all those considered by the Foucauldians to be traditional historians. Furthermore, while it may be true that many non-Foucauldian historians place an emphasis on economic-rationalist explanations of accounting change, to suggest that they totally ignore other contextual factors is somewhat disingenuous.

Loft (1995), for example, while suggesting that there are four main schools of thought in accounting history - traditional, neoclassical revisionist, labour process and Foucauldian - also recognises that such a categorisation may oversimplify reality. Indeed, some historians do not fit neatly into any one particular school and, if accounting history is to continue to develop, interchange between members of such schools is likely to be vital, especially since there is no single 'correct' methodological approach to historical research. As Funnell (1996) has argued, it is through the interchange of ideas and concepts between those from different historical research methodologies, through a collaborative rather than a combative approach to their subject, that the quality of accounting history will be enhanced and thereby also our understanding of accounting's development.

The authors of this book consider themselves essentially to be members of Loft's 'neoclassical revisionist' school, but we are acutely aware that economic factors may not be the only influences behind the adoption of particular practices or modes of accounting at specific points in time. Thus, while operating from an economic-deterministic standpoint, we are nevertheless willing to acknowledge the potential influence of other factors, including the socio-political and historical contexts of a period. We hope that, in the analysis that follows, we are able to combine both economic and other explanations to provide a better understanding of the birth of industrial accounting in France and Britain prior to c.1880.

The role of comparative studies

Methodological issues

The usefulness of comparative research is not something which is accepted, at least unreservedly, by all historians. Thus, in the field of economic history, some writers have urged an element of caution, and their arguments would appear to have some validity in respect of comparative research in accounting history. Crafts (1977), for example, has argued that it is incorrect for historians to consider that the economic supremacy of one country over another is inevitable. Therefore, there is little sense in historians spending their time searching for those factors in a countries' past development which may explain why it has grown faster. For Crafts, economic development is a stochastic process, where the *ex ante* probabilities of any country developing in a particular way are more or less the same. This is not to argue that economic development is the result of a lottery or that no causal relationships are involved, but rather to argue that one should not perpetuate the common mistake of *post hoc ergo propter hoc*.

Crafts therefore warns against expecting too much of comparative history, suggesting that "some of the uncontrolled experiments that history performed were unique, non-repeatable events" (1977, p.441). For other writers, however, comparative history has its place. In the context of French and British economic and technological development, writers such as Crouzet and Harris have written at length on the similarities and differences between the two countries. For them there is little doubt that comparative history has a role, but in the fields of accounting and business history little work of a comparative nature has yet been attempted. The need for such work is receiving increased recognition, however, particularly in the light of recent revisionist views of French economic development in the eighteenth and nineteenth century, and the view that the impact of French developments on the rest of continental Europe may have been greater than previously thought. Thus, for Cassis (1995, p.9), the replacement of notions of French backwardness and decline, when compared to Britain, by those of difference or specificity, increases the need for comparative analysis of developments in the two countries, in order to establish what have been the main similarities and differences. Furthermore, he considers that, in relation to the rise of business in the late nineteenth and twentieth centuries, such analysis is likely to be more beneficial than the usual comparisons between Britain and either the USA or Japan:

> Anglo-French comparisons should be particularly interesting . . . The homogeneity between the two countries, far greater than [that of Britain] with the United States or Japan, together with the lack of synchronization in their periods of stronger or weaker economic performance, provides a valuable ground for testing the validity of many variables of economic performance, especially . . . those concerning business activity." (Cassis, 1995, p.8)

This book, notwithstanding the arguments and warnings of Crafts, is very much within the tradition exemplified by Cassis, Crouzet, Harris and others, which accepts that comparative history is a valid methodological tool, if handled with care. Furthermore, we argue that a comparative historical study of accounting development in France and Britain could be particularly informative, and of interest to modern practitioners, in the light not only of the moves towards greater harmonisation of accounting rules currently underway, but also because of the generally perceived differences in the accounting models developed within the two countries over the last two centuries. We will now illustrate, in a general sense, the nature of these differences in order to provide a *raison d'être* for the approach adopted in this book.

British and French accounting: an historiography

Early research into the development of accounting has tended to focus not on individual countries, but on the evolution of accounting more generally. These works, due to first British and then American economic dominance, and the linkage perceived by early writers between accounting and economic development, tended to emphasise developments in those countries. Whilst they threw much light on the development of accounting in the Anglo-Saxon world, many of these works were written by non-British authors. Indeed it has been argued that British contributions to the study of accounting history prior to 1939 did "not include studies that could compare with the best works of Continental scholars" (Parker & Yamey, 1994, p.3). During and immediately after the Second World War, little was published and interest in accounting history did not revive until the 1950s. In 1952, in his *Studies in Costing* (1952), David Solomons published a paper entitled 'The historical development of costing', and this was followed in 1956 by Littleton and Yamey's *Studies in the History of Accounting*, which brought together twenty-four articles on accounting from the ancient world to the nineteenth century. Accounting history had begun to take hold in Britain and work specifically on the development of British accounting began to be carried out, a notable landmark being the appearance in 1954 of Nicholas Stacey's book, *English Accountancy: A Study in Social and Economic History, 1800-1954*. From that time, and more especially from the 1970s, the development of accounting in Britain has been studied in ever greater depth by historians, in marked contrast to the position in France where it is only in recent years that the development of accounting in that country has become a focus of study.

In part, this somewhat belated concern with the history of French accounting stems from the perceived wisdom which, until recently, argued that the significance of France in the development of accounting generally was tiny. For example, the first major work examining the international development of accounting, Richard Brown's, *A History of Accounting and Accountants*, published in 1905, considered that France had only played a minor role. According to Fogo (in Brown (1905, p.145)), this could be explained by the fact that "at an early date the legislature [in France] . . . saw fit to make an attempt to check fraud by issuing stringent laws regulating the methods of keeping accounts. The necessity of conforming to these requirements naturally hampered improvement ... " It was assessments such as this, and previous, now largely rejected, views of French economic backwardness in the nineteenth century that led Chatfield (1974), in his *A History of Accounting Thought*, to ignore France since it was not considered economically significant.

Despite these negative views, there were some French authors who concerned themselves with aspects of the history of accounting prior to 1946. Early progenitors of modern French accounting historians include George Reymondin (1909) and Albert Dupont, whose lectures were published between 1925 and 1931 in the *Revue de la Société de Comptabilité de France*. In 1947 and 1956 respectively, there then appeared two historical works which, for the first time, dealt in a significant manner with French accounting: Pierre Garnier, *La comptabilité, algèbre du droit* (1947) and the work by the Belgian,

Joseph Vlaemminck, *Histoire et doctrines de la comptabilité* (1956).
Prior to Vlaemminck, French accounting developments from the end of
the seventeenth century were considered to be unimportant, a typical
view being that of Fogo who did not consider any French writings after
Irson's 1678 text worthy of mention. However, whilst Vlaemminck
found little to admire in seventeenth century French accounting
literature, he was much more taken with the French literature in the
eighteenth and nineteenth centuries, devoting over forty pages of his
work to it. Nevertheless, general works on the international aspects of
accounting development continued to suggest that France played a very
small role in the history of accounting, either because this was indeed
the case or because a lack of research into French accounting history
meant that the French contribution remained obscured and hidden
(Lemarchand and Parker, 1996, p.xxxv). Even before 1980, however, a
few works suggested that the latter might be the more correct
interpretation. R.S. Edwards (1937c), for example, had shown that,
during the nineteenth century, French cost accounting literature was
more advanced than that in Britain. More recently, Lemarchand and
Parker have pointed out that in most European languages other than
English, the French terms *actif* and *passif* have been adopted as the
main headings in balance sheets (1996, p.xxxv).

Research into the history of accounting in France, like that in
Britain, has gathered pace in the last twenty years. Between 1977 and
1982, seven bulletins were published by *L'Institut National des
Historiens Comptables de France* and, since 1988, the *'Groupe
d'histoire de la comptabilité'* has met annually at the CRD. Furthermore,
since 1995, three annual *Journées d'histoire de la comptabilité* have
been held under the auspices of the *Association Française de
Comptabilité*. Recent work, particularly by French accounting
historians such as Colasse, Durand, Lemarchand and Nikitin, as well as
by non-French historians, has generated a more detailed understanding
of the development of accounting within France, and a much wider
recognition of the significance of the French accounting model within
the European context. There is still much to be learnt, however, both in
France and Britain, not least because one deficiency of much of the
research into the development of accounting prior to 1970, as noted by
Raymond de Roover (1974), was that it had been built almost entirely
upon descriptions of the techniques expounded in accounting textbooks.
Whilst this research is obviously important if we are to understand the
development of accounting, the virtual absence of historical studies of

accounting practice meant that our knowledge base was not only limited but also somewhat biased. Since the 1970s in Britain, and the late 1980s and early 1990s in France, however, the study of accounting practice has been steadily gaining momentum. The work of authors such as Yamey, Parker, J.R. Edwards, Fleischman and their associates, has vastly increased our understanding of British developments, whilst in France, the work of a small number of authors, including Lemarchand and Nikitin, has led to a significant improvement of our understanding of the development of French accounting practice.

The raison d'être for a comparative study of France and Britain

It is widely accepted that modern Continental European and Anglo-Saxon accounting systems are predicated on different principles. Most noticeably, the former tends to be based on the application of strict rules to achieve uniformity, as exemplified in the use in the late twentieth century of prescribed charts of accounts by all businesses, whilst the latter has been based, at least in Britain up until 1980/81, on minimalist regulation which allows great flexibility in accounting choice, as long as the accounts provide a 'true and fair' view of the accounting entity. In the context of Anglo-Saxon accounting, the British influence has been significant, the British model[1] having spread throughout the countries of the British Empire. The British model, however, made little or no impact on the European mainland where, in the light of the recent research of accounting historians, the French model appears to have played a significant role. Indeed, both Walton (1993) and Lemarchand and Parker (1996) consider that France has been the most significant country generating and disseminating accounting ideas within Europe. For Walton, the Savary inspired Ordonnance of 1673, part of the Colbertian programme of national administrative reforms in France, should be awarded the accolade of "most important contribution to European accounting statutes" because it:

> established the idea of an annual balance sheet, and that accounting requirements were a consequence of business activity, not related to the legal form under which business was carried out. (Walton, 1993, p.288)

Whilst Savary's contribution was important, Walton considers that Napoleon, because of the 1807 Code de Commerce, should also be presented with an award, this time as the 'most successful promulgator' of accounting ideas (1993, pp.287-8). Through the incorporation of Savary's statute into the Napoleonic Code of 1807, French accounting ideas were exported, on a compulsory basis, throughout the Napoleonic Empire, including Belgium and the Netherlands, and also later, on a voluntary basis, to countries such as Germany and Sweden. The consequence has been that, in mainland Europe, 'generally accepted accounting principles' have developed independent of corporate reporting, in contrast to the situation in Britain, where statutory rules have been linked almost entirely to limited liability and incorporation.[2] However, in Walton's view, this commonality of accounting origins within mainland Europe should not be construed as indicating the existence today of a 'continental European' accounting model, since local factors, including social, economic and cultural ones, have subsequently influenced the development of accounting systems, leading to the creation of differences. Indeed, Walton has suggested that:

> even a cursory glance at the history of accounting in just one or two European countries reveals that most law makers observed what was happening to their neighbours and borrowed and adapted from them. (1993, p.286)

Lemarchand and Parker, whilst noting that developments in French commercial and company law have influenced other countries in Europe, have also suggested that, France imported as well as exported accounting ideas (1996, p.xl). But why was there such an interchange on the mainland of Europe, and why did French ideas have the greatest impact? Given the current state of knowledge, definitive answers to these questions are not possible. Indeed, in Walton's view, it is "difficult to do more than speculate about the reasons for the adoption of the French Commercial Code..." by other European countries (1993, p.289). It is clear, therefore, that there is still much research that needs to be carried out in order to better understand the influence of the French accounting model on the mainland of Europe and why, despite the French influence, there is no single 'Continental European' model. If, however, the views of writers like Walton and Lemarchand and Parker regarding the significance of France are correct, then a comparative study of accounting development in Britain and France during the eighteenth and nineteenth centuries would seem relevant to achieving a better understanding of the wider development of accounting. As the two most economically-advanced nations of the time, the finding that they developed different and distinct accounting models, and that their models had a different impact on other countries within Europe, are issues which prima facie would appear worth investigating.

To understand fully both the similarities and differences of British and French accounting development, it is insufficient, however, to rely on a detailed examination of the accounting literature together with the rules and regulations laid down by the state. It is important to examine also the development of accounting practice through a detailed examination of business archives. In the field of accounting history, such an examination is in its infancy but it is already beginning to throw up some interesting results, as will be indicated below in chapter 4 of this study. For Crouzet, archival research plays a key role in historical investigation, since it provides fresh raw materials for historians, thus preventing them from continually reprocessing the same information (1990, pp.95-6). Thus the archival based work reported in chapter 4 attempts to emulate, in the realm of accounting development, the work of Harris (1992) on the development of coal-fuel technology in Britain and France during the eighteenth century.

The results of the examination of accounting practice, when married to those from the survey of the literature carried out in chapter 3, make it possible not only to compare both practice and the development of the literature between France and Britain but also the link between practice and literature in each country. While it is hoped that the analysis carried out below will enable us to identify certain factors which help to explain similarities and differences in the development of accounting in France and Britain, it should be recognised that this work is only a beginning. By identifying what appear to be key influences we intend that this book should stimulate and focus further investigations into the comparative development of accounting in these two countries.[3] Further, we hope to encourage those accounting historians who have shown an interest in the history of their discipline, to think not only about accounting development within their own country, but also more generally.

Such work, it is hoped, will help us to understand how and why these two countries may have developed different systems, and to locate accurately the timing of any divergence. Furthermore, an explanation may emerge as to why, despite the fact that British accounting methods have been taken up in English and non-English speaking countries elsewhere in the world, it was the French method of accounting rather than the British which achieved a position of pre-eminence on the mainland of Europe. Such studies gain importance from the fact that, today, the French and British accounting models are seen to provide alternatives from which developing countries may choose. Such issues clearly indicate the important light which historical research can throw on modern practices and hence that the findings of this book, in terms of helping us to understand the differences and similarities between current French and British accounting methods, should be of interest to not only accounting historians but also to modern accounting practitioners.

The scope of the book

We have seen that there are a large number of important issues in relation to the development of the British and French accounting models, and their wider importance, which need to be addressed by historians. It should be clear that, despite the length of this book, it is impossible to address all of these issues in great detail, particularly given the relatively small amount of detailed archival research that has been carried out up to this point in time. It was therefore necessary to focus our work on certain issues. In the light of some of the arguments discussed above, and given their backgrounds and areas of historical expertise, the authors of this book have focused attention on an examination of the development of both accounting thought, as applied to industrial/manufacturing activity, and the accounting practices of industrial enterprises in France and Britain during the period up to c.1870. Through the use of both archival material and a review of the contemporary and more recent accounting literature, the aim has been to seek to identify factors which would help to explain both the similarities and differences found.

Up till now, the development of accounting has largely been viewed as proceeding through a number of stages. In Britain, for example, a generalised view of 'management' accounting developments between the eighteenth century and today may characterise it as having passed through the following phases: cost recording; costing; cost accounting; managerial accounting; management accounting. Although assigning these labels to specific time periods is difficult, there is the suggestion of an evolution from one form of accounting to the next over time, as first one then the next form became dominant. Thus, over time, the way in which cost information was generated by accounting systems, and the purposes for which it has been used, is seen to have changed. Sometimes these changes occurred in an evolutionary fashion, whilst at other times they occurred in a more abrupt, or discontinuous, manner. Even with the hindsight of the historian, however, judging whether a change is evolutionary or sudden is usually a matter of individual perspective - one historian's sudden change is another's speeding up of a longer evolutionary development. Sometimes, for some historians, such as the Foucauldians, a change, although not occurring necessarily particularly rapidly, can nevertheless be seen as a crucial discontinuity in the development not only of accounting but also that of modern society.

A traditional view of Anglo-Saxon historians has been that developments within accounting have arisen from two sources. On the one hand, financial accounting developed out of merchant double entry bookkeeping whilst, on the other, cost accounting emerged much later, from the end of the nineteenth century, outside the double entry framework through the influence of engineers. Thus at the end of the twentieth century there is a distinction within the Anglo-Saxon world between financial accounting and cost/management accounting, a distinction which, in part, has been enshrined by legislation in France since the introduction of the *Plan Comptable* in 1947, i.e. between *comptabilité analytique d'exploitation* and *comptabilité générale*. It has long been recognised in both countries that, since they are dealing with the same thing, only viewed from different perspectives, periodic cost/management accounting reports are necessarily linked to and should be reconcilable with the financial accounts[4], but the extent to which such linkages exist and the degree to which they can be reconciled, varies across enterprises, both within each country and between them, and over time. Hence there is concern within both countries to examine the reasons for differences in these areas. There is, however, an implicit premise in the concern with accounting integration, namely that the two branches of accounting started off separately and thus, at some subsequent stage in accounting's development, there was a need for them to become integrated. One result of our work is to question this belief and to open up the possibility that, in the early stages of industrial development in both

Britain and France during the eighteenth and nineteenth centuries, the calculation of costs for managerial control purposes was carried out within the same accounting system that was used for what would today be described as financial purposes.

It is therefore argued that the traditional view of accounting's development in the Anglo-Saxon world may have failed to detect a significant development in the late eighteenth century and first half of the nineteenth century. Blinded to some extent by the conventional wisdom in respect of the emergence of costing in America post-1870, historians have possibly failed to observe, or fully appreciate, the nature of earlier important costing developments, particularly in Britain. Even where this costing has been noted (Fleischman and Parker, 1990, 1991), the full implications have not been recognised because they have been interpreted within a teleological framework which assumes that cost and financial accounting developed from different and independent roots.[5] The research presented and analysed in this book has identified a phenomenon which should be seen as a significant influence on accounting's history in the nineteenth century and beyond. In order to distinguish these phenomena from other developments previously examined and discussed within the accounting history literature, we will refer to it as 'industrial accounting'. This phrase is, of course, a translation of the French term '*comptabilité industrielle*', which was first used by Mézières (1842) and later became an accepted part of French accounting terminology. The term seems to us an ideal phrase for the purposes of this book since, in regard to the Anglo-Saxon literature, it does not carry with it any prior intellectual connotations, as do terms such as 'cost accounting', 'managerial accounting' and 'financial accounting'.

By 'industrial accounting' then, we mean the practice of cost calculation *within* an accounting system based on double entry bookkeeping, developed by industrial enterprises for managerial purposes. Hence, for the period and firms studied, there was a single, integrated accounting system; there was no distinction between what today we would describe as the 'cost' and 'financial' accounting systems. Therefore, we do not feel that the use of these latter terms, and the distinction that they imply, is helpful to an understanding of the development of accounting systems within eighteenth and nineteenth century French and British industrial enterprises.

The finding that routine cost calculation was embedded within the general accounting system rather than having been developed separately, outside the system, requires historians to alter the perspective from which subsequent accounting developments should be considered. Rather than cost accounting and financial accounting being seen as having developed from different sources, thus generating the need for them to be subsequently integrated or made reconcilable, it suggests that, at some stage, accounting systems which initially provided both cost and financial information, were usurped or diverted, requiring a subsequent re-integration. This leads to the interesting questions of why and how the former integrated system may have been usurped - what were the forces that made this possible? One answer might be that accounting, at some stage in its past, possibly during the late nineteenth and early twentieth centuries, lost its way, enabling ideas from outside to capture ground which might legitimately be considered to be part of accounting's intellectual domain.

In the light of recent research by Scapens *et al* (1996), an alternative possibility emerges. These authors have found, in contrast to the Johnson and Kaplan (1987) thesis, no evidence that the management accounting practices of British firms towards the close of the twentieth century are dominated by financial reporting requirements. More significantly, in the light of the findings reported here for the nineteenth century, they have found that a single accounting information system is used for both internal and external purposes. This therefore raises the question of whether or not accounting systems were ever dis-integrated in Britain. Very little is known of the accounting practices of industry in the first half of the twentieth century so it is impossible to address this question given our current state of knowledge, but the finding that, in Britain, industry has always used a single, integrated system of accounting over the past two centuries, has important ramifications for much of the conventional wisdom in regard to the development of Anglo-Saxon accounting in the twentieth century. In particular it raises the strong possibility that there may have been different development paths within the Anglo-Saxon accounting model, if indeed the use of such a term could any longer be justified, namely a specific American model, where cost/management accounting and financial accounting developed separately, and a British model, where accounting was integrated.

A few words of caution and explanation

Whilst this book is based on a study of both the accounting literature and accounting practice, it needs to be recognised that, in relation to the latter there is much that still needs to be done. Before major gaps in our knowledge can be filled there is a need for a much more systematic analysis of surviving business archives for the eighteenth and nineteenth centuries in both Britain and France (Lemarchand, 1996). It is intended that this study, by drawing together the findings of research into both accounting practice and the accounting literature in both countries, should help to identify the major issues which need to be addressed, and provide a stimulus to the carrying out of more archival based research. We recognise that archival research is time-consuming, but it is considered vital if we are to understand fully the process of accounting development during the eighteenth and nineteenth century and, just as importantly, why various differences and similarities can be observed on each side of the Channel.

Structure of the book / main findings

In chapter 2 we examine briefly the economic and social development of France and Britain from the beginning of the seventeenth century through to the end of the nineteenth century. The first part of chapter 2 summarises the current interpretation by economic historians of the extent and rate of growth of the two countries over the research period and is then followed by a brief discussion of some of the possible causes of the observed differences. One important factor underlying both economic and social developments in the two countries, including that of accounting, of course, was the gradual move from mercantilism in the eighteenth century to a more *laissez-faire* philosophy in the nineteenth century. Chapter 2 therefore provides a general background against which the development of accounting in the two countries can be analysed, both in economic and socio-cultural terms. Chapter 3 analyses the development of accounting literature in both Britain and France, whilst chapter 4 analyses recent work by accounting historians on the development of accounting practice in the two countries. It is found that, whereas the French accounting literature was markedly in advance of that in Britain, in terms of practice the opposite was the case. This raises the interesting question of how, despite an absence of relevant literature on industrial accounting, businesses within Britain were able to develop accounting systems appropriate to their needs. Chapter 5 attempts to evaluate different possible explanations as well as to provide a better understanding of the reasons for the differences and similarities in accounting development in Britain and France. We conclude with an indication of areas where we consider that further historical research would be beneficial.

Notes

1	Most modern writers on accounting history refer to the 'Anglo-Saxon model' of accounting rather than the 'British model'. For the period dealt with in this report, and possibly later periods as well, we are unhappy with the implication that all countries within the English-speaking world used the same accounting model. In particular, we are not convinced that the British and American systems, particularly from around the 1870s, but possibly even earlier, developed along similar paths. It may be that there was a single system (the Anglo-Saxon model), with two important and different variants (the 'British' and the 'American'), but it is also possible that, especially after the 1870s, they were distinct systems. However, since this is not the place to examine such possibilities (for more on this point, see Boyns and Edwards (1996c), and in order to avoid any confusion over what we may mean, for the period under study here, we will throughout out study use the phrase 'British model' in preference to the phrase 'Anglo-Saxon model'.
2	"The ordonnance established the idea of an annual balance sheet, and that accounting requirements were a consequence of business activity, not related to the legal form under which business was carried out. When new legal vehicles were introduced, therefore, they sometimes carried additional disclosure requirements but relating to this separate accounting base." (Walton, 1993, p. 288)
3	In a recently published work, Youssef Cassis has noted that, in relation to British business history and the explanation for Britain's relative economic decline since the late nineteenth century, Anglo-French comparisons have been very limited

and "have only played a marginal, and very recent, role in the perception, measurement and analysis of the British decline, far less than comparisons with the United States, Germany, and Japan" (Cassis et al, 1995, p. 7). One reason for this lack of comparison, of course, was that, until the work of recent revisionist historians, France was considered to have been backward in its economic development when compared to Britain, and therefore little presumably would have been gained from comparative studies. This view, however, can no longer be sustained.

4   This need not be the case, of course, with *ad hoc* cost/management reports.

5   The teleological approach is based on a knowledge of engineering practices as conveyed by the late nineteenth century journal literature, and argues that cost accounting developed from the need for engineers to make technical estimates of cost, independently of the accounting system.

Chapter 2 - Economic development and the development of accounting

The first part of this chapter outlines modern views as to the comparative economic development of Britain and France during the eighteenth and nineteenth centuries. We then go on to examine possible explanations, both economic and social, for the differences observed. Since the underlying political economy of the period is seen by many, including Foucauldian accounting historians, as being an important factor underlying most explanations, we pay particular attention to the implications of mercantilism for the development of legislation relating to both business and accounting. This will then provide a backcloth for the remainder of the study, and one against which similarities and differences in the development of accounting, both in terms of the accounting literature and accounting practice, in Britain and France can be considered and compared in subsequent chapters.

I.   The economic development of Britain[1] and France, c.1700-c.1880

The extent of the economic development of both France and Britain during the eighteenth and nineteenth centuries has been the subject of much debate amongst economic historians. When François Crouzet suggested, over thirty years ago, that previous writers had somewhat exaggerated the economic superiority of Britain over France at the commencement of the industrial revolution, his views were met with much disbelief (Crouzet, 1967, 1990). Whilst it is still generally accepted that Britain passed through its industrial revolution before France did so, subsequent revisionist research has suggested that Britain's economic progress may not have been so far in advance of that of France during the eighteenth and nineteenth centuries as was once thought, though the gap between them was nevertheless significant. However, as Crouzet himself has admitted, these results do not mean that there were no differences between the two countries during these two centuries, but rather that any differences were long-standing. Indeed he has recently reiterated his view that the gap in economic development between the two countries was not of "sudden or recent appearance" (Crouzet, 1990, p.12) but existed at the time of the death of Louis XIV in 1715. In his assessment, France's relative backwardness at the beginning of the eighteenth century can be explained by the fact that she suffered a long period of stagnation and decline during the period 1630-1720 (the *longue durée*), whilst England did not. In Crouzet's view, therefore, "Colbert's policy of industrialisation [in the late seventeenth century] was really nothing but a desperate effort to counteract this declining trend." (Crouzet, 1990, p.14) Colbert's policy appears to have had a limited effect, however, with any increase in total industrial output during his government being, at best, small: "whilst some of his new industrial undertakings survived and developed later, many others declined and quickly disappeared" (Crouzet, 1990, p.14).

By the beginning of the eighteenth century then, England led France in agriculture, in industrial technology, and in the commercial and financial fields. Given this widespread lead, it is not altogether surprising that when France at last began to develop significantly, it was unable to reduce the gap which existed between herself and Britain. Thus, although French industrial performance after 1720 compares favourably with that of England, the gap, already established, remained. Furthermore the two economies developed somewhat differently:

> France was producing less coal, non-ferrous metals, ships and cotton goods than Britain, but more woollens, linens and silks, as well as more iron. French total industrial production was appreciably higher than the English, but production per head remained smaller, as it had already been in the seventeenth century. (Crouzet, 1990, p.23)

Thus even though in the 1770s, as in the seventeenth century, French economic power was "clearly superior in mercantilist terms, England was still the more "developed", the richer country, with certainly a higher average income per head" (Crouzet, 1990, p.26). Part of the problem was that French economic development in the eighteenth century continued to be based on traditional organizational structures and methods of manufacture. Whilst Britain developed new technologies and new products to meet the bottlenecks consequent upon the conjunction of the increasing pressure of demand and a shortage of labour, France merely produced more of the same goods in the same old way, largely unaffected by similar pressures. This is partly explained by the different types of markets for which the respective industrialists catered: in Britain they concentrated on producing products for the average person, whilst in France they produced goods for the rich.[2]

For Crouzet, the reason that the industrial revolution did not begin in France in the late eighteenth century was because there was no discernible force in the country "tending to effect a thoroughgoing transformation of economic structures" (1990, p.102). Furthermore, he notes that the process by which the industrial revolution occurred can be likened to the launching of a two-stage rocket, with an initial stage of unbalanced growth followed by a secondary stage of balanced growth. Although Crouzet considers that the Peace of Versailles in the 1780s provided a detonator for the second stage, he noted that France had failed to undergo the first stage of change. Thus it was:

> only natural that she should have experienced some difficulty in her attempts to imitate England's second innovatory push, a difficulty that was exacerbated by the troubled condition of her economy in the 1780s. (Crouzet, 1990, p.104)

Indeed, France's attempts to 'catch up' with Britain were crucially thwarted by the effects of the French revolution:

> At this date [the 1780s] English industry had a clear superiority, but was only just entering the stage of fast growth and widespread revolutionary changes; France was not disastrously behind, and the Industrial revolution might have taken off there with only a few years' delay in relation to England. But the 'national catastrophe' which the French Revolution and the twenty years war meant to the French economy would intensify the discrepancy and make it irremediable. In 1815 it would be more pronounced than in 1789, because during this quarter of a century, despite a delaying effect due to the wars, the British economy had continued to change and to make rapid growth. (Crouzet, 1990, p.43)

By the time Britain's industrial revolution was reaching a phase of maturity around 1830, French industrial development was only just gaining pace. Interestingly, however, it has been estimated that, expressed in per capita terms, the rates of growth of commodity output in the Britain and France between 1780 and 1914 do not appear to have been so very different (O'Brien & Keyder, 1978, p.196). Further, whilst labour productivity in French agriculture remained throughout the nineteenth century consistently below that in Britain, output and labour productivity in French industry grew at a long run rate comparable to that of British industry.[3] Progress in neither country was smooth, with periods of more rapid industrial advance being separated by more quiescent periods. According to Caron (1979, p.135), the period between the 1830s and 1860s represented a period of rapid industrial growth in France, though it was characterised by a high degree of diversity in both methods of production and in the nature of the goods produced.

Given that France lagged behind Britain in the early eighteenth century, Britain remained the more economically advanced of the two countries towards the end of the nineteenth century, despite equivalent rates of growth over the previous one hundred years or so. Thus Maddison (1991) has calculated the following figures for 1870:

($)	GDP	GDP per head
GB	81,934m	2,610
France	60,397m	1,571

In a major sector such as iron and steel production, France substantially lagged behind Britain in 1880:

(000 tons)	pig iron	steel
GB	7,873	1,316
France	1,725	389

(Cassis, 1995, p.11)

Although France was clearly behind Britain c.1870-1880 in terms of overall wealth, level of industrialization, and scale of business activities, she was not 'backward'. Rather, historians at the end of the twentieth century view the economic development of Britain and France in the eighteenth and nineteenth centuries as having been comparable, even though the two countries, due to specific factors, took somewhat different courses.[4]

A detailed examination of why France lagged behind Britain in 1700 lies outside the scope of this investigation, but certain developments at the end of the seventeenth century, most notably the system of regulation of industry developed under Colbert, are germane to an understanding of the economic and socio-political context within which business, industry and accounting techniques developed in the eighteenth and nineteenth centuries. Before examining in detail the development of accounting in both France and Britain, it will therefore be necessary to examine the nature of the economic and social development of both Britain and France during the eighteenth and nineteenth centuries and to survey the various explanations that have been put forward for their different growth paths. This will then help to provide us with a framework for understanding similarities and differences in regard to respective attitudes towards business and the role of accounting in the two countries.

II.   Explaining differences in economic development

Differences in British and French economic performance have long been recognised, and it is not only modern historians who have attempted to provide explanations. Thus, at the end of the eighteenth century, many contemporary Frenchmen, mainly travellers and polemicists, were clearly aware of the nature of the economic differences between the two countries, and put forward explanations which have been subsequently taken up by historians. Indeed, in Crouzet's view, as far as explanations for Britain's supremacy are concerned, *rien de nouveau sous le soleil* . Thus French observers and writers of the late eighteenth century mentioned, as possible explanations:

> the role of foreign trade, supported by sea power, as an
> engine of growth; the precocious improvement of
> agriculture; political and economic freedom; the absence of
> legal barriers within a mobile society; a system of 'social
> values' which was congenial to economic progress; the
> making of consumption goods for the many rather than of
> luxury articles [for the few]; the rapid accumulation of

capital, low interest rates, an elaborate credit system. (Crouzet, 1990, p.146)

In searching for explanations for Britain's economic supremacy over France in the eighteenth and nineteenth centuries, historians have not surprisingly focused on a number of factors, some economic, some social, and some political. In many respects, of course, these factors are inter-related to such an extent that identifying their relative significance is sometimes extremely difficult. For Crouzet, however, contextual factors such as social structure and capitalist mentality, only play a secondary role in providing an explanation for why France was technically behind Britain on the eve of the industrial revolution. For him:

technical progress is closely bound up with economic phenomena, and the explanation we are looking for must [therefore] be first and foremost an economic one. The contention is that the French did not innovate because, unlike the British, they were not made to do so by the strong pressure of economic forces. (Crouzet, 1990, p.32)

Whilst economic explanations for the different paths of economic development in Britain and France are numerous, they can essentially be divided into demand-side or supply-side explanations. On the supply side, the most significant explanatory factor championed is the different factor endowments of the two countries, though differing social attitudes towards industry and capitalism are also cited. On the demand side, the class structure and the distribution of income are deemed by some to have played an important role. Most of the explanatory factors, with the exception of factor endowments of raw materials, are in some way connected with the prevailing doctrine of political economy. Hence we first undertake a detailed examination of mercantilism before briefly reviewing the factor endowment hypothesis. We then briefly discuss the move from mercantilism to laissez-faire before examining other factors, both supply side and demand side, which have been suggested as possible explanations for the different paths of British and French economic development.

Mercantilism

The term 'mercantilism' has been applied retrospectively to describe the underlying philosophical and economic system prevailing in many countries in north-western Europe between the middle of the sixteenth century and the late eighteenth century, but there were undoubtedly significant differences in the way that mercantilism developed, especially in France and Britain. It is often argued that it is these differences, rather than the common elements, which help to explain variations in the scale and scope of industrialisation in the two countries prior to 1820, and they may also provide an insight to the differing attitudes that developed towards accounting. Before examining the differences, however, it is necessary to establish the common elements of mercantilism

For Bronowski and Mazlish (1960, p.337) although "there was no unified economic system or philosophy of mercantilism . . . only a loose set of beliefs", they did recognise that mercantilism had a core element. The essence of this "was the developing territorial, or national, state, and the main purpose of mercantilist theory was to make economic activity subservient to the requirements of the state" (Bronowski and Mazlish, 1960, p.337). Under mercantilist thought, state power was considered to depend upon its wealth, which was determined by the amount of precious metals, in particular gold, held by the state treasury. For states which were not endowed by nature with supplies of precious metals, the main means of obtaining wealth comprised either conquest of wealthy nations (e.g. the Aztec and Inca states of South America by the Spanish), or by trade.

Under mercantilist ideas, the quantity of money (bullion) in the world was considered to be constant and therefore so too was the total amount of wealth. Hence whilst one country or state could become wealthier through trade, since trade was considered to be a zero-sum activity it would be at the expense of another country or state. Thus, whilst an inflow of bullion through a surplus of exports over imports directly raised the wealth of one state, by simultaneously reducing that of the state or states whose imports were greater than their exports, trade had a double impact upon the relative wealth, and hence the power and prosperity, of the various states. Not surprisingly, therefore, states saw trade as a way of improving their wealth and power, and undertook measures to ensure a favourable trade balance.

Generally speaking, mercantilism resolved itself into two elements: a monetary system and a protectionist system. Whereas the latter was designed to protect a country from being flooded with imports and a consequent outflow of bullion and hence loss of wealth, the former was designed to encourage the production of exports, to ensure an inflow of bullion. States encouraged exports in two main ways: the direct state fostering of production, through the use of bounties, subsidies, etc., and through the encouragement of commercial activities, so that manufactured goods could be exchanged for precious metals. One way of encouraging both production and trade was through the granting of monopoly rights by the state.

Whilst mercantilist thought held the high ground throughout the seventeenth and much of the eighteenth century, it gradually came under attack from proponents of a new economic philosophy, *laissez faire*. These attacks began in France around the middle of the eighteenth century through the work of the 'Economists', or Physiocrats as they are more commonly known today, and were built upon in England by Adam Smith in *The Wealth of Nations* published in 1776. Whilst mercantilism saw wealth as being generated through trade, the physiocrats saw land as its basis. For them, rent was the centre of wealth in the community, and since rent was derived from land, agriculture was considered to be a productive activity whilst industry was considered to be sterile. Smith, however, went further than this, and although he recognised the importance of land in the creation of wealth, he also saw labour as an important factor, leading to the development of his labour theory of value.

Mercantilism in France

One of the most important aspects of French economic policy during the mercantilist period which roughly lasted up to the French Revolution was that of *fiscalisme*. Thus, under the "more or less false pretence of guiding industry along the right lines", the French state wished to create large sources of revenue for itself, not least to finance wars and the lavish expenditure of the court (Heckscher, 1955, p.178). This fiscal influence, however, was carried on largely outside the framework of the *règlements*, which show "fewer signs of fiscal tendencies than other parts of industrial policy" (Heckscher, 1955, pp.183-4). Although previous attempts to create regulations had been made, these had proved ineffectual, and it was only under Colbert, from 1665, that an effective system of *règlements* was established. Initially put in place between 1665 and 1669, following a number of enquiries ordered by Colbert into the state of French industry, these were subsequently multiplied, completed and extended throughout the remainder of the mercantilist era. They provided the basic mechanism for the control of industry (Heckscher, 1955, p.158).

The first aim of the *règlements* was to unify the treatment of industry over the whole country, the term industry being, in this connection, principally confined to the various branches and stages of textile manufacture (Heckscher, 1955, p.158). Later, however, their influence was extended into the areas of mining, and paper and glass manufacture. The *règlements*, only introduced after consultation with the craftsmen of various localities, were highly detailed and established a system of inspection designed to control the quality of industrial production, by preserving what was considered to be best practice as enshrined in methods which had been established over the centuries (Heckscher, 1955, p.165). In the realm of textiles, the regulations established, for example, the dimensions of various cloths (in terms of numbers of threads in the warp and weft respectively), specified the number of categories (three) of dyers that could exist, forbade members of certain guilds to live in the same house as members of other guilds and specified how linen was to be carried, laid in fields, soaked, etc. (Heckscher, 1955, pp.160-2)

In order to ensure the greatest possible respect for the regulations, a complex system of administrative machinery was erected to oversee their operation. Whilst inspection of production to ensure compliance with the regulations was essentially in the hands of the guilds, especially their wardens, a system of industrial judges (*juges des manufactures*) and inspectors (*inspecteurs,* or *commis, des manufactures*) was created to oversee them. The most crucial role in the administrative system, and the link between the production areas and the central administrative machinery of the state, was played by the *intendants*. They were responsible for the administration of their district and were in contact with the minister of finance, the *controleur général*, and the *conseil de commerce* which had central responsibility for industrial policy. According to Heckscher (1955, pp.152-3), the *intendants* represent the only element within the French administrative system of the mercantilist era where there was no conflict between appearance and reality and that without their constant supervision, regulation of industry, including that of the privileged industries, would have been impossible. It is of interest to note from the accounting point of view that, "the two Savarys, father and son, authors respectively of the two works, *Le parfait négociant* and *Dictionnaire universel du commerce*, our principal sources of knowledge about contemporary trade" were both *inspecteurs*, as were Dupont de Nemours, the leading physiocrat, and Roland de la Platière, "author of the remarkable exposition of industry in the *Encyclopédie Méthodique*, later Girondin minister ... " (Heckscher, 1955, pp.154-5). Heckscher has suggested that a government department which could attract such talent was probably far in advance of other branches of state service of the *ancien régime*" (1955, p.155).

Despite the formal nature of the system of regulating industry, for example, towards the end of the *ancien régime* each piece of manufactured cloth required six different authenticating marks, regulations in France do not seem to have been strictly enforced, and the degree of enforcement probably declined as the eighteenth century wore on. In Heckscher's assessment, "it certainly cannot be said that, judged by modern standards, a high degree of orderliness, honesty or lawfulness prevailed" (1955, p.153). It is undoubtedly the case, however, that the regulation of industry hindered technological change and also the development of new industries, leading one author to describe the state of industrial equipment in France c.1750-1760 as "medieval in character" (Price, 1975, p.93). One important factor holding back developments was the power granted by the state to the various corporations that existed in many French towns. Under the mercantilist system in France, these corporations possessed the legal power to regulate a trade, and often used their powers to limit competition as well as to protect consumers through controlling quality (Price, 1975, pp.93 and 159). Entry to the trade and the quantity of production were both restricted and, until the 1730s-1750s, when the power of urban corporations began to decline, unorganised professions had pressure exerted on them to form corporations.

Prior to the middle of the eighteenth century, the routes by which industrial development could take place were somewhat limited. Although in the rural areas, where corporations were less significant, industry was able to develop more rapidly and cheaply (Price, 1975, p.93), the general environment up to 1750 in France was not particularly conducive to industrial development. Indeed, in some areas where industrial development was considered desirable by the state, such as in the glass industry, where most glass had to be imported, especially from Venice, direct encouragement had to be provided. This led to the establishment of the *Manufacture Royale des Glaces de Miroirs* in 1665 and the *Manufacture Royale de Grandes Glaces* in 1688, these two enterprises being subsequently merged by royal decree in 1695 as the *Manufacture des Glaces de France* or, as known today, Saint-Gobain.[5] Elsewhere, the securing of royal privileges was often vital if a rich landowner or merchant wishing to develop new industrial enterprises was to be able to assemble the requisite workforce to commence operations. Given the absolute power of the French Kings, the development of industry in France in the seventeenth and eighteenth centuries relied largely on the granting of royal privileges. Thus the state both directly encouraged the formation of new enterprises and permitted the establishment of others through a system of royal privileges. Therefore there emerged at this time:

> a many-sided system of favours upon which the new structures were erected, such as subsidies, protection against foreign competition and other benefits to the undertakings themselves, besides personal privileges of different kinds for the manager and his subordinates. The majority of these undertakings were in private hands and the name of *Manufactures royales*, conferred upon the most favoured of them . . . did not signify state ownership. There were also, however, a few state undertakings. (Heckscher, 1955, pp.187-8)

Often these enterprises were "large-scale undertakings, even in the very frequent cases where they were not really large industrial plants" (Heckscher, 1955, p.188). Some plants could be very large, e.g. the cloth-mill of Abbeville in Picardy, owned by the Dutch van Robais family, employed between 1200 and 1700 workers during the early eighteenth century. The system of royal privileges thus led to a growth in the formation of large industrial units, especially in textiles where such operations had been much smaller than, say, in mining and metallurgy (Heckscher, 1955, p.189). Initially, however, the system of privileges encouraged the development of enterprises in the fields of textiles and luxury goods. Not all of them proved successful. Furthermore, there is little evidence that the enterprises created by the granting of royal privileges paved the way for significant long-term economic development. Indeed, France continued to lag behind Britain in terms of industrial and economic development and increasingly looked across the Channel for both technical knowledge and inspiration.

Thus, key workers, technicians, engineers, etc. were head-hunted from Britain, and privileges "were very often granted for the production of all sorts of articles made 'on the English model'" (Heckscher, 1955, p.194). Whilst the industrial policy in France, compared with that in Britain, may not have been culpable for the inferiority of France's mining and metallurgical industries before the introduction of the steam engine and iron-made machinery, from that point onwards Heckscher considers that it was. The French system of industrial regulation and royal privileges which continued to favour the production of luxury goods such as glass, porcelain, silk, etc., rather than common goods such as iron acted as a force for conservatism in a period of rapid technological change (Heckscher, 1955, pp.197-9).

By the second half of the eighteenth century, if not before, the regulatory framework in France, concerned as it was with qualitatively superior methods, proved a hindrance rather than a help to the development of the French economy. But there were some signs of change even prior to 1750, with reformist tendencies, fostered by the airing of views in *salons* (of which there were few, if any, counterparts in England), and new administrative tendencies led to 'reformed mercantilism' (Heckscher, 1955, p.213). As early as 1720 there was "already a disposition in the *Bureau du Commerce* to oppose and even to reverse existing tendencies ... " (Heckscher, 1955, p.213), and by the middle of the eighteenth century the power of urban corporations was beginning to decline and many of them were beginning to change their administrative practices. A growing groundswell of opinion against regulation was thus beginning to manifest itself in the middle decades of the eighteenth century in France. One important change brought about by increased pressure for reform came with the ordinance of 1779 which reformed the *règlements*, and abolished the use of the title *manufacture royale* for all enterprises that were not unique (Heckscher, 1955, p.219). Nevertheless, despite the changes which occurred in the period prior to the French Revolution in 1789, these:

> were far less attempts at a new ordering of industrial life, than a confused medley of activities and concessions on the part of officials very often ignorant of what they

> wanted, what they were able to do and what rules they had
> to follow. (Heckscher, 1955, p.219-20)

Overall, Heckscher also noted that the retardatory effects of state involvement in industry did not end with the French revolution. Whilst:

> mercantilist regulation in France had placed obstacles in
> the path of all innovations which had somehow succeeded
> in becoming established in England, . . . the Continental
> System, together with the general unrest that prevailed on
> the continent until 1815, again retarded fresh development
> in France. (Heckscher, 1955, p.203)

Mercantilism in Britain

During the mercantilist era, the British state shared similar broad aims to those pursued by the French state, but the means by which mercantilist policy manifested itself was somewhat different. As elsewhere in Europe, control of industry in England was effected through a local authorities and legislation, but:

> In two important respects economic legislation was . . . less
> influenced by municipal policy than on the continent. First,
> all branches of industry were uniformily regulated
> throughout the country and great care was taken to
> maintain a regular supply of labour for agriculture.
> Secondly, the agents which the law prescribed for the
> administration of its rules were the same for town and
> country. (Heckscher, 1955, p.233)

Compared with other countries, this resulted in both a greater uniformity of measures throughout the length and breadth of the nation, and a greater interest in non-urban branches of industry (Heckscher, 1955, pp.224-5). Whilst the former undoubtedly contributed to a greater degree of mobility of economic forces, the main driving force here was the absence of internal customs barriers.

> The circumstance that no single branch of economic life
> was preferentially treated in England laid the foundation of

a deep-set difference between English and continental
policy, a difference which found its last expression in the
specifically English form of mercantilist protection, the
protection of agriculture and industry combined, or the
'system of solidarity'. It was, however, only at a
comparatively late period that a protectionist system of this
kind arose ... (Heckscher, 1955, p.226).

Statutes affecting industry did not go any further than the
regulation of labour conditions. Thus, the Elizabethan Statute of
Artificers (5 Eliz. c.4), and its subsequent modifications, created a
national regulation of wages, of conditions of apprenticeship, and
methods of determining the giving of notice and the hours of labour.
Thus the regulation of handicrafts was left largely to the guilds, with the
state encouraging the development of new handicrafts (Heckscher,
1955, pp.236-7). Whilst it is true that, prior to the Municipal
Corporations Act of 1835, the guilds played an important part in local
administration, they never attained in England the same presence as did
their counterparts in France. British guilds also differed from their
French equivalents in that they often covered many and varied crafts
within a single organization, something which undoubtedly contributed
to a lessening of their effectiveness. In Heckscher's view, this, along
with other traits, probably led to "the exceptionally early decline of the
old industrial code in England" (1955, p.245). The attitude of Elizabeth
and the older Stuarts, especially Charles I, in creating monopolist
privileges in favour of courtiers and other outsiders, clearly also helped
to undermine the position of the guilds.

Within the English constitutional framework, the Justice of the
Peace (JP) occupied a unique position as the agent of "unified industrial
legislation" (Heckscher, 1955, p.246). The activity of JPs, unlike that of
guilds, was not limited to towns but covered the whole country. They
were responsible for many things: technical control of various branches
of industry (only a small fraction of their work); the supervision of all
branches of domestic trade and the fixing of prices; control of the
general conditions of labour and fixing wages; control of middlemen's
activities; inspection of weights and measures. It is clear that:

the state placed superhuman demands on the J.P.s, and ...
they could not possibly carry them all out. It is equally
apparent that both the will and the ability varied greatly

and that their control of industry was particularly variable. (Heckscher, 1955, p.250)

The effectiveness of JPs was clearly lessened by the fact that they were unpaid, rendering them susceptible to bribes, and that much of their control was effected through largely honorary, i.e. unpaid, subordinates who furthermore lacked the prestige afforded to the JPs (Heckscher, 1955, p.247). The variability of the control effected by JPs was particularly marked in regard to industry, where they could be both a force for implementing rules, and for resisting their implementation. As agents of local administration, JPs represented the outlook of the local population and whilst they would happily implement policy where it coincided with local opinion, where it did not they could often effectively resist it. Ultimately, therefore, the power of the state and parliament could be undermined at the grassroots level. For Heckscher, however, a more crucial determinant of the course of English industrial, and consequently social and economic development, was the removal of the Stuarts from power. Given their capacity for interfering with social life, which was unique in English history, a major influence on industrial development was removed, allowing England to develop in a way not possible on the European continent during the eighteenth century (Heckscher, 1955, p.261).

Those industrial regulations which existed in England were mainly concerned with the technique of manufacture, but they were "always confined to a modest number of clauses" (Heckscher, 1955, p.266). More rapidly than in France, however, the English system of regulating industry

collapsed from within. Only a few of its prescriptions were specifically abolished in the 18th century, and one of the few measures which did have this aim was unable to attain it . . . But among the ruling classes the general opinion that it was impossible to carry out the system effectively gained wider and wider currency. The English mode of jurisdiction, a mobile system built up on legal practice, together with the impotence of the central and local administration, combined to do away with the political hindrances obstructing those developments which were to make England the theatre of the Industrial Revolution. There were extremely few measures definitely assisting

industrial progress along these lines, and even the
dissolution of the old order was carried out without plan or
system. These circumstances gave English social life its
peculiar character and distinguished it from that of the
continent. Nevertheless in spite of the absence of any plan
the changes which took place had a profound effect.
(Heckscher, 1955, p.325)

Contrasting mercantilism in Britain and France

In his overall summary of the development of mercantilism, Heckscher
has commented that:

It must never be lost sight of that the basic ideas of French
regulation held for England as well as for most countries of
Western Europe. . . . [However] On common foundations
were erected two edifices which nevertheless were
different in England and France; and the differences are as
important as the similarities. As an approximate
generalization we may say that the resemblances were
greater in form than in content, though quite extensive in
both. (1955, p.222)

In relation to English developments, Heckscher notes the use by
Cunningham of the phrase 'Parliamentary Colbertism' to describe the
period between the revolution of 1688 and the publication of the *Wealth
of Nations* in 1776. Whilst Heckscher considers that, from some points
of view, this designation is comprehensible, particularly as regards
foreign trade and colonial policy, it is a description which requires
some additional comments:

In the first place it was a Colbertism without a Colbert. . . .
After 1688 there was less than ever anyone in England to
be compared with Colbert. Secondly - and this was the
vital point - England after the Restoration lacked the whole
system of general administration which in France had
come to full flower under and through Colbert. Without his
intendants in every part of the country, the French minister
could not have kept the machinery at work for a single day.

England on the other hand could not boast of any better executive agents in the counties than the Lord Lieutenants, who at the best correspond to the French provincial governors, whose general uselessness and particular inefficiency for the purposes of the new state regulation had precisely caused the far-sighted French statesmen to create and support the institution of intendants. Thirdly, neither before nor after 1688 was there in England a paid *ad hoc* bureaucracy to supervise the enforcement of industrial legislation which Colbert had been at pains to create in France. During this, while France built up a new bureaucracy under centralized control both for administrative work in general and industrial regulation in particular, in England the administration which had served the older Stuarts was on the contrary breaking down and nothing was being set up in its place. This explains the development of the general European development of economic life. In other words, England before the 19th century acquired no civil service - no state-paid officialdom. (1955, pp.262-3)

In relation to the regulation of industry, there were certainly some symptomatic differences in principle between France and England, in particular "that many important districts were set free from the application of the statutes in England, while in France nothing remained unregulated in principle, apart from purely accidental exceptions on subordinate points" (Heckscher, 1955, p.266). The most significant difference between the two countries, however, relates to manufactures:

Not only was there no counterpart in England to the *établissements* of the luxury industry in the hands of the state, but also - and what is much more important - the numerous and extensive private *manufactures royales* endowed with every possible privilege, and similar industrial forms to be found in France, were absent in England. . . . In so far as great enterprises did arise in England they came in the guise of companies and in this way they had a more direct relation to market demand. (Heckscher, 1955, p.221)

For Heckscher, whilst differences in trade and industrial regulation, and the absence of state supervised manufacture of luxuries in England, undoubtedly play a role in explaining the relative industrial positions of the two countries over the seventeenth and eighteenth centuries, it was not the sole determining factor, or even necessarily the most important factor. He also notes that it was also partly dependent on the character of the people: "a less aristocratic life being better adapted to the new type of economic structure" (Heckscher, 1955, p.223). Significantly, however, he considers that the most important cause of differences in industrial and economic performance was the different endowment of natural resources.

Different factor endowments

One key factor in world economic development over the last three centuries has been the availability of energy and raw materials. The industrial revolution in most countries in the eighteenth and nineteenth centuries was based on the development of steam power, and was closely associated with the development of metal smelting industries, either directly or indirectly. Thus although the British industrial revolution is most closely associated with the development of the cotton textile industry, that industry could not have developed as it did without the development of new machines and supplies of coal to produce the steam which powered them. Many economic historians, but most particularly J.R. Harris, have pointed to Britain's superior endowments of raw materials, when compared with France, particularly in regard to reserves of coal, as a major factor explaining her more rapid industrialisation. This, he argues, led Britain to develop a highly-integrated coal-fuel technology which was to be at the heart of industrial development at the end of the eighteenth century (Harris, 1972, pp.9-17). Only in the 1780s, according to Harris (1972, p.16), did Frenchmen become fully aware of the fact that British technology was advancing on a broad front and that it would take France a long time before it was in a position to compete. Indeed, solutions could not be found readily because of the highly integrated nature of this technology, and early French attempts to introduce new techniques on a piece-meal basis prior to the nineteenth century proved unsuccessful. It was only after 1815, with the arrival of immigrants possessing the necessary expertise, that France began to address the problem in a meaningful way.[6]

Whilst endowments of raw materials are determined by nature, and states can do little to alter this, though they can, of course, attempt to gain access to greater supplies through the acquisition of more territory through war and conquest, and/or obtain them through trade, other possible explanatory factors are more susceptible to direct influence by a state. Most of the other major factors considered to help provide an explanation of the differing paths of economic development in Britain and France are generally considered in some way or another to be linked to the prevailing underlying philosophy of the period and changes therein. It is to a consideration of some of these factors, and the impact on them of mercantilism and the movement towards laissez-faire, that we will now turn our attention.

From mercantilism to laissez-faire

The impact of mercantilism was clearly different in France compared with Britain, and probably played some part in explaining the more advanced nature of economic development in Britain even before the advent of the industrial revolution c.1780. Furthermore, since mercantilism was not an isolated philosophy relating to the regulation of industry, but a social and philosophical movement which underlay most aspects of life in the seventeenth century, its earlier demise in Britain permitted a framework which was more conducive to rapid industrial expansion. The demise of mercantilism was, of course, accompanied by the rise of an alternative economic and social philosophy, that of *laissez-faire*.

The movement from mercantilism to laissez-faire did not occur suddenly, however, and changes in competition and industrial structure were not wrought overnight. In France, traditional methods of manufacture could continue to survive well into the nineteenth century, due both to the interventionist policies of the state, and the lack of an effective national transport system (Price, 1981, pp.163-64). Although not all industries were free from outside influence, relative isolation and state regulation often reinforced local monopoly positions. It was this which made it possible for industries, particularly those processing high quality manufactures, to survive in France using outdated technology (O'Brien & Keyder, 1978, p.192). After 1815, however, the picture in France begins to change. Whilst some sectors benefited from tariff protection, and some of the former direct and strong interventionist policies continued in place, others did not. Furthermore, the development of canals helped to break down natural regional monopolies, though it was not until the 1850s, when the main elements of a national railway system were put in place, that the full impact of competitive forces began to be felt throughout businesses the length and breadth of France.[7] Once again, however, change was not immediate, certain market imperfections continuing to retard the diffusion of new techniques until well into the second half of the nineteenth century. Thus, it has been noted that:

> "Industrial companies, especially in metallurgy, often engaged in price alignment and the division of markets, whilst competition was further reduced by a common unwillingness on the part of the more efficient producers to squeeze the less efficient out of existence. They preferred instead, at least when demand was high, to accept the high price levels set by the latter." (Price, 1981, p.137)

Innovation and the social class system

The economic growth of a country is undoubtedly dependent on the rate of technological progress which is itself a product of the pace of innovation. Innovation, however, has two dimensions: supply-side and demand-side. On the supply-side, there needs to be both the creation of new technology and a group of individuals willing and able to utilise these inventions. Thus, there needs to be both a culture of scientific and/or practical investigation and invention, coupled with a capitalist attitude to exploit the advantages provided by new techniques, including lower production costs (and hence prices) and new or better quality products, which will allow an extension of the market. On the demand-side, the increased needs of consumers, reflected in rising prices and growing bottlenecks in existing supply processes, can stimulate the search by both businessmen and inventors for new techniques to increase and/or speed up production. Whilst analyses of the different growth paths in France and Britain have considered both supply-side and demand-side possibilities, one factor which has been considered as having had an all-pervading influence is the social class system.

Differences in the social class systems of France and Britain during the eighteenth and nineteenth century have been suggested as a factor which may help to explain the relative retardation of French industrial techniques. In France, to a much greater extent than in Britain, the ruling classes engaged in an extremely lavish lifestyle made possible by a highly skewed distribution of wealth, often maintained through high rates of taxation on the majority of the population. Thus a mass market for consumer products was unable to develop in France in the way that it did in Britain, thereby denying the opportunity for businesses to make money by supplying large quantities of cheap, mass produced products utilising new technology. Instead, French businesses continued to concentrate mainly on the production of fine quality products manufactured in the traditional way for the ruling classes though, as already noted, there is evidence to suggest that change did begin to occur in the late eighteenth and early nineteenth centuries.[8]

The social class system in France in the eighteenth century undoubtedly had a demand-side effect on the rate of innovation and technology, and it is also though to have had a supply-side influence. Thus, with respect to innovation and technological change, Davis (1973) has argued that English society provided a more congenial climate for innovation than French society. There were two aspects to this: the French mode of thought favoured theorizing over practical experiment, which possibly retarded innovation; and French social attitudes towards industry and the capitalist ethos. It seems clear that the British were far more inventive than the French in the eighteenth century when it came to industrial affairs. One explanation put forward for this is the importance of the Newtonian approach, developed in Britain, that industrial progress was possible through observation and experiment. It is certainly true that French and British attitudes towards industrial innovation differed significantly from one another, but to what extent this influenced economic development in the eighteenth century is far from clear.

The French mode of thought in the eighteenth century, as it still is today, was strongly based on the ideas of Descartes (1596-1650). Essentially, Cartesian philosophy is the concept of doubt - everything must be doubted until a rational explanation can be found. The French rationalist approach therefore was to question everything, and to attempt to deduce rational explanations, since they believed that every effect must have an identifiable cause (Bronowski and Mazlish, 1960, p.228). French rationalist thought therefore was concerned more with the essence of things, rather than with practicalities. By contrast, British thought in the eighteenth century, following in the traditions of Newton, Locke, Bacon, etc., was much more pragmatic and was based on empirical inductivism (Bronowski and Mazlish, 1960, p.229). For the British, it was facts that were important, and from these principles or 'laws' could be induced. This empirical analytical tradition, based firmly in the pragmatic approach, was thus in direct contrast with French theorizing which was more concerned with causes. In reality, of course:

> science cannot develop without the constant combination
> of these two methods. Bacon's notion that experiment will
> give results of itself is obviously ill founded. So, equally, is
> Descartes' notion that the universe can be constructed by
> thinking alone. The empirical method and the rational
> method have to go hand in hand to make a science which is
> both realistic and orderly. (Bronowski and Mazlish, 1960,
> p.229)

Although the basic approaches of the French and British initially represented two opposing viewpoints, there was some movement towards each other during the eighteenth century. Under the influence of Newton, the Royal Society began to give definitive form to a method of analysis which consisted of a combination of rational deduction and empirical induction (Bronowski and Mazlish, 1960, p.249). These ideas were gradually taken over to France and developed there, most notably by Voltaire and Diderot, and this led to something of an 'Anglicization' of French thought. Voltaire had been attracted to Newtonian ideas whilst spending a three year period of enforced exile in England between 1726 and 1729, during which time Newton died. On his return to France Voltaire began to expound the elements of Newtonian philosophy. In doing so:

> Voltaire extrapolated from the master's work and proposed
> the application of the Newtonian method of analysis to all
> knowledge. He advocated a concern with how things work
> and not with their 'essence'. For Voltaire, as for Newton,
> the fact came before the principle . . .
>   . . . The French, after Voltaire, wished to deal with
> 'practical' matters. Such problems as the freedom of the

will and the nature of grace were dismissed as meaningless. (Bronowski and Mazlish, 1960, p.249)

The desire for reform in France in the middle decades of the eighteenth century was a response to the absolutism of Louis XIV, which "had left a France morally and physically weakened." (Bronowski and Mazlish, 1960, p.250) Although a few voices were raised against the king in the seventeenth century, it was not however until the eighteenth century that thinkers such as Voltaire and d'Alembert "provided the intellectual and metaphysical support behind the desire for economic and political reform entertained by practical men like d'Argenson and, in general, by the middle class." (Bronowski and Mazlish, 1960, p.250) The most obvious manifestation of the changing emphasis of French thinking was the *Encyclopédie*.

Directly prompted by Chambers' *Cyclopaedia*, published in England in 1728, the *Encyclopédie*, edited by Diderot, attempted to summarize, mainly English, technical achievement at the time. In the event, however, the *Encyclopédie*, which was published only slowly between 1751 and 1780, due in part to opposition and censorship, grew until it embraced "not only the presentation of technological achievements but the general state of contemporary culture" (Bronowski and Mazlish, 1960, p.250) Indeed:

> Diderot declared expressedly that the purpose of the *Encyclopedia* was not only to communicate a definite body of information but to produce a change in the way of thinking: "*pour changer la façon commune de penser*". (Bronowski and Mazlish, 1960, pp.250-1)

In Bronowski and Mazlish's view, then, the *Encyclopédie* reflects the striking juxtaposition between the English empirical approach and the French method of doubt consciously present in Diderot's mind.

For many in authority, the *Encyclopédie* was a source of disturbing ideas and a possible revolutionary force. Although Voltaire wrote only a few contributions for the *Encyclopédie*, "it was the inspiration which he brought from England which made distinguished Frenchmen feel that the real change which would transform the French social system was the type of free intellectual approach which the *Encyclopedia* fostered" (Bronowski and Mazlish, 1960, p.252). Whilst Voltaire may not have had revolutionary intentions, his ideas were revolutionary, and "His combination of English empiricism with the French method of doubt was an explosive one" (Bronowski and Mazlish, 1960, p.263). Since it is generally agreed that the French revolution retarded economic development in France, it could be argued that any Anglicization of French thought in the eighteenth century was unhelpful to economic progress. The extent of the British influence on French thought, however, is a matter for debate, as is the impact of the latter on the techniques used within French industry.

Crouzet, for example, considers that, although it was developed in Britain, the philosophical and scientific movement was just as powerful in France, which had plenty of scientists, some engaged in industrial research, and numerous scientific academies and societies, which numbered businessmen amongst their members. Furthermore he argues that the belief in progress and the wish to improve man's material condition were as widespread in France as in Britain, with Diderot's *Encyclopédie* indicating clearly the French interest in technology. However, Harris (1976) urges caution in viewing the existence of a large French technical literature as necessarily indicating that the technology was being utilised or that the country was in advance of, or at least keeping up with, other nations. He notes, for example, that:

> In the case of France, some of her main publications on mines and metals were produced by propagandists wishing to bring France up to the standards prevalent abroad, and some of the works were wholly or largely translations of foreign authors. . . . many writers of the eighteenth century were part of the intelligentsia, savants to whom the esteem of the learned world was the first concern. It was more important to them to follow scholarly authorities and to cite the well-known works of the past - since failure to do so would reveal academic ignorance - than to make a simple enquiry of someone engaged in the day-to-day conduct of an industry. (Harris, 1992, p.20)

The social class system in France has also been criticised for generating an anti-capitalist spirit. Some historians, for example, have stressed the greater social mobility in England than in France, but as Crouzet has noted, the French nobility was not a closed caste (1990, p.29). Nevertheless, commenting on the results of his examination of

French   archives,   Harris   uncovered   many   cases:

> not looking to rise to an entrepreneurial role, the noble
> requiring a royal privilege to preserve his status before he
> would enter in anything so demeaning as industrial
> enterprise. (1972, p.9; quoted in Crouzet, 1990, p.74)

Overall it seems clear that the social prestige of business was lower in
France than in Britain. For Crouzet, the important factor here is not so
much the social differences *per se*, but rather the lack of a 'capitalist'
spirit in France. Thus, although the French social and psychological
environment was not basically hostile to innovation, there would appear
to have been a different mentality amongst those employed in business
in France and Britain:

> In English society there was a more 'capitalist', a more
> commercial, a more acquisitive spirit; and according to
> contemporary accounts there was in England a harshness, a
> ruthlessness, a concentration on the pursuit of gain, which
> was absent in the more easy-going France of the *Ancien
> Régime*. (Crouzet, 1990, p.29)

Harris sees one part of the problem being the fact that "The
magnificent illogicality of the French tax, tariff and toll structure
created a world of economic Kafkaism, with the entrepreneur as anti-
hero" (Harris, 1972, p.9). This helped to contribute to a much lower
level of innovation and entrepreneurial activity in France as compared
to Britain in the eighteenth century. Rostow (1975) has also noted that a
disproportionate number of the innovators who were instrumental in
developing and implementing new production methods in Britain were
dissenters. Furthermore, most, if not all, of the key innovations which
ultimately enabled the British industrial revolution were developed in
that country. In France, despite possessing many marvellous craftsmen,
and excellent technicians in the fields of shipbuilding, ordnance and
public works, this talent was not applied to the improvement of
industrial techniques. In Crouzet's view 'French industry only
developed on the technical side through taking up foreign machines and
techniques, and to assimilate them usually required the help of foreign
technicians, most of them British, though some were Swiss or German'
(1990, p.27).

Thus, despite an apparent broadly similar level of interest in technology, the lower rate of practical innovations in France possibly stemmed from both the anti-capitalist ethos prevalent in the country and the fact that science was considered to be a purely intellectual matter, rather than being one for practising industrialists. A potentially important role in reinforcing this divide was the nature of the education system.

The education system

Crouzet (1990) has pointed out that Britain had a higher literacy rate than France in the eighteenth century. The reason for this would appear to have been that the majority of the French population received little or no formal education at that time. In both Britain and France, such education was essentially the province of the rich, since there was no national system of education in the eighteenth century. However, the development of economic activity in Britain was accompanied by a growth in the number and range of educational establishments. Gradually, there was a shift away from the provision of merely a classical education to the provision of vocational and practical training. Whilst the latter tended to be taught more in the emerging private and dissenting academies, there were also signs of this beginning to occur in the private schools, the grammar schools and the universities, though developments amongst the latter institutions were generally more gradual.

Whilst the provision of vocational training, especially in the fields of business and commerce increased in Britain in the eighteenth century, there is a general view that technical education in Britain lagged behind best European practice in the eighteenth and nineteenth centuries. Much has been made of the lack of major educational institutions in Britain catering for industry, even towards the end of the nineteenth century. In contrast, the French *grandes écoles*, established in the eighteenth century, are generally considered to have been superior to anything that could be found in Britain in that period. However, these institutions were not numerous: the first, the *Ecoles des ponts et chaussées*, was established in 1715, but this was not followed until 1783, when the *Ecole des mines* was founded, and 1794 when the *Ecole polytechnique* was established. Whilst these provided scientific and technical education, there is little evidence that they helped provide a more advanced business élite in France, or that they represented any shift in the prevailing ethos towards industry. Indeed, these schools were established largely to provide a supply of engineers for the state rather than for industry. Employment by the state continued to hold social prestige far into the nineteenth century, and training engineers for industry was not considered to be a fit task for professors at such establishments (Shaw, 1995, pp.164-5).

Partly in an attempt to overcome this attitude, and the deficiency of trained engineers in industry, Napoleon established a number of *écoles des arts et métiers* in the provinces. Perhaps significantly, they were originally intended to cater for the sons of the lower ranks of the army, and the graduates of these schools were clearly considered to be the inferiors of those from the *grandes écoles*. During the nineteenth century, however, there is evidence of gradual change. As the French economy began to develop more rapidly, and the demand for people with the necessary skills to organise and run business enterprises increased, graduates from the *grandes écoles* and the *écoles des arts et métiers* began to play an increasingly significant role in French industry. Price notes, for example, that, whereas the *grandes écoles* provided specialists who occupied managerial and engineering roles, the five *écoles des arts et métiers* provided individuals capable of occupying lower level positions within large business organizations (1975, p.169). Despite this, there were many complaints in France in the second half of the nineteenth century that French technical education was insufficient, even though it appears to have been much in advance of that in Britain. The fact that Britain was able to industrialise earlier, and to maintain her lead over France, despite the latter's apparent lead in terms of scientific and technical education, rather implies that formal education was not a major factor in explaining differences in the economic development of the two countries.

Indeed, studies of British entrepreneurs of the industrial revolution and later periods suggest that they came from a wide variety of different educational backgrounds, as was the case with French entrepreneurs. Their education was either very rudimentary or classical in nature. If France was behind Britain in terms of literacy in the eighteenth century, changes in the French education system in the nineteenth century seem to have changed this balance, placing the French system somewhat in advance of Britain by 1880, with little or no evidence that this change had any major influence in helping to close any gap in economic development that may already have opened up between the two countries.

Institutional factors

Innovation undoubtedly requires a supply of new ideas and inventions, and a demand for new and improved products, but it is also important that there is in place a framework of legislation relating to business structures which enables innovators or entrepreneurs full reign to exploit perceived opportunities. It has already been seen that there was a greater degree of regulation exercised by the French state during the mercantilist era than was the case in Britain. Most significantly, in Britain "the powers of the king were limited and he did not interfere with business" (Crouzet, 1990, p.143). Thus state regulation of industry was largely abandoned in practice during the seventeenth century, though the relevant laws still remained on the statute book, whilst the guild system fell into decay. In France, by way of contrast, a bureaucratic system of regulation covered many aspects of industrial life. In respect to business structures, and the nature of their financial systems, however, the French and British systems exhibit possibly less significant differences.

Formal business structures

The move from mercantilism to *laissez-faire* during the eighteenth and nineteenth centuries was accompanied by changes, some subtle, some the result of legislative action, in the formal structure of business organization. The nature of French legislation suggests that there was greater flexibility in France than in Britain, where the alternatives, unlimited partnerships and joint-stock companies, with or without limited liability, were much more polarised. In practice, however, there is evidence that the differences may not have been so great, and probably did not have any major impact upon the relative pace of economic development of the two countries.

The development of legislation relating to French business structures[9] began as early as the twelfth century, when *sociétés générales* (general companies) were established with identical characteristics to today's *sociétés en nom collectif*: the partners had unlimited liability. In about the seventeenth century *sociétés de command* appeared, containing two of the main characteristics of today's *sociétés en commandite*, namely: (a) people (now known as *commanditaires*) who subscribed capital and could scrutinize the management carried out by partners, and had limited liability; and (b) partners (now known as *commandités*) who had unlimited liability.[10] At the beginning of the eighteenth century there appeared the *grandes compagnies* (or *compagnies coloniales*) which were share-issuing companies enjoying privileges granted by the king. The 1807 Code de Commerce, which was the first of its kind in France, provided for three types of company: (a) *société anonyme* (limited company), which were the successors to the *grandes compagnies*; (b) *sociétés en commandite* (limited partnership), which succeeded the *sociétés de command*; and (c) *sociétés en nom collectif* (general, i.e. unlimited partnership), which succeeded the *sociétés générales*. The *société anonyme* (SA) of 1807 had the same essential characteristics as the SA of today: no limit on the number of shareholders or amount of capital, limited liability and the annual shareholders' meeting being the source of all power.

In Britain in the early nineteenth century, the choice of business forms was between a joint stock company (with or without limited liability) or an unlimited partnership. Joint stock companies could be formed through two alternative routes. The first, the chartered company, created by Royal Charter, dates from the sixteenth century, a well-known example being the East India Company established in 1600. The second route was through the formation of a statutory company via a private act of parliament, an example of this type being the Bank of England which was formed in 1694. As promoters in Britain recognised the scope provided by a joint stock for the expansion of business activities beyond the financial resources of the management group, the practice developed of raising finance from the public through informal arrangements. The scope which this provided for deception and fraud was also recognised by some, and a series of frauds and speculations culminated in the notorious collapse of the South Sea Company (incidentally, an entirely legitimate enterprise) in 1719. The governments response was suppression rather than regulation of this new type of enterprise. Under the Royal Exchange and London Assurance Corporation Act of 1720 (more usually referred to as 'The Bubble Act'), any grouping of more than six individuals wishing to form a business but also wishing to retain the right to transfer shares could only do so by obtaining a charter or private act of parliament. The utilisation of the latter form, i.e. the statutory company, for trading purposes dates from the canal construction movement beginning in about 1760. It was during the 1830s and 1840s, when canals were replaced by the economically much more efficient railway system, that we observe the high point in the creation of the statutory company for business purposes.

British legislation on company formation at the beginning of the nineteenth century was, therefore, somewhat restrictive. There was no equivalent legal form during the eighteenth and early nineteenth centuries to that of the French *société en commandite*, which lay somewhere between the two extreme British forms and provided France with a greater flexibility of business forms. Nevertheless, the absence of such a legal form did not prevent Britain from experiencing a period of rapid economic development. Indeed, during most of the period which is conventionally assigned to the industrial revolution in Britain, c.1780-c.1830, these restrictive arrangements remained in place. However, their impact was perhaps not as significant as might first be thought since at this time, and prior to advances in legislation from 1825, an alternative form of business organization, occupying a similar position to that of the French *société en commandite*, emerged. Although of uncertain legal standing, the deed of settlement company was developed to occupy an intermediate position between the limited liability enjoyed by many chartered and statutory companies and the unlimited liability status of common law partnerships. Perhaps in recognition of this, and the need for somewhat greater flexibility, the restrictions on the formation of joint stock companies were removed by the repeal of the 'Bubble' Act in 1825.   With the precise legality of deed of settlement enterprises at common law largely unclear, and the inherent opportunities provided for fraudulent behaviour in relation to joint-stock companies restored, there was a need for further regulation. During the 1830s the British government began to explore the possibility of developing a more formal structure for the conduct of business activity through a select committee chaired by Belenden Ker which reported in 1837. This favoured the creation of a limited liability partnership along the lines of the French *société en commandite*, but no action was taken at this time and it was not until 1907 that this structure was legitimated in the United Kingdom. The need for the limited liability partnership, however, had by 1907 been long since overtaken by events set in train by William Gladstone. A series of irregularities, involving mainly insurance companies, resulted in the establishment of a government select committee chaired by Gladstone in 1841. It recommended the creation of the joint stock company by simple registration under a companies act and compliance with a limited range of formalities. These recommendations were incorporated in the Joint Stock Companies Act 1844. The Limited Liability Act 1855 gave promoters the option of registering with limited liability and the consolidating Companies Act 1862 formed the basis for corporate registrations for almost half a century thereafter.

Whilst some in Britain clearly looked across the Channel for inspiration in developing legislation relating to business forms, it is clear that some in France were similarly observing developments in Britain. Indeed, developments in France during the nineteenth century were along lines not too dissimilar from those in Britain, despite the apparent greater flexibility of legal forms that already existed. The French system, however, was far from adequate for the purposes of the time. Although the 1807 *Code de Commerce* clarified certain distinctions between societies of persons and those of capital which had emerged during the eighteenth century, and firmly established the principle of limited responsibility, both in partnerships and wider associations, it nevertheless had its limitations. In particular, company law, as defined in the 1807 *Code*, is generally considered not to have been particularly conducive to the mobilisation of capital. The requirement that prospective companies should undergo certain formalities, including an investigation by a Committee of the *Conseil d'Etat*, which was both time consuming and expensive, undoubtedly increased the reluctance of some groups to apply for authorisation (Price, 1975, p.146). Thus changes in company legislation were introduced during the middle decades of the nineteenth century. A law of 17 July 1856 substantially revised the articles in the 1807 Code relating to *sociétés en commandite*, giving rise to the *société en commandite par action* (the share-issuing limited partnership), whilst a law of 24 July 1867 modified the 1807 Code as it applied to *sociétés anonymes*. The latter regulation also repealed those sections of the law of 23 May 1863 which had established the *sociétés à responsabilité limitée* (SARL), a business with at least seven members, all having unlimited liability, but whose capital could not exceed FF 20 million.[11]

Despite the advances in legal forms in France and Britain, it is worth noting that the family-run business continued to dominate economic affairs until the end of the nineteenth century and beyond (O'Brien & Keyder, 1978; Wilson, 1995). This was particularly so in the textile industry where, due to the lack of mechanisation, even as late as 1840 it was possible to set up in weaving cloth with about 3000 francs (Price, 1975, p.148). In iron and steel making and mining, however, large capitals and large business organisations began to emerge at a much earlier stage of economic development (the late eighteenth and early nineteenth centuries in Britain, and from the middle decades of the nineteenth century in France) (Caron, 1979). The most usual business form in France throughout the nineteenth century was the *société en nom collectif*. Prior to the legislative changes of 1867, *sociétés anonymes* were rare, only 616 being formed between 1817 and 1867, with 60 per cent of these being railway or canal companies, and 28 per cent in banking and insurance (Caron, 1979, p.78). Of 19,258 companies formed in the 1840-50 period, only 221 (1.05 per cent) were *sociétés anonymes* (Price, 1975, p.146). The lack of legislative control over business formation in Britain prior to 1844 unfortunately makes it impossible to provide comprehensive comparative figures for Britain until the middle of the nineteenth century, although Hunt (1936, p.76) notes that 300 companies were floated between 1834 and 1836. Shannon's study of the first 5,000 limited companies has shown that under the 1844 Companies Act, of the 3,942 companies which provisionally registered without limited liability between November 1844 and July 1856, only 956, 910 English and 46 Irish, completed the second stage and were formally registered (1932, p.397). Under the 1855 Limited Liability Act, 6,161 companies were registered with limited liability between 1856 and 1865, of which 741 had been formed prior to 14 July 1856 (Shannon, 1932, p.421).

The growth of large firms, however, did not alter significantly, at least not before 1870, the preference of French or British business, large or small, for financing expansion out of ploughed-back profits. Self-financing was a function of two things: the inadequacy of the financial system and the desire of owners to retain control over their business. During the eighteenth and early nineteenth century the financial requirements of much of business were relatively modest. In Britain they were supplied from the following sources: personal savings, bank finance, retained profits, loans, trade credit and the admission of additional partners. In France, similar networks proved important:

> The vast majority of businesses were family enterprises, using the savings of family and perhaps friends, and growing, if at all, by means of the re-investment of profits. . . . self-investment was usually a necessity, given the general unwillingness of those with capital to lend or risk it

in the insecure world of the small businessman. (Price,
1975, p.148)

The more highly skewed income distribution in France may have made
it more difficult for certain businesses to obtain funds, and hence
implement innovatory practices, than was the case in Britain.

As industry grew, and with it the need for large amounts of
fixed capital, it is likely that the existing networks proved increasingly
inadequate. The British banking system of the eighteenth and
nineteenth centuries concentrated chiefly on the provision of short-term
loans for the purposes of working capital rather than long-term loans
for fixed capital investment. The lack of involvement of British banks
in capital investment has often been singled out as being a factor in
Britain's lack of dynamism and relative economic decline from the end
of the nineteenth century, but there is still much debate as to whether
under-investment reflected a lack of demand from industry for outside
funds or the failure of the financial institutions to provide an adequate
supply. In France, prior to the 1860s, the banking system was
characterised by three essential traits: geographical fragmentation; an
orientation towards commerce rather than industry; and the
involvement of banks with a very limited range of social groups (Price,
1975, p.152). Traditional, private networks therefore continued to be
more important than the banks up to 1860, but there is some evidence
that financial institutions in general subsequently became more
involved in the supply of industrial finance. In Britain, in the second
half of the nineteenth century, provincial stock exchanges began to
emerge, in addition to that in London, but shares in only a small
number of limited companies were traded prior to 1880, and the main
function of these exchanges was to serve as a secondary market rather
than to help raise new finance.

Throughout the period covered by this study, then, self-
financing remained a key element of much of business development.
However, as Lemarchand (1993a,b) has pointed out in the context of
French business development, it is more difficult to grow through self-
financing within public companies than it is in the case of a family-run
business.[12] Whilst many were forced to call for external investment
and loans, Lemarchand has shown how some industrial concerns,
through the use of appropriate accounting tools, were able to maximise
the 'hidden' part of the profit, in order to provide for the optimal

retention of funds, thereby making self-financing a more feasible proposition.[13]

Legislative requirements relating to accounting

On the face of the legislative requirements, France was prescriptive in relation to accounting long before this was the case in Britain. The first move in France came when, between 1661 and 1683, during the reign of Louis XIV, Colbert embarked upon a number of reforms which were aimed to increase the wealth of the nation through improving industrial activity. According to Miller (1990), a key component of Colbert's innovations related to private enterprise accounting, namely the *Ordonnance de Commerce* of 1673. The architect of this *Ordonnance* was Jacques Savary, and the key element of it, in respect of accounting, was that specified categories of merchants were required to 'keep books'. According to Miller the *Ordonnance*:

> stipulated the types of books to be kept, procedures to be observed in making entries, authentification by a public official, the making of periodic inventories, and the preservation of correspondence. . . .
>
>   . . . Tradesmen, merchants, exchange dealers and bankers were required to keep a journal in the modern sense, a *livre journal* or book of original entry. These books were to be signed on the first and last page by a consul, mayor or alderman, and the pages initialled by his representative (Savary, 1676, p.478). Journals were to be written up consecutively in date order without blank spaces and with nothing written in the margin. New journals were to be opened every six months, at the same time making an inventory of all their effects, and of their accounts receivable and payable. All correspondence was to be kept and filed. (1990, p.324)

Unfortunately, at this stage of research by historians, it is far from clear whether the *Ordonnance* sought to lead business practice or, as in the case of the industrial *règlements*, it merely reflected existing best practice.

In his text *Le Parfait Négociant* (1676), Savary recommended the keeping of different arrays of books depending on whether the merchant was one of substance or alternatively engaged in *commerce médiocre*. Furthermore the array recommended for the former exceeded those stipulated in the 1673 *Ordonnance*. The practical effect of the latter, however, is doubtful. Miller acknowledges, for example, that there:

> were disparities between these programmes for the keeping
> of books [as advocated by authors such as Savary, Irson
> (1678), de la Porte (1685) and Barrême (1680)] and the
> actual practices of merchants. Enforcement of the legal
> requirements was a particular problem. The Ordinance of
> 1673, and even the *Code de Commerce* of 1807 provided
> no administrative machinery for the enforcement of the
> accounting rules it prescribed. Effective control could only
> be exercised *ex post* rather than in a preventative manner.
> (1990, p.326)

The accounting rules laid down by the *Ordonnance* of 1673, and continued in the 1807 *Code de Commerce*, at best provided only an overarching framework for accounting. Books had to be kept, but the exact type of books, and the way in which the entries should be entered up in the ledger, for example, were not covered by the regulations. Therefore, industrial companies which emerged in the eighteenth and nineteenth century, some of which we discuss in chapter 4, were essentially free to establish whatever form of internal accounting system they wished. Moreover, until the law of 1863, there was no legal requirement for a company's accounts to be audited, and even then there was no requirement for the audit to be undertaken by an independent person. It merely required the appointment of one or more auditors who were charged with making a "report to the following annual general meeting on the company's situation, the balance sheets and accounts presented by the directors" (article 15 of the law of 23 May 1863, subsequently retained as article 32 of the 1867 law). It was not until the decree-law of 8 August 1935, that the auditor was required to be a competent, independent professional.

The French Companies Act of 1867 required the communication of a balance sheet and a profit and loss account to the shareholders at the date of the annual general meeting. Article 34 of the

1867 law required each *société anonyme* to prepare a summary of assets
and liabilities every six months and hold it available for the auditor,
relaxing the three month requirement laid down in article 17 of the
1863 law. Furthermore article 34 required each *société anonyme* to
prepare annually: (a) an inventory showing the value of fixed and
movable assets; (b) a balance sheet; and (c) a profit and loss account
(*compte de pertes et profits*, now called the *compte de résultat*).

In Britain, the position during the eighteenth and much of the
nineteenth century was, in theory at least, very much different, and even
when legislation was brought to bear, as in France it related solely to
what we today consider as aspects of financial accounting rather than
with issues of cost calculation. There were two main routes in the
development of accounting requirements in Britain during the period
covered by this study. It was perfectly open for royal charters and
private acts of parliament to impose requirements for accountability on
the managements of these enterprises. Quite naturally, investors who
were increasingly divorced from the organisation which they financed
insisted upon a degree of accountability. The early charters of the East
India Company, for example, contained requirements to account[14], and
the private statutes of canals and railway companies included
increasingly onerous accounting and reporting provisions in the third
and fourth decades of the nineteenth century.

The Companies Clauses Consolidation Act 1845 set out some
indicative provisions which represented a convenient range of
provisions relating to accountability which might be adopted by
companies subsequently incorporating under their own Act of
Parliament. The creation of the registered company in 1844 saw the
immediate introduction of fairly extensive requirements relating to
accountability, including obligations to publish an audited balance
sheet, file it with the Registrar of Companies and circulate it to
members (variable by deed of covenant) 21 days before the general
meeting. These statutory requirements were replaced by more extensive
'adoptive' provisions by the Joint Stock Companies Act 1856. For the
remainder of the nineteenth century, the regulation of registered
companies, in general, was a matter for private negotiation between
owners and management for inclusion in the articles of association.
During this period, however, statutory provisions for accountability
were introduced for particular categories of company (e.g. railway
companies in 1867/8, life assurance companies in 1870, gas companies
in 1871, banks in 1879, and electricity companies in 1882). It is

interesting to note, in the context of this study, that standardised accounting requirements were introduced in a number of these cases in order to improve comparability between companies and years, despite the fact that this type of framework was not introduced for companies in general until the passage of a major Companies Act in 1981. At this latter date, the initiative was designed to give local effect to the provisions of the Fourth Directive on Company Law issued by the European Parliament.

Overall we would contend that, despite the longer tradition of government legislation relating to business structures and accounting, there is little evidence to support the view that industrial enterprises in France should have kept their accounts in a manner different from that of similar enterprises in Britain. There was nothing in the French legislation handed down from Colbert that required the use of any particular form of accounting, leaving the issue entirely up to those running the business, as was the case in Britain.

III.   Conclusion

This chapter has examined modern views as to the relative economic performance of France and Britain up to the end of the nineteenth century, and investigated possible explanations for the similarities and differences. Attention has been focused on the underlying economic and social factors associated with the prevailing orthodoxy of mercantilism in the seventeenth and eighteenth centuries and the gradual move towards a *laissez-faire* approach in the nineteenth century. The impact of these orthodoxies in a number of areas, including business legislation, including that relating to accounting, provides the background for our comparative study of the development of accounting literature and accounting practice in industrial enterprises up to 1880. Two key findings are worth remembering before we embark upon these investigations: Britain's industrial development dates from c.1780, whereas that in France only dates from c.1830; and that despite the greater regulation of industry in France under mercantilism, there is little direct evidence that this had any real influence on the way in which French firms kept their accounts.

Notes

1   Within this chapter, the reader will note that the references are
     often to England rather than Britain. This is not out of any
     deliberate attempt to slight the Celtic fringes of Britain
     (Scotland, Ireland and Wales), but rather to reflect the tenor of
     the literature cited. Many historians of economic development
     and/or mercantilism, when referring to the eighteenth or
     nineteenth centuries, invariably refer to England rather than
     Britain. Since it can not always be assumed that the points
     made will necessarily apply equally to the Celtic fringes,
     where authors refer to England, when there work is discussed,
     our references will be to this entity rather than Britain.
     Elsewhere in this chapter, where more general points are being
     made, as elsewhere in the book, Britain will be used.

2   This view was recognised at the time, for example, by the
     Marquis de Biencourt (quoted in Crouzet, 1990, p. 142).

3   Cassis (1995, p. 5) considers that O'Brien & Keyder's claim
     that French productivity remained higher than in Britain until
     the 1890s is based on figures which are overestimates.
     However, he goes on to indicate that they are "at least an
     indication that France's productivity levels in manufacturing
     industry were not far behind Britain's in the nineteenth
     century."

4   Despite these differences, and Britain's lead, however, both
     Britain and France were facing a similar threat at the end of the
     nineteenth century, namely they "were already losing their
     position as the two leading industrial nations" (Cassis, 1995, p.
     28).

5   For further details relating to the development of this
     company, see chapter 4.

6   As the study of Decazeville in chapter 4 below shows,
     however, the use of immigrants, whilst often necessary, at least
     in the initial stages of establishing an enterprise or industry,
     could be something of a two edged sword. As well as bringing
     technology and skills, they also brought different cultures and
     work practices which were not always ideally suited to their
     host country. Thus, once they had fulfilled their task, by
     establishing plants and training local workers, they might then
     be discarded because of their 'disruptive' ideas.

7   In many respects, of course, the impact of canals and railways was similar in Britain, although again it can be argued that developments in Britain pre-dated those in France by a few decades, the canal era, for example, really dating from the late eighteenth century, rather than the early nineteenth century. There was, therefore, a difference of degree here once again in favour of more economic development in Britain.

8   In his study of the development of the Tubeuf industrial enterprise in the late eighteenth century, Lewis (1993) notes the fact that many of the textile manufacturers in the Nimes and Lyon area began to produce cheaper, poorer quality cloths in order to survive.

9   The information on French legislation contained in this section is based largely on Mikol (1993).

10   These *sociétés* were established in large measure to allow nobles to become involved, albeit at arms length, with industrial development. Strictly speaking, prior to 1789, nobles in France were not supposed to be engaged in activities whose essential purpose was the making of money. Since the position of a noble was one of honour, gained through service to the king, especially in the field of arms, any noble found to be engaged in making money and transgressing the judicial concept of *dérogeance* would lose his noble status. Whilst in the case of old established families such loss of status only applied during the lifetime of the transgressor, since it also involved the loss of very real tax privileges guaranteed by noble status, degrading activity was generally avoided. Over time, however, involvement in certain money-making activities, such as sea-borne commerce (1669), large-scale commerce (1701), mining, glass-making and metallurgy (1722), were exempted from *dérogeance*. The creation of *sociétés en commandite*, enabled nobles to become sleeping partners, i.e. they could provide finance, and hence enjoy dividends, without having any responsibility for, or direct concern in, the day-to-day affairs of the business (Price, 1975, pp. 142-3).

11   The SARL of 1863 is generally considered to have been based on the model of the British joint stock company, though the modern French SARL is based on the German GmbH.

---

12   The same was the case in Britain. At the Dowlais ironworks in
         Wales, for example, G.T. Clark, the managing trustee who
         controlled the business from 1856 through to the 1890s, noted
         that because the works was family-owned, he was able to
         retain funds for the purpose of investment which would not
         have been possible if the enterprise had been a joint stock
         concern with shareholders pressing for the distribution of
         dividend payments.

13   In Britain, however, the use of secret reserves is seen to have
         been rather more of a twentieth century phenomenon (Edwards
         and Boyns, 1994).

14   In France, the statutes of companies such as that of Saint-
         Gobain carried detailed provisions relating to accounting from
         the beginning of the eighteenth century (see chapter 4 below).

Chapter 3 - The development of accounting literature prior to 1880

I.   The contribution of double entry bookkeeping

Historical studies of the accounting literature have emphasised the importance of texts espousing the virtues of double entry bookkeeping, though noting that, alternative methods, such as single-entry, have been put forward by certain authors from time to time. Double entry methods remain in widespread use today, testimony to the fact that proposed alternative methods were never able to usurp the position it had established within the accounting literature over several centuries. The longevity of double entry bookkeeping methods suggests some obvious superiority over the alternatives, though it is not entirely clear to some authors exactly what these advantages might be. Is it due to certain inherent beneficial characteristics of the method, or is its longevity merely a reflection of the methods flexibility in adjusting to the different needs of various groups at different points in history?

Yamey has noted claims that double entry has three main advantages over the earlier methods of record-keeping:

> First the records are more comprehensive and orderly; second, the duality of entries provides a convenient check on the accuracy or completeness of the ledger; third, the ledger including as it does personal, real and nominal accounts in an integrated whole, contains the materials for developing, as part of the system, statements of profit-and-loss and of capital, assets and liabilities. (Littleton and Yamey, 1956, p.7)

Despite this, it is questioned whether any or all of these attributes were likely to have provided the spur for the development of double entry bookkeeping. Whilst it is recognised that the first two qualities 'were much appreciated', Yamey is far from convinced that the third played a significant role. Whilst some writers have suggested that double entry has advantages in relation to the recording of capital and the calculation of overall profit, Yamey's view is that the total capital of an enterprise and the periodic profit made "can be derived independently of a system of double-entry bookkeeping" (1964, p.120). Indeed, in these respects, he argues that double entry has no inherent superiority over other types of record keeping. Moreover :

> the double-entry system does little more than provide a framework into which accounting data can be fitted and within which the data can be arranged, grouped or re-grouped. The system does not, by itself determine the range of data to be included in a particular setting, nor impose a particular pattern of internal ordering and re-ordering of the data. (Yamey, 1964, p.127)

The greatest advantage of double entry bookkeeping then "lies in its comprehensiveness and its possibilities for the orderly arrangement of data" (Yamey, 1964, p.133). Whilst this aids routine administration and the control of assets, Yamey urges caution over emphasising the superiority of double entry in such respects: "A system of single entry, with personal accounts for debtors and creditors as well as a cash account, provides a large part of the information necessary in routine administration" (1964, p.134). Much is often made of the fact that the double entry system provides an arithmetical check on the accuracy of account books. though Yamey does not consider this to be 'a major consideration' in relation to its use by business. In many respects, the checks, he believes, can be provided by records kept under systems other than double entry (1964, pp.135-6).

With regard to the issue of using accounting information as a basis for making decisions, Yamey is sceptical of the ability of double entry bookkeeping to provide any help. Indeed, he stresses that the methods advocated in the accounting literature were best suited to the activities of merchants, with their generally discontinuous series of diverse transactions. Thus "*particularized* merchandise accounting" is seen as a form of 'perpetual inventory' rather than as a means of calculating profit on individual transactions or consignments (1949, p.113). Since the next activity of the merchant may be unrelated to the last, there was no way in which any analysis of past profits could provide a guide to future results. Only when "the economic activities of the firm are more or less continuous and specialized to a limited range" (Yamey, 1949, p.113) could the past provide a guide to the future, and hence would the calculation of costs and profits of various items provide information with the potential for decision-making purposes. For the texts examined, Yamey concluded that the writers "placed no great value on double-entry on account of the subdivision of the profit which it made possible" (Yamey, 1949, p.112). This last observation, at least, appears somewhat biased. Whilst Yamey stresses that the illustrative examples contained in these texts concentrated on one-off activities, i.e. situations where successful operation depended upon making profits whenever, wherever, and in whatever line opportunity offered (1949, p.113), there are, in fact, a number of texts which show the calculation of profits from different products.

As a result of his studies, Yamey is not convinced by the thesis put forward by Sombart that the growth and development of double entry bookkeeping was closely tied up with the rise of capitalism. Under the Sombart thesis, systematic or scientific accounting, identified with double entry bookkeeping, is seen to have played a significant role in the development of capitalism, either as a causal or, at least, a predisposing factor. This thesis rests on three planks: by transforming assets into abstract values and by expressing quantitatively the results of business activities, double entry bookkeeping clarified the aims of acquisitive business; it provided the rational basis on which the capitalist could choose the directions in which to employ his capital to best advantage; and it made possible the separation of the business firm from its owners and hence the growth of large joint-stock businesses (based on Yamey, 1964, p.117; 1949, p.100). Yamey attempts to show that, in all three regards, the impact of double entry was small. On the issue of 'abstraction', Yamey argues that the transferring of actualities ("the true realities of commerce") into money values ("book-keeping ciphers"), would make decision-making more, rather than less, difficult (1964, p.123). Yamey's examination of double entry ledgers for the seventeenth and eighteenth century convinced him that, rather than leading to a withering away of the commercial realities, the detailed entries, buttressed by those in the journals, enabled businessmen to keep a close check on them (1964, pp.124-5).[1] On the link between the development of double entry and the separation of the 'firm' from its proprietors, Yamey is also somewhat sceptical. He notes, for example, that many partnerships or firms existed before double entry was invented and many others were able to survive afterwards without its use. Indeed:

> some capitalistic joint-stock companies have functioned for long periods without double entry; these include the Dutch East India Company, the Sun Fire Insurance Office of London, the Whitin Machine Company in the United States, and the Capital and Counties Bank in England. (Yamey, 1964, p.126)

Nevertheless, Yamey notes that partnerships could have important influences on accounting practices, such as the need for a clear distinction between business expenses on the one hand and personal or household expenses on the other. In sole proprietorships, the mingling of personal and business accounts was often of no real account, but in a partnership any mingling might make difficult the identification of the respective rights of each investor. However, this need for separation in partnerships occurs, "irrespective of the type of bookkeeping employed" (Yamey, 1964, p.127) and is not an issue specifically related to the rise of double entry.

    Yamey's criticism of the Sombart view is that double-entry bookkeeping was not fundamental to the development of capitalism, since it does not appear to have been a necessary condition. More recently, Hoskin and Macve (1988a) have suggested that the development of accounting since the end of the eighteenth century cannot be seen in economic rationalist terms. For them the rise of accounting was not the practical response of men faced with new entrepreneurial and organizational challenges, since "no 'practical' man would have invented modern accounting practice [the outputs of which are not obviously what is needed for such purposes...]" (1988a, p.68). They are particularly critical of the problems associated with measuring overall financial performance through the calculation of profit and loss and the attempts which have been made to try and reduce the limitations of such measurements. For Hoskin and Macve, refinement of profit and loss measures is a waste of time, and should be abandoned (1988, p.68). Their explanation for the continued fixation of accounting with attempts to perfect profit and loss measures is that accounting represents a mode of 'writing the world', embodying "the power relations and the knowledge relations of a disciplinary and self-disciplinary culture" (1988, p.68).

Whilst they do not necessarily accept wholeheartedly the Sombart thesis, many accounting historians have clearly indicated a link between the development of accounting, especially that of accounting for costs, and the rise of industrial activity. Although double entry bookkeeping was first developed to serve the needs of merchants in the fourteenth and fifteenth centuries, it is clear that accounting developments were generated, albeit slowly, perhaps somewhat too slowly, as a result of industrialisation. As industrialisation began to gain pace in parts of Europe during the eighteenth century, there was a need for developments in accounting ideas to cope with the changing needs of users. There are times, however, when the accounting literature seems to have had difficulty in keeping up with such changes. If one is to accept the conclusions of previous writers then the major problems occurred during the late eighteenth and nineteenth century, at the time when the main industrialisation drive was beginning to develop in Europe. Solomons (1952, p.1), for example, notes that during the period prior to industrialisation, when the merchant was king and economic activity was restricted largely to buying and selling, accounting texts were perfectly adequate since they were written solely with the merchant in mind. Furthermore, since "manufacturing processes were [largely] in the hands of small craftsmen closely controlled by the rules of their guilds, there was little scope for anything worthy of the name of industrial accounting" (1952, p.1). During the eighteenth and nineteenth centuries, however, the advent of industrialisation led to different demands being placed upon accounting, but these failed to be reflected in the accounting literature. Solomons therefore identifies two phases in the development of accounting literature:

> The first part, covering the period from the early fourteenth century down to the third quarter of the nineteenth is largely, though by no means only, concerned with bringing the records of industrial activity within the compass of double-entry book-keeping, and of extending the scope of that system to cover transactions, such as the transfer of materials from process to process *within* a business, which its early practitioners had never had in view. By 1875 or thereabouts, that technical problem had been completely solved. The second part of the story, which spans the three-quarters of a century down to our own day, is concerned, not with a rather narrow technical problem in book-

keeping, but with the broader issue of making the
accounting records mean something, of making them
flexible and capable of providing information which would
be significant not for one purpose (say, the measurement of
profit or loss) or two (say, in addition, the fixing of selling
prices) but for any of the purposes which, in modern
business, figures may be called upon to serve. In the earlier
period, there is really a single line of development which it
is not too difficult to trace. In the later period, however, the
trail divides . . . (1952, p.2)

There is a clear indication then, that the needs created by
industrialisation were not being served by the accounting literature of
the late eighteenth and early nineteenth centuries. With Britain being
the first country to experience rapid industrialisation from c.1760, it
was there that the needs were felt most but, perhaps somewhat
surprisingly, it was in other countries that the literature in relation to the
development of industrial accounting seems to have evolved most
rapidly. Initially, of course, the publication of books describing double
entry in one country were influenced by books published in other
countries. Thus (1977), for example, has noted that prior to the
seventeenth century, and indeed up to the 1630s, it is possible to discern
a foreign influence upon English bookkeeping manuals describing
double entry bookkeeping. Thereafter, however, despite the fact that
they often lagged behind practice, English treatises were "based
essentially on the English experience" (Chatfield, 1977, p.57). Few of
these texts indicated any major concern with the accounting needs of
industry, however, continuing to explain double entry bookkeeping in
relation to the commercial activity of merchants.

Despite French economic development lagging behind that in
Britain, however, both Edwards and Solomons have noted that the
French accounting literature of the early nineteenth century was
somewhat in advance of the British literature, both in the areas of farm
accounting and industrial accounting (Solomons, 1952, pp.12-16).
Authors such as Payen, Godard-Desmarest and Mézières, in the first
half of the nineteenth century, began to write texts containing ideas and
discussions that were clearly in advance of any British texts. In
Solomons' view, during the same period, "Little seems to have been
published in England . . . which could be dignified by the name of
industrial accounting" (1952, p.16). Indeed, most accounting texts

merely imitated earlier works. Thus, in a study of the link between the rise of scientific bookkeeping and capitalism, Yamey noted that "The accounting manuals in the period under review [i.e. up to the 1840s] reveal striking uniformities in accounting technique in the nature of the examples used in illustration, and in their general tone" (1949, p.100). It has been argued by Chatfield that the impact of textbooks during the seventeenth and eighteenth century was to standardise accounting practice. Thus:

> By the eighteenth century Italian bookkeeping had become dominant and fairly uniform throughout Western Europe . . . Most of the methods described in early accounting treatises were like those used today. But record keeping was emphasized rather than analysis, and description rather than tabulation. The important topics in modern books - asset valuation, income finding, financial statements - took up very little space in most texts written before 1850. Cost accounting was hardly mentioned; double entry bookkeeping was considered almost entirely from the viewpoint of mercantile traders. (Chatfield, 1977, p.58)

During the last three decades of the nineteenth century, however, Solomons discerns evidence of a significant change, as a result of the occurrence of "what can only be described as a costing renaissance in the English speaking world" (1952, p.17). Following Solomons' line of argument, Chatfield (1977) has argued that, in the English-speaking world, texts on cost accounting did not appear until the end of the nineteenth century. The first such text is identified by him as being that by the American, Captain Henry Metcalfe (1885), *The cost of manufactures*. Two years later this was followed by the first text in Britain, *Factory Accounts*, by Garcke and Fells (1887), itself followed two years later by Norton's *Textile Manufacturers' Bookkeeping*. Wells (1977, p.48), however, considers that the accolade for the first text published in Britain should really go to Thomas Battersby, a Manchester public accountant, who published a book in 1878 entitled *The perfect double entry book-keeper (abridged), and the perfect prime cost and profit demonstrator (on the departmental system), for iron and brass founders, machinists, engineers, ship-builders, manufacturers, etc.*

II.   The development of the accounting literature in
Britain to 1880

The conventional wisdom

According to Chatfield, by 1800 over 100 treatises had been published in England, many in multiple editions. Most advocated double entry bookkeeping, but some were critical of this method, Edward Jones' *English system of bookkeeping by single or double entry* (1796) being probably the most well known of these (Yamey, 1956). Although Chatfield considered that the aims which motivated Jones to write his book, namely to try and combine the simplicity of single entry bookkeeping with the comprehensiveness of the Italian method, were 'on the right track', he notes that the "English system was never widely used in England (or anywhere), and was later repudiated by its author" (1977, p.57). However, in Chatfield's assessment, the popularity of Jones' book did lead to an examination and criticism of traditional accounting procedures which ultimately "furthered the tendency of bookkeeping to become statistical rather than descriptive" (1977, p.58). Overall, however, texts on single entry did not generate any serious threat to double entry bookkeeping and the literature came to be dominated by texts on the latter subject.

The English texts on accounting, whether published in the eighteenth or nineteenth centuries, however, largely ignored the problems of manufacturers, concentrating instead on the activities of merchants and traders. Thus, in his review of the development of the cost accounting literature, R.S. Edwards noted that:

> The bookkeeping literature of the 18th and 19th centuries abounds with examples of consignment accounts, voyage accounts and accounts showing the profit on the sale of different types of commodities by the same business. These types of transactions had required recording for centuries and Italian, German, Dutch, French and English writers have left a legacy of textbooks to show that the needs of the day were met. (1937b, p.193)

Until the nineteenth century, then, the accounting problems faced were considered by Edwards "not [to be] beyond the competence of the bookkeeper trained in the rather simple rules of 'double-entry'" (1937b, p.193). Indeed, even in manufacturing businesses, until industry was revolutionised by power machinery and the growth of communications, their activities were generally easy to cater for. It was with "the development of iron manufacture, engineering, coal mining and the textiles, [that] the accountants' problems began" (Edwards, 1937b, p.193). In the late eighteenth century the size of enterprises in iron manufacture began to rise. Often vertically integrated, such enterprises involved the investment of a large amount of fixed capital, generating a new set of problems for accounting:

> A series of costly processes between the raw material and the finished product, a dead weight of fixed cost which could not be shifted in bad times, a large body of labour to be paid and watched. The iron master would want to have details of his raw materials on hand at all times in order to be sure that production was not going to be held up; on the other hand he would wish to see that capital was not being tied up unnecessarily by holding stocks which were too large. He would require information as to the expenditure and output of the different processes, in order to keep a check on waste and inefficiency. He would need a system of check in order to prevent the fraud and error possible with a large pay roll. In ascertaining his profit or loss at the end of the year, the problem of depreciation of the factory and plant would arise. Lastly it would be necessary to know the minimum to which prices should be cut in bad times and this would involve a knowledge of the variable, or so-called 'prime' costs, per unit of output. The problem of 'overhead' had come into being. (1937b, p.193)

According to Edwards, it was the engineering trades, after the mid-nineteenth century, that provided the most fruitful field for cost accounting, since here, although firms were not large, estimating and tendering for contracts were key features of the trade, leading to job or contract costing (Edwards, 1937b, p.194).

Despite the growth of industrial activity throughout the eighteenth century, few early accounting texts undertook any significant consideration of the accounting issues related to manufacturing activity. The conventional wisdom, based primarily on the seminal writings of

Edwards (1937a, 1937b) and Solomons (1952)[2] is that just ten English language texts focused on aspects of cost/industrial accounting prior to the costing renaissance which is seen to commence circa 1870.[3] These were: John Collins (1697), Roger North (1714), James Dodson (1750), John Mair (1760), Wardhaugh Thompson (1777), Robert Hamilton (1777/9), Frederick William Cronhelm (1818), George Jackson (1836), Frederick Charles Krepp (1858) and Joseph Sawyer (1862).

Collins (1697) demonstrated the application of double entry bookkeeping to the internal transfer of raw materials employed in dying from a stock account to a process account.[4] Dodson (1750) provided a remarkably clear illustration of a shoe-maker's accounts, wherein he recommends the segregation of different kinds of transactions through the use of separate books, e.g. a workman's ledger, a cash sales book, etc., something which "was by no means a commonplace feature of accounting systems of his time" (Solomons, 1952, p.3). Whilst Dodson's example dealt with what is now referred to as 'batch' costing, Wardhaugh Thompson, in 1777, provided an early description of process costing through the use of an example of the manufacture of 'thread-hosiery' under the putting-out system. Thompson, like Dodson, was not concerned with internal transactions, but with transactions with outsiders, and according to Edwards (1937b, p.253) there was no question of the need to allocate the costs of a factory between different activities.[5]

Though they failed to deal with the issue of internal transfers, Dodson and Thompson's works, written as they were prior to the advent of the factory and power machinery, were clearly adequate for the circumstances of the period (Edwards, 1937b, p.253). It was left to later works, however, for the issue of internal transfers to be considered. Thus Cronhelm (1818) illustrated internal transfers within the activities of a woollen cloth manufacturer, but in terms only of physical quantities,[6] while Jackson (1836) emphasised the need to open a manufacturing account to record resources consumed, including transfers of raw materials from the stock account. Krepp (1858), on the other hand, argued the need to maintain books for raw materials and finished goods in terms of both quantities and values,[7] while Sawyer (1862) reflected on the appropriate method of costing transfers of hides in the process of tanning. Despite the inclusion of these later works, it was the text of Hamilton (1777/9) which was by far the most advanced (Mepham, 1988) in demonstrating the process cost accounts associated with the manufacture of linen, including the use of transfer prices based on market value and an interest charge to reflect the cost of capital employed.

The original assessment of Hamilton's work, most notably that of Edwards (1937b), was based on the contents of the second edition of his text, *An Introduction to Merchandise*, published in 1788. Consequently, Edwards' view of Hamilton's work (see also Solomons, 1952, p.7) does not adequately reflect the advanced nature of the latter's thoughts on costing issues, since the section on costs in the second edition was a much condensed version of the material presented in the first edition (Mepham, 1988). Using present day terminology, Mepham shows that the range of topics addressed by Hamilton included: flow production and process costings; transfer pricing (where market price was favoured); joint costs and decision-making; rate of return calculations; residual income; and interest as an opportunity cost. Mepham suggests that the costing material was removed from his second edition due to a lack of space following the reduction from two volumes to a single one.[8]   The essence of Hamilton's approach is alternatively summed up in his own words:

> When a person is engaged in several branches of manufacture, whether on different materials, or on the same materials through several successive stages, he should keep his books in such a manner as to *exhibit the gain or loss* on each . . .
> If all these branches of business were necessarily connected, and the manufacturer had no other choice than to purchase the rough flax, and carry on the successive operations, it would be sufficient to keep his books in a form that should exhibit the gain or loss on the whole; but if he has the *opportunity of beginning or desisting at any stage of the manufacture*, his books should exhibit the gain or loss on each operation separately. (1788, pp.487-8 - emphasis added)

Basing his assessment on the contents of the second edition, Edwards criticised Hamilton for failing to provide any "details of the particular application, and the number and form of the subsidiary books as these 'will be different, according to the nature and extent of the business'" (1937b, p.253). Thus, in his first edition, Hamilton had shown what Edwards suspected, namely that, given the "clarity of other examples in the same book, one might well believe that Dr. Hamilton could have put his general principles into practice" (Edwards, 1937b, p.253).

It is perhaps of interest to note that the first edition of Hamilton's book sets, as an exercise through which the reader can develop his skills based on the material contained in the book, the following:

> a brewer purchases barley, and converts it into malt; he also occasionally purchases and sells malt; he carries on the different branches of strong-ale - small beer, and porter-brewing; and desires a form of book-keeping that shall exhibit his expenses and sales, his debts and credits, the quantities malt obtained from barley, the quantities bought, sold, or consumed, the quantities beer of different kinds obtained from malt, and compared with the price of the barley, and in comparison of the profit on different branches of his business?

Although this exercise has roots based in farming, brewing is clearly a manufacturing activity, and this illustrates Hamilton's view that the brewer would be concerned with calculating profits on different products. Hamilton apart, it was not until well into the nineteenth century that other writers began to refer to this issue. One writer who exhorted manufacturers to be able to correctly analyse the expense of the several processes of any manufacture was Babbage (1832), but again he provided little guidance as to how this objective was to be achieved. In Solomons' judgement, it must be doubted if accountants of that time would have been "commonly able to provide the cost information which Babbage so clearly saw to be desirable.." (1952, p.9).

Referring to developments, or more correctly the lack of development, in the nineteenth century, Edwards considered it "difficult to account for the absence of works on industrial accountancy during the next eighty or ninety years [after Hamilton]" (1937b, p.254). Works such as those of Cronhelm (1818); Jackson (1836); Krepp (1858); and Sawyer (1862) did consider some aspects of the problems facing manufacturers, but generally these were minor works and outside the mainstream of accounting texts which ignored industrial accounting and concentrated on commercial accounting. Edwards considers that an obscure book by Battersby (1878) was a noteworthy attempt to bring into job costing expenses which cannot be traced directly to individual contracts. Edwards' overall conclusion, however, was that these works merely indicated a lack of concern with the problems of manufacturers, resulting in a wide variety of practice of industrial accounting, much of which was incapable of dealing with the problems faced:

> It would appear that the late eighteenth century had produced an accounting technique adequate to deal with industry built up on the domestic system, but the Industrial Revolution had not yet [by the 1870s] brought in its train an accounting service aimed at resolving the 'fixed cost problem'. (Edwards, 1937b, p.255)

The early British literature revisited

Through an examination of the contents of The Herwood Library of Accountancy[9] and the rare book collection of the Institute of Chartered Accountants in England and Wales, we have been able to determine whether or not the findings of Edwards and Solomons, as supplemented by Mepham, remain a fair reflection of the state of the British literature now available for the period of study. The starting point for our investigation was those books whose title indicated the possible inclusion of material on accounting for the transactions of a 'factory' or a 'manufacturer', although we also examined books where the title contained a phrase which indicated that the methods being advanced were applicable to all kinds of business. Our investigation soon revealed that inclusion of the word factory in the title was unlikely to signal that the book dealt with accounting in a manufacturing context. Throughout the eighteenth century and into the nineteenth century, the term factor was used to describe an agent working overseas on behalf of a UK trader, and the derivative term 'factory' was used to signify the operations of such a factor. Books which used the term manufacturer or manufactory in the title, however, turned out to yield important evidence, such as those by Gordon (1770), Wood (c. 1777), Comins (1814) Smith (1840), Henderson (1841), Tuck (1856), and Hamilton and Ball (1869). The contribution which these, and later, publications make to our understanding of the way in which costing transactions were incorporated in the books of account will now be considered.

In general, the accounting texts published up to the middle of the nineteenth century are devoted to extolling the virtues of double entry bookkeeping,[10] though some recognise the continued merit of single entry bookkeeping for smaller organisations, typically retailers. The principal focus of these texts is transactions undertaken by merchants but, over time, there is a growing attempt to expand their appeal in three separate ways. This enables us to divide these texts into three separate categories, depending on the method of expansion used:

(1)   Those books which include, in addition to merchants' accounts, exercises or sections of the text detailing procedures appropriate for one or more of: wholesalers (e.g. Tuck, 1843); retailers (e.g. Monteage, 1675); and factors (e.g. Carpenter, 1632) or agents acting on behalf of principals. They neither refer to nor tackle manufacturing activities.

(2)   Those books which are specially prepared for particular types of activities and entities including: rent gatherers (Monteage, 1683); landed estates (North, 1714); shipping (Liddel, 1803); banking (Lowrie, 1809); schools (Morrison, 1810); executors (Highmore, 1821); housekeepers (Kitchener, c. 1830); tanners (Sawyer, 1862).[11] It is not until the costing renaissance that we find books specifically devoted to the affairs of manufacturers.

(3)   Those books where authors, in an endeavour to obtain a wider readership for primarily merchant-based texts, outline the 'general principles' (usually illustrated using the accounts of a merchant) of accounting and claim that, once these are mastered, they can be applied to a wide range of businesses, which are sometimes specified (e.g. Gordon (1770), Wood (c. 1777), Comins (1814) Smith (1840), Henderson (1841), Tuck (1856), and Hamilton and Ball (1869)). Even where books do refer specifically to manufacturers, the numerical examples provided are nearly always based on the activities of merchants, retailers or wholesalers, i. e. they rarely use a manufacturing organisation for illustrative purposes, thereby avoiding the problem of accounting for internal transfers by confining their example to external transactions.

Of these three categories, clearly only the third is of relevance to this study, and the relatively few examples of this form demonstrate the relative paucity of material relating to industrial accounting in Britain prior to c.1870. There is, however, something of a paradox here in that, despite the lack of texts dealing with industrial accounting, many writers clearly recognised the increasing importance to Britain of manufacturing. Henry Tuck, for example, made reference to:

> the whole of the wealth of this country derived from mines, collieries, fisheries, colonies, agriculture, and manufacturers, as well as the produce brought from foreign lands ... . (1856 p.12)

However, his book, published under the promising title, *The manual of book-keeping; or, practical instructions to the manufacturer*, even as late as the eighth edition contains no practical examples based on the activities of a manufacturer, or even any additional narrative direction as to how manufacturers should tackle their peculiar problems. The impression that there are no specific problems peculiar to manufacturers is also conveyed by Krepp:

> "the MANUFACTURERS' SYSTEM, in its main features, is identical to that drawn up for Tradesmen, except for more extensive manufacturers, who probably find it to their advantage to follow the MERCHANTS' SYSTEM" . (1858, p.151)

The idea that manufacturers' bookkeeping requirements were similar to those of traders or merchants also received explicit recognition from Hamilton and Ball (1869, p.32) who concluded that 'commercial accounts' are not really different. Given the assumption that records should be confined to external transactions, this is a reasonable conclusion which, moreover, explains the lack of specific attention to the bookkeeping practices of manufacturing concerns in the accounting texts before 1880.

Not all the texts of the pre-1880 period unearthed in the course of our search take this line. In several cases, these texts contain a discussion of how double entry bookkeeping can be utilised to cope with the special accounting problems facing a manufacturer. According to Smith:

> In the several works that have been published, I have never noticed any observations relative to a DR and CR Manufacturing Account, and as I am perfectly convinced Double Entry Book-Keeping would be found of the very *utmost utility* to manufacturers, and particularly those in extensive business, it will be no more than right to allude to the subject.

> In an DR and CR MANUFACTURE ACCOUNT you debit all *material*, *wages*, and *other expenses*, in getting up the goods, and credit the account with the *amount of your sales* - the difference is your profit; but in those cases where a manufacturer is also a merchant - when he ships his own manufactures - has two distinct concerns - and wishes to see his profit arising from *each*,[12] it is advisable to pursue the above plan as regards his manufactory, and when the goods are transferred into his mercantile warehouse, GENERAL GOODS ACCOUNT must have debit for the amount, the same receiving credit by any ultimate customer. (1840)

And Henderson:

> It is sometimes thought, that double entry may be a proper mode of book-keeping for merchants; it cannot be advantageously applied to such modes of business as manufacturing, retailing, etc. This I conceive to be a mistake. It appears to me that it *can* and *ought* to be applied to *every* mode of business whatever, since, in all, its use would be attended with advantages which can never appertain to single entry ... .

> In the case of a manufacturer, the profits are, of course, the difference between the cost of the raw material, wages of labour, wear and tear of machinery, rent of buildings, &c. , and the price obtained for the manufactured article. Take, as an example, a cotton

spinner. Here nominal accounts may be opened for each article of expenditure, as cotton, wages, machinery, &c, all being balanced by a 'twist account', which receives on its Credit side all the sales of twist, and on its Dr. side all the various expenses; the nominal accounts of general expenses, bills, cash, discount and interest, profit and loss, and stock, existing as matters of course. In all cases of manufacturing, the wear and tear of machinery form important items of cost, and much care should be taken, in balancing the books, to estimate it as correctly as possible ... . Many extensive manufacturers keep their books on double-entry, though it is by no means so general as it might be (1841, p.105).

Wood (c. 1778), in a chapter on manufacturer's accounts (pp.185-200), provided an indicative list of books that a manufacturer ought to keep, recognising that no "two houses proceed exactly in the same manner, or make use of the same books" (p.187).[13] However, as in the case of most other texts, Wood is silent on the practical operation of the system described.

Our research has also shown that the British literature contains examples, additional to those indicated by Edwards and Solomons, of attempts to build up cost figures where goods are transferred between operations. Gordon (1770, pp.260-7), for example, gives an example of operations under the 'putting out' system. Two individuals, Abraham and Benjamin, join in partnership to purchase linen, lawns, gauzes and Holland, which are then to be bleached and sold. The goods are 'put out' to Alexander Colvin for bleaching. A separate account is opened for each of the four products, and the cost of bleaching is debited and sales proceeds credited; each of the accounts also contains columns for physical quantities as debit and credit. The balances on the four accounts are transferred to a profit and loss account at the end of the year and divided equally between the partners after crediting them (debit profit and loss) with charges paid on behalf of the firm.

In the preface to *The science of commerce ... To which is added a selection of new systems, plans, and forms of accounts, for anonymous co-partnership, manufacturers* (1814), Comins makes numerous references to manufacturing activities which include: "I shew the learner how to buy, cure, manufacture, and export beef, pork, butter, hides, skins, linen, corn" (xix); and "I have written a new and most

useful system of conducting the Butter business; and for the particular
advantage and convenience of Manufacturers, Wholesale Warehouses
and Shopkeepers" (xx). The book traces the transactions of a business at
various stages in its development through the year 1807-1808. Of
particular interest are pages 157-97 which give:

> a general view of the most mercantile mode of conducting
> and carrying on the whole import and export trade of
> Ireland, particularly that of beef, pork, butter, hides and
> skins, corn and linen business, will be seen by a reference
> to, and a perusal of the invoice-book, page 71, and sales-
> book, page 91. The former shews the exports, the latter the
> imports; the method of calculating the first cost, charges,
> and loss or gain on a given quantity, (or on any quantity
> proportioned thereto) of beef, pork, butter, hides, and
> skins, which I bought, manufactured, and exported; the
> various pieces it was cut in, the casks they were put in, the
> number of pieces put into each cask, and the iron hoops
> that bound them; the quantity and kinds of provisions the
> green beef and pork should produce when manufactured,
> suitable for the army, navy, Indies and merchants' use or
> service, and how to keep a complete check on the entire
> quantity manufactured and exported. (Comins, 1814,
> pp.xlviii-xlix)

The elements of profit (other than 5% on investment in pork - see
below) recognised at 31 August 1807 are journalised (Journal Entry I)
on p.167:

<u>Journal Entry I</u>

	£	s	d
Merchandise	1,988.	16.	3
Charges	1,170.	5.	4
Pork	566.	10.	0
Roe and Ramsey, gained on exchange	83.	18.	3
Butter	143.	9.	4
Commission	1,761.	9.	11
	5,714.	19.	1

The use of transfer prices by Comins may be illustrated by reference to the calculation of the profit on pork. The ledger account for pork naturally includes purchases of pigs and the sales proceeds from their produce. Also, as is often the case, the ledger account includes quantity columns for control purposes. The journal entry (Journal Entry II) dated 31st August, however, which debits pork and credits salt, charges, casks, interest, profit and commission with the following amounts, is of most significance.

Certain inferences may be drawn and observations made concerning the logic underlying the calculations presented in Journal Entry II. First, the salt and saltpetre appear to be issued to pork at cost as the balance on hand at the end of the period on the salt and saltpetre account is stated to be at cost. Second, it might be concluded that 'charges' are made at figures which are, overall, above purchase cost, as we know that transactions on this account give rise to a profit over the year to 31 August 1807 of £1,170. 5. 4 (see Journal Entry I). Finally, that interest is charged at 1½% (possibly the cost of capital) and profit at 5% (arguably the normal rate of return)[14] on £4744. 3. 4 which represents the 'first cost' of the pigs (in the pigs ledger) plus the cost of salt petre and charges included in the journal entry. Commission is then charged at 2½% on costs plus interest and 'normal' profit.

Whilst a few examples can therefore be found of British texts attempting to deal with the accounting issues in relation to manufacturing prior to 1880, overall the literature c.1880 represents something of a paradox. On the one hand authors recognised,sometimes tacitly but sometimes more explicitly, the need to consider the problems facing manufacturers, but at the same time were reluctant to provide detailed examples showing how the accounts could actually be kept. Thus the specific problems facing manufacturers failed to be addressed, in the main, though some authors continued to take the view that there were no specific problems facing those engaged in industrial activities. Evidence of this paradox can be observed in the book by Barnes (1872), entitled *A new and improved universal system of book-keeping, suitable to be used in all businesses. . . .* The extremely long title of Barnes' book clearly indicates an intention to deal with manufacturing, since it includes the phrase "adapted respectively to the accounts of a retail, a wholesale, and a manufacturing business..".

Journal Entry II

	£	£
Salt and salt-petre used 198 barrels of St Ubes salt, at 22s. 9d per barrel	225. 4. 6	
Ditto - 1 ounce of salt-petre per tierce and half an ounce of do per barrel, on 250 tierces and 595 barrels, is 34¼ lbs, at 100s per cwt	1. 10. 7	
		226. 15. 1

Charges

For mens' labour, to salt pack, pound, pickle, and fit for shipping, 1230 pigs, allowing 14 men and 3 boys to every 40 pigs, including allowance to them, and 2lbs of pork to each for dinner.	76. 9. 4	
Brokerage 6d cutting 2d is 18 per on 1230 pigs, being bought of countrymen and not butchers	41. 0. 0	
Offal of said pigs given to the salters, averaging £13 per pig, make 15990lbs, at 3½d per	233. 3. 9	
6 iron hoops on 250 tierces, a 3s. 6d	43. 15. 0	
For binding ditto and nails at 2s. 3d	28. 2. 6	
4 iron hoops on 385 barrels, at 2s. 4d	44. 18. 4	
For binding ditto and nails, at 1s. 7d	30. 9. 7	
Wood binding 210 barrels of Newfoundland pork, at 1s. 7	16. 12. 6	
Turf used to brand the entire	5. 11. 5	
Proportion of cost of brand irons	0. 16. 0	
Branding it	1. 18. 0	
Trecks, tin plates, bungs, and bung cloths	2. 6. 9	
Proportion of clerk's salary and storage	62. 10. 0	
		587. 13. 2

Empty casks used

150 India tierces at 17s	127. 10. 0	
100 contract do. at 14s.	70. 0. 0	
595 barrels at 9s. 9d	290. 1. 3	
		487. 11. 3
Interest, on £4744. 3. 4 being amount first cost of the pork and the above charges on it for 3 months, at 1½ per cent	71. 3. 3	
Profit and loss - for manufacturing profit on £4744. 3s. 4d. at 5 per cent	237. 4. 1	
Commission on £5052. 10s. 8d being the whole amount, at 2½ per cent	126. 6. 3	
		1,736. 13. 1

Barnes' text refers to both a 'Cost Prices Book' and 'Factory Books'. The nature of the latter is unclear, though there is an indication that they record, in the context of a cloth manufacturer, the physical amount of cloth produced. The nature of the Cost Prices Book, however, is described in some detail:

> In businesses where many large or small articles are *made to order*, it is desirable to have an entry book, for present guidance and future reference, in which the actual cost out of pocket, which probably will include several, or numerous different items, may be stated. This cannot be done in the *Day Book*, nor with any special convenience in any book which forms a part of the system of accounts to be carried into the Ledger; and it is desirable to keep a separate book for the purpose, with references to the Day Book.
>
> Another description of Cost Prices Book will often be found very serviceable, the contents consisting of an alphabetical or arranged list, of all the articles which the firm may require to purchase, with a note of the various prices at which they have been or can be obtained.
>
> *Note.* - It is much less trouble to make a brief entry in a book of this character, than to copy out at full length, all Invoices received, in the *Bought Book*, as is sometimes done for the sake of securing a memorandum of the prices.
> (Barnes, 1872, p.37)

Despite this description, when Barnes comes to describe the model set of books required for a manufacturer (he uses the example of someone producing manufactured cloth), in Chapter IX, there is no specific mention of the Cost Prices Book, his model set comprises eleven items: Day Book, Bought Book, Journal, Daily Cash Book, Banking Account Book, Cash Book, Petty Cash Book, Wages and Salaries Book, Bill Book, Ledger, and Balances Book. The omission is, however, not all that surprising since he does not consider it to be part of the main accounting system. Within his discussion of the manufacturers accounts (1872, pp.230-40), Barnes only refers to manufacturing costs in relation to the Ledger where he notes that:

> The various manufacturing accounts are so arranged as to
> show the exact and entire cost of the manufacture, in raw
> material and wages. By opening a separate account for
> each item of the cost of the *Cloth*, the *Manufacturing
> Account* is made to show, when the Ledger is balanced, the
> totals of each of these on one side, while on the other side
> it is credited with the number of yards of cloth that have
> been made, which will be obtained from the Factory
> Books.
> The balance of this account thus shows the entire quantity
> made, and cost of making, and can be carried, in one line,
> to the *debit* of the *Trading Account*. (1872, p.238)

Barnes' work, in that it recognised the need to collect together
and identify the cost of manufacture, was undoubtedly something of a
step forward. Furthermore, it also acknowledges the fact that
manufacturers could usefully keep sets of books, e.g. Cost Prices Books
and Factory Books, outside of the normal double entry bookkeeping
system. Whilst recognising their existence, and indicating something of
their function, he does not describe them in detail. Furthermore it is far
from clear that his cost prices book is in any significant way related to
the concept of cost calculation, indeed they would appear to be a record
of the cost of items purchased and those produced, perhaps to be used
for purposes such as tendering/pricing. Costs only enter into the
accounting system through the manufacturing account in the ledger, and
hence are firmly enshrined within the double entry books. There is little
hard evidence from Barnes' work, therefore, of any real move towards
cost accounting in the sense of a completely separate system of books
kept for purposes of cost calculation outside of the double entry
accounting framework, though the 'Factory Books' may hint at some
movement in that direction.

Conclusion

Most British accounting texts prior to 1880 totally ignored the
accounting problems faced by manufacturers. Virtually none discuss
key issues of concern to manufacturers, such as transfer prices,
depreciation and overhead allocation. There is growing evidence of

accounting texts paying lip service to business activity and to the preparation of accounts for businesses involved in manufacturing, but practical worked examples are usually conspicuous by their absence. Only one text, the first edition of Hamilton published in 1777/9, examined effectively the issue of internal flows within the firm and provided worked examples, but this unique occurrence was not repeated in any of the subsequent four editions of his work. Though we have discovered some early examples of works discussing issues of costing within double entry bookkeeping in relation to textiles (i.e. undertaking operations under the putting out system) and brewing (included in texts on farm accounts), the overall conclusion of Edwards and Solomons, that there was nothing of any real significance published in the accounting literature relating to costs in manufacturing business prior to the 1870s/80s, remains valid. In the next section we turn our attention to the consideration of these issues in the French literature, where industrial accounting developed into the dominant accounting doctrine during the nineteenth century.

III. The development of the accounting literature in France to 1880

An overview

Prior to the beginning of the nineteenth century, French accounting texts were largely restricted to a discussion and explanation of double entry bookkeeping in the Italian style, i.e. as applied to mercantile activities. Whilst there were some advanced texts relating to agricultural accounting, there was almost no discussion within the literature of the accounting requirements of industry. Although most accounting texts espoused the double entry method of bookkeeping, there was a good deal of interest shown in the literature with single entry systems as an alternative to double-entry in the first few decades of the nineteenth century. This appears to have been stimulated to some extent by the publication in Britain of E.T.Jones' work entitled *English system of book-keeping, by single or double entry* (1796). Unusually for the time, Jones' work was translated into French, not once but twice (the first in 1803). The intuitive appeal of Jones' book, especially to newly emerging businessmen, seems to have lain in his attempt at trying to find an accounting method that would provide the same information as a double entry system but with less effort. Thus Reymondin (1928) has argued that single entry systems were something of an expedient measure, providing a simplified form of accounting for the majority of small firms who could not afford to employ qualified accountants.

Certainly, for a time, Jones' 'English system' was à la mode, spawning a number of French texts advocating single entry systems. Even authors who preferred double entry, nevertheless often made reference to single entry. Within a couple of decades, however, enthusiasm for single entry began to wane, and though texts espousing single entry continued to be written, those advocating double entry once again began to predominate by the middle of the nineteenth century. By the end of the nineteenth century all French accounting texts espoused the double entry system, with single entry no longer mentioned. In the view of Reymondin, the enthusiasm for single entry was a transitory phenomenon, representing a partial solution to the problem faced by industrialists. When a more comprehensive solution, i.e. an effective management/accounting tool, was developed, it withered away. Single entry systems thus began to disappear, as industrial accounting (*comptabilité industrielle*) began to develop.

Industrial accounting is a system in which cost calculation is carried out within the double entry system. In the early nineteenth century it was a term used to represent the method by which the traditional form of mercantile double entry bookkeeping was adapted to suit the needs of industrial activities. Although some merchants who had moved into industrial activities during the eighteenth century may have utilised double entry systems in their businesses, accounting texts before 1800 in France, as in Britain, largely ignored the issues facing industrial concerns. There were, however, a few authors who recognised that industrialists faced particular accounting problems, though they rarely, if ever, attempted to provide technical solutions in their texts. Martin-Sylvestr Boulard, for example, in his text *Manuel de l'imprimeur* (1791), noted the entrepreneur's need for cost calculation to provide data for decision making purposes, but he provided no technical solution.

Writing in 1801[15], Edmond Degranges senior also drew attention to this problem, but spent only half of one page discussing the issue. Nevertheless he provided a clear indication of how the merchant system of double entry bookkeeping could easily be developed for use by industrialists, despite the fact that they faced a more complex situation than that faced by merchants. For the manufacturer then, it was not a case of merely purchasing from one source and selling to another, but of having to produce the good from raw material inputs before it could be sold. To reflect this increased complexity, Degranges senior advocated the creation of factory and production cost accounts as subdivisions of the 'General Goods' account. Although no mention is made of stocks within these production accounts, possibly for purposes of simplification, they do figure in his 'General Goods' account.[16]

In the view of Nikitin (1992), the accounting works published in France between 1801 and 1880 can be divided into four categories, in part based on a chronological division, and partly in terms of their long-term role in the development of the new accounting doctrine of industrial accounting. The four categories are as follows:

1   Texts on single-entry bookkeeping, such as those advocating Jones' 'English system', which represented the final throes of a system which could not cope with the demands of industry.

2   Texts advocating cost calculation within a double entry framework which were somewhat idiosyncratic and not built upon by later authors, e.g. those of Jean-Baptiste Payen (1817) and de Cazaux (1824).

3   Texts which developed the work of Degranges senior (1801). These were instrumental in establishing the doctrine of industrial accounting and enabling cost calculation to be mastered: for example, from the works of Godard-Desmarest (1827) and Mézières (1842) through to the school texts of Joseph Barré (1872) and others.

4   Texts on the development of industrial economics which, in France, were an early predecessor of modern management accounting. These post-1860 publications dealt with techniques such as: break-even analysis, inventory valuation, and the regrouping of accounts into categories (the last-named being the forerunner of charts of accounts and the ideas to be later enshrined in the *Plan comptable général*).

The year 1801 saw the publication of the first text making any significant reference to the idea of industrial accounting, and by 1880 most of the ideas which comprised industrial accounting had been clearly established and had become enshrined in the accounting texts of the period. These texts, firmly advocating the double entry system of bookkeeping, usually dealt with all general accounting issues, including their application in specific areas such as commercial accounting, and industrial accounting.

Until the recent work of French accounting historians, our understanding of accounting developments in France had been based largely on the work of Anglo-Saxon writers. Nikitin believes that we should be indebted to the work of Edwards (1937c) and Garner (1954) for drawing our attention to the importance of French literature in the field of costing during the early nineteenth century, but he considers their analyses to be biased in certain respects, since they saw *comptabilité industrielle* as merely a French version of Anglo-Saxon cost accounting. In order to examine this proposition more fully it is necessary to investigate further the work of the authors previously examined by Edwards and Garner, as well as the work of other authors not considered by them.

Single-entry texts on industrial accounting

Few of the single entry systems put forward during the early nineteenth century offered solutions to the problems faced by industrial enterprises, but an important exception to this rule was the *Méthode complète de la tenue des livres* (*Complete method of book-keeping*) by F.N.Simon (1830). *Régisseur* (steward) of the Marmont ironworks, and one who, on his own admission, had applied single entry techniques in relation to the forges for a number of years, Simon was a firm believer in its viability, arguing that it made possible relatively complicated accounting without a profound knowledge of accounting theory. The bulk of this work, extending to two volumes and over 1000 pages, was devoted to an explanation of the single entry system, though in the final 130 pages of the work he did explain the method of double entry bookkeeping.

In common with Edward Jones, Simon was concerned to provide a simple system that would generate the same results as the double entry system. Simon was prepared to admit that single entry had its limitations, but pointed to the fact that some businessmen adopted it because they were incapable of understanding double entry. Indeed, Simon stated that his book was:

> particularly meant to give information to those who do not
> know that single entry systems only have one column, and
> also those who use double entry to keep their books, [and
> to this end] I am going to offer a new method for keeping
> the day book in single entry form, in such a way that you
> obtain all the results as in double entry for all general
> goods but by only doing one third of the work. (1830, p.5)

In attempting to prove that you obtain the same results with
single as with double entry bookkeeping, Simon completely changed
the nature of the former, creating a system containing many of the
features of double entry bookkeeping and one that has little to do with
the simple registering of debts and amounts due:

> It will be seen that we can obtain from single entry
> bookkeeping all the general accounts of each type of
> merchandise, if one thinks one has need of it, which will
> reveal the inflows and outflows of merchandise at the same
> time as one finds the profit or the loss on each of them.
> One can also manage to report, in the single entry system,
> all the most complicated elements of double entry, such as
> sundry items going to miscellaneous, etc. . . . (1830, p.6)

Simon's proposals in relation to cost calculation note the
difficulty of recording all relevant details in the Day Book, such as the
consumption of raw materials, their transformation into the finished
product, and the production of each worker. He advocated the
maintenance of a monthly notebook or journal to solve this problem.
This would contain details of the factory's production, indicating
amounts of raw materials consumed and goods produced by the forges
and blast furnaces, a weekly and monthly statement of the day
labourers, and a statement of individual production for each piece
worker. Simon also suggested that it would be wise, at the end of each
month, to report in the Day Book the results of the different accounts
set out in the notebook. This would enable the cost of the products of
each furnace, forge and works to be obtained. He did not, however, see
any purpose in using transfer prices in relation to internal flows
between departments (vol. 2, p.139): "the cast iron, coal, ores, iron etc.
... can be sent from one factory to another, but it is pointless to place a

price on these goods." In the absence of transfer prices, it is impossible to calculate the cost of intermediate products or to recognise the contribution of each stage of production to the overall profit of the business.[17]

In Nikitin's view, Simon's work represents something of a rearguard action. It was an attempt, through advocating additional accounting calculations, to persuade others that the single entry system could be made to produce the same results as double entry. Further support for single entry came from the society of master joiners in Dijon who adopted, in 1838, the method as laid out in D.Clousier's *Traité de la comptabilité du menuisier* (*Treatise on accounting for joiners*). Whilst only a rudimentary form of cost calculation is contained in this work, it is of interest to note that, in recognition of the need to allow wood several years to dry out, Clousier's calculation of the cost of wood used contained interest at 6 per cent per annum to allow for the capital tied up in this process.

Nikitin (1992) has argued that advocates of single entry bookkeeping methods can be seen to have developed some important ideas in relation to the calculation of costs, even though the system itself was in the process of being overshadowed by *comptabilité industrielle*. However, as Yamey has long argued, double-entry bookkeeping is not essential for businesses success, many businessmen in the past, and even today, still use single entry systems which prove quite adequate for their needs. It was, and is, however, in the larger businesses that double entry methods have played a more important role. The development of ideas by the three groups of writers who espoused the double entry system will now be examined.

The idiosyncratic writers

Edwards (1937c) believes that the work of Payen (1817), *Essai sur la tenue des livres d'un manufacturier*, is one of the most significant works in relation to the development of industrial accounting in France. For Nikitin (1992), however, the book is idiosyncratic and therefore unlikely to have significantly influenced later writers on the subject. The book was written not by Anselme Payen, as indicated by Edwards, but by his father, Jean-Baptiste (b.1759) who, having qualified as a lawyer in 1792, went into the chemical industry. His business activities proved successful and he became very interested in chemistry, his son later becoming a well-respected chemist. In 1817, Jean-Baptiste published a book which described a system of accounting, based on his own industrial experiences, for use in an industrial setting. Although it attempted to link double entry and cost calculation, the technical manner in which this was accomplished is not always easy to follow, most notably in regard to how the various postings were effected. Because of its deficiencies, Payen's system, whilst an early forerunner of 'industrial accounting', was significantly different from the arrangement that eventually became recognisable under that title.

The work of de Cazaux (1824), *De la comptabilité dans une entreprise industrielle et spécialement dans une exploitation rurale* (Accounting in an industrial enterprise, especially in a rural setting), falls into the same category. Like Payen, de Cazaux was not an accountant and the idiosyncratic nature of some of his ideas likewise meant that he spawned few, if any, disciples. Although the title of de Cazaux's text (1824) clearly refers to accounting in an industrial enterprise, he was mainly interested in developing accounting ideas in relation to economic activities within the agricultural sector. Thus, whilst he mentions, as do many British writers of the same era, that his ideas can be adapted for use in relation to industrial activities, he provides no technical illustration of how this outcome can be achieved. Nevertheless, important issues relating to the problems of accounting for industrial activity - such as the method of apportioning overheads, the calculation of depreciation, and the source of profit - and which involved concepts that were to be subsequently incorporated within industrial accounting, were discussed by de Cazaux.

The mainstream influences on the development of industrial accounting

The main influence on the long-term development of French industrial accounting was the line of thought which passed from Degranges senior (1801), through Godard-Desmarest (1827) and Mézières (1842) to the writers of the second half of the nineteenth century such as Barlet[18] (1861), Heudicourt (1862), and Guilbault (1865). Written by authors who had an accounting background, these texts discussed key issues in relation to cost calculation firmly embedded within double entry bookkeeping methods. The work of these and other authors can be seen as part of a transition from the traditional mercantile accounting of the eighteenth century to the industrial accounting of the post-1860 era.

Although few in number, and with probably a limited circulation (most French texts of this time were published in only a single edition), the texts written by these authors provided the basis from which a new accounting doctrine was to emerge. Of greatest significance were works which attempted to provide general principles, such as those of Godard-Desmarest and Mézières. However, it was not until the publication of the latter's book, in 1842, that the term industrial accounting (*comptabilité industrielle*) came to be used in France. Godard-Desmarest's 1827 work, for example, referred merely to 'commercial accounting' (*la comptabilité commerciale*), whereas the full title of Mézières' work was *Comptabilité commerciale, industrielle et manufacturière*. The titles of both books clearly indicate a concern to provide a set of accounting principles applicable to all areas of economic activity, but in contrast to similarly titled contemporary British texts, they did in fact devote sections of their work to industry. Thus Godard-Desmarest's work is concerned with general accounting principles, with various parts of his text being devoted to different issues. In the fifth part of his book, for example, he deals with the finances of public administration, where he advocates ideas which differ quite markedly from those put forward in an earlier work (1821) written by him on this subject. It is the fourth part of his 1827 treatise, however, that provides applications of his general accounting principles to various forms of economic activity: their application to banks is covered in 2 pages; agriculture, c.10 pages; and industry, c.20 pages. In the section relating to industry, Godard-Desmarest adds flesh to the bones of the principles sketched out in Degranges (1801), an approach which was also adopted by Jeannin (1828).

In addition to the general texts, a sizeable literature developed setting out accounting systems for use in specific sectors or industries.[19] The vast bulk of this literature comprised monographs or a series of monographs indicating the application of industrial accounting within a particular sector of economic activity. The sectors or types of manufacturing establishment covered (the number of texts, if greater than one, being indicated in parenthesis) were: iron works (4); tanning (3); printing (3); brewing (3); mechanical engineering (3); coal mining (3); public buildings and works (2); mines and quarries (2); silk factories (2); construction workshops; manufacture of metal boxes; sugar manufacture; jewellery; ceramics; architecture; flour milling;

carpentry; iron production; gas manufacture; and the weaving of braid.[20] These industry/sector-specific works take the double entry bookkeeping system and apply it to the issue of cost calculation given the production process typically found in that type of business. Some texts, however, were more ambitious, attempting to build on the sectoral model in order to develop a system which had more general applicability. In most cases, however, they failed because of the inability of the authors to escape completely from the specifics of the industry/sector within which their particular system had been placed.

The earliest of these works, published during the 1820s and 1830s, included those by Degranges junior (1824) and Pillet-Will (1832) dealing with the issue of accounting in ironworks. The work of the former seems to have grown out of a series of lectures delivered in response to an approach from a group of iron manufacturers. The book by Count Michel-Frédéric Pillet-Will (1832), who was one of the directors of the business, describes the management and record-keeping system at the newly established Decazeville ironworks.

By the end of the nineteenth century, the emphasis within French accounting texts was the process by which, in an industrial setting, cost calculation could be carried out within the double entry system. Unlike the bulk of the literature of the eighteenth century which had concentrated on financial issues and the external flows as applicable to mercantile activity, the focus of nineteenth century French accounting literature was on internal flows and analytical issues related to the production process. It is not until the twentieth century that 'general accounting' comes to be developed, as a result of which the accounting literature begins to focus once again on external flows and financial accounting, a process which culminates in the division of financial accounting from management accounting (*comptabilité analytique*) enshrined with the *Plan comptable général*.

Post-1860 developments and their links to modern French accounting

The importance of the early works on industrial accounting mentioned above needs to be seen in terms of providing a springboard for further development in the second half of the nineteenth century, rather than in terms of numbers sold or their immediate impact on actual accounting methods employed in industry. Until the publication of Mézières book, for example, none of the works specifically detailing industrial accounting (save that by Degranges senior) were published in more than a single edition. Whilst it does not necessarily follow that such books were only sold in small quantities or had a limited circulation, such an inference may not be unwarranted. Mézières book, however, published in at least five editions, the first of which appeared in 1842 and the last in 1862, seems to signal a growth in the importance of industrial accounting as an accounting doctrine. This is perhaps confirmed by the fact that subsequent works proved to be more imitative and much less innovatory than those of, for example, Payen and Godard-Desmarest. Thus, whilst Mézières could write in 1842 that he did not know of any other book which united commercial accounting with industrial and manufacturing accounting (pp.iii-iv), by the end of the 1870s a number of other such books had entered into print.

In 1854 the economist, Courcelle-Seneuil, published a *Manuel des affaires* (*Business manual*) in which accounting was dealt with, but only as a side-issue. In 1861 Charles-Henri Barlet wrote *Tenue des livres appliquée à la comptabilité des mines de houille, des hauts-fourneaux et des usines à fer* (*Book-keeping applied to coal mining accounting, smelting furnaces and steelworks*), whilst in 1862 Heudicourt saw his *Etudes sur la comptabilité industrielle* (*Studies on industrial accounting*) published. Three years later, in 1865, Adolphe Guilbault's *Traité de comptabilité et d'administration industrielles* (*Treatise on industrial accounting and administration*), was published in Paris. The publication of these and other works marked the establishment of the new accounting doctrine of industrial accounting. In marked contrast to most earlier works, multiple editions of these texts were published. Indeed, judging by the number of editions published of these and other similar texts from the 1870s (Barré (1872), Dugué (1874), Godart (1875), Coq (1876), Guilbault (1877), de Valdrôme (1878), Durand (1879)), industrial accounting had become much more widely disseminated and firmly established in France by the late nineteenth century.

This consolidation of industrial accounting post-1860 can be seen as part of a wider development in the second half of the nineteenth century in France, and within Continental Europe more generally, namely the emergence of industrial (or business) economics, the forerunner of modern management studies. The link between the two would appear natural: industrial accounting provided the basic information upon which the decision making studied by industrial economics was to be based. However, in Britain, and throughout the Anglo-Saxon world, the earlier development of an accounting profession appears to created a barrier between economics and accounting.[21] In France, the closeness of the links is clearly indicated in the works of people like Guilbault. Following the success of his 1865 accounting text, and prior to the publication of the second edition in 1880, Guilbault published a *Traité d'économie et d'organisation industrielles* (*Treatise on industrial economics and organisation*) in 1877. In this he developed certain indispensable concepts and general rules to serve as a guide to research into costs.

Guilbault's book does not concern itself with the detailed recording of industrial transactions, but with explanations for the efficient use and handling of the accounting techniques "to make sure that everything comes into place, there is neither time lost or movement without a purpose, nor effort without a result . . . ". For him, industrial economics was a practical version of political economy. Whilst the latter, as advocated for example in Godard-Desmarest's 1835 work *De l'économie politique en matière commerciale* (*Political economy as applied to commercial matters*), was too far removed from the practical preoccupations of managers, industrial economics was "economics from the particular viewpoint of industrial operations". The growing importance of industrial economics in the second half of the nineteenth century is reflected in the fact that it became the object of special training provided at the *Ecole Supérieure de Commerce de Paris* in the 1860s. The integration of accountancy within industrial economics, according to Nikitin, illustrates a growing concern with the outputs of the accounting system rather than merely with the technique itself. In part this reflected an increasing familiarisation with the technique, even though it continued to be refined over time. Thus, as the nineteenth century wore on, French (industrial) accounting increasingly became coordinated with the needs of business decision makers.

Within accounting itself, however, two strands of development can be discerned in the late nineteenth and early twentieth centuries. On the one hand there were those who were concerned to determine general principles upon which an accounting plan (*plan de comptes*) could be constructed, and on the other those who sought to determine accounting systems for each sector/industry which mirrored as closely as possible the underlying production process. The former search was linked to the desire of some authors to determine a scientific basis for accounting, which led to a growing concern in the twentieth century, and particularly between 1910 and 1920, with the issue of standardisation. According to Colasse and Durand (1994, p.42) "the issue of standardisation has stood at the very core of twentieth-century French theoretical ideas on accounting". For them, this search can be traced back to that of Guilbault, whom they describe as "a man of extensive practical experience in both accounting and engineering". According to Nikitin, Guilbault (1865) was one of the first authors to indicate a distinction between industrial and commercial accounting, though it was Heudicourt (1862) who first noted that they were distinct entities though "mixed together in general accounting".

In the view of Colasse and Durand, Guilbault's significance in relation to the development of French accounting stems mainly from a later work, published in 1885, *La science des comptes à la portée de tous* (*Accounting for all*), which they consider opened up new orientations for French accounting. Together with his colleague, Léautey, Guilbault perceived of accounting as a science, and their work gave rise, within French accounting theory, to a concentration upon two key issues: standardisation, and the role of the account as a central feature of economic valuation (Colasse and Durand, 1994, p.44). Subsequent work, in the early years of the twentieth century, by Faure, who, in his role as a consultant, devised valuable accounting charts, represented an attempt to develop scientific accounting principles from a practical base. In a similar vein Bournisien espoused his belief "in the capacity of accounting procedures to control technical and financial congruence to precise standards" (Colasse and Durand, 1994, p.44).

According to Colasse and Durand, Dumarchey believed that "thinkers such as Léautey, Guilbault, Cerboni and Faure were mere metaphysicians: they had not been able to separate the scientific aspects of accounting from its more trivial practical concerns" (1994, p.45). He instead advocated the application of up-to-date scientific approaches based, logically for a Frenchman, on the ideas descended from Descartes and Auguste Comte. For Dumarchey, it was time that accounting entered the age of positivism. Accounting was a social science which made use of mathematics and was related to philosophy, economics and sociology. Indeed, Dumarchey also saw accounting as the core of economics, since economics is the science of society's accounts (Colasse and Durand, 1994, p.45). In the forefront of the drive for standardisation was the desire to develop general principles for the construction of a *plans de comptes*, which was eventually formalised in the legislation which enacted the *Plan comptable général* in 1947.

Implicit within this development was the attempt to find an acceptable classification of accounts, based on an increasingly detailed nomenclature which would be widely applicable.

Key aspects of the doctrine of industrial accounting

The term *comptabilité industrielle*, in the early French literature, clearly meant a system whereby cost calculation was integrated within the traditional merchant system of double-entry bookkeeping. Obviously the main difference between the activities of the merchant and those of the manufacturer, which industrial accounting had to address, concerns the movement of goods through the enterprise, from one stage of economic activity to another. In this section we examine the development of thought in relation to a number of key issues and problems faced by industrialists, especially concerning the calculation of cost price.

The classification of accounts

There has been a tendency in Continental Europe to develop a positive/descriptive form of accounting. In the eighteenth and nineteenth century, French writers (de la Porte (1685), Ricard, de Barrême (1721), Giraudeau, Degranges, sr. (1795, 1801) and Vannier (1840)) played a major part in this process and, according to Zan, the French tradition of accounts' personification can be seen as "a first effort at constructing a 'logical explanation' or theory of accounting" (Zan, 1994, p.273). He goes on to note that "What seems to characterize the French tradition is the effort devoted to developing a taxonomy of accounts as a means of handling the accounting process of keeping and closing the books." Writing from the Italian context, Zan argues that this initiative had a significant effect on the development of accounting in Italy in the eighteenth and nineteenth centuries and, contrary to earlier writers, he is not convinced that this influence was necessarily detrimental.

Italian historians usually identify three steps in the evolution of the French tradition: the rise of accounts' personification (step I); the emergence of the so-called '*cinquecontisti*' (or five accounts) (step II); and the theory of fictitious personification (step III) (Zan, 1994, p.273). Step I of the evolutionary process goes back to de la Porte (1685, 1712) in whose works accounts are classified mostly in terms of the 'person' to whom they refer. A distinction is made between accounts relating to the proprietor (*comptes du chef*, i.e. *capital, profits et pertes, dépenses, commissions* - capital, profit and loss, expenditure and commissions), those accounts relating to things or 'effects in kind' (*effets en nature*, i.e. *disponibilités, marchandises et immobilisations)* (liquid assets, goods and fixed assets), and those accounts referring to persons or correspondents (*comptes de correspondants*, i.e. creditors and debtors).[22] Around the end of the eighteenth century, step II commenced, and is largely associated with the writings of the two Degranges, Edmond sr. and his son Edmond jr. Writing in 1795 and 1804 respectively, the two Degranges' advocated a division between personal accounts (*les comptes ouverts aux personnes*) on the one hand, comprising accounts for creditors and debtors, and general or impersonal accounts on the other. These general accounts, five in number (hence the use of the term *cinquecontisti* by Italian historians), are referred to as the proprietor's, and comprised *caisse, marchandises générales, billets à recevoir, billets à payer, et pertes & profits* (cash, general goods, bills receivable, bills payable, and profits and loss). Within the Degranges' system, the 'objects' received by or provided by the proprietor were credited and debited according to the basic rule of "crediting the one who gets and debiting the one who gives" (Zan, 1994, p.273). The final stage of the evolution of the French tradition of personification of accounts, step III, is associated with the contribution of Vannier (1840), who proposed the 'theory of fictitious personification'. For Vannier there were three classes of accounts: accounts due to the merchant (capital, losses and profits); accounts referring to commercial activities and values (cash, goods, bills receivable and bills payable, fixtures and fittings, start-up costs, and trading funds); and accounts related to correspondents (debtors and creditors). In the case of the first and last classes, there is an obvious person or persons to whom the account refers: for the first it is the merchant and for the last the correspondent. In the case of the second class of accounts, however, Vannier proposes a fictitious personification. "They are treated as if they refer to the persons or consignees - whether actual or fictitious - deemed responsible for them (the cashier for cash, the storekeeper for goods, etc.). By such a fiction, all the accounts in this framework are referred to persons" (Zan, 1994, p.276).

As Zan points out, however, the view of Italian historians that the Degranges' 'five accounts' theory comprised the whole of the French tradition of 'personalist' or personification theory, understates the true complexity of the evolutionary process. Indeed, many French authors, including those who wrote on the issue of industrial accounting, displayed views relating to the classification of accounts which differed from that of the two Degranges'. Godard-Desmarest (1827), for example, argued that there were only three main accounts, to which all others were subservient: *capital, caisse et marchandises* (capital, cash and goods). Other authors suggested different classifications: Jeannin (1828) proposed four, Mézières (1842) five and Guilbault (1865) six. Writing in 1878, Chevandier de Valdrôme proposed ten classes!

Clearly, then, the personification debate was important in the development of accounting in Continental Europe during the eighteenth and nineteenth centuries but Zan considers that it was largely ignored in the Anglo-Saxon world (1994, p.278). Chatfield (1977, p.219), however, notes that personification of accounts, which he argues remained the accepted way to set forth general rules of bookkeeping from the seventeenth to the twentieth centuries, was initially strengthened in the process of translating Italian textbooks into English due to the lack of corresponding terms. Thus there developed the "connotation of inanimate objects possessing human qualities ... [which helped to] explain movements of value in nonpersonal accounts" (1977, p.219). According to Chatfield, three main forms of account personification have developed (1977, p.219): accounts treated as living persons; accounts treated as representing the owner of the business; and accounts thought of as separate from the owner but responsible to him. Although English writers did play some part, it was French authors, as Zan has suggested, who were in the forefront of developments, at least in the Italian context:

> the French tradition could be seen as the first effort - however incomplete and/or unsatisfactory - to develop a *logical explanation of the 'why'* of the process of bookkeeping and closure . . . the first effort to develop the *basic rules for a synthetic structure of accounting entries*, a crucial stage in the development of a theory of bookkeeping ... (1994, pp.276-7)

In the developing French literature on industrial accounting in the first half of the nineteenth century it seems clear that production and/or cost accounts were seen as being essentially a class of accounts which subservient to the main accounts. This can be seen from the second edition of the work by Degranges senior (1801), which indicates clearly how the ideas used in mercantile accounting can be adapted to the needs of industrialists. Degranges proposed, in circumstances where the businessman is not content to purchase goods and re-sell them, but wished to produce them himself, accounts for production and production costs as sub-divisions of the 'General Goods' account. The form of the account proposed was:

Production Account

Debit   Credit

Purchase of raw materials   Value of finished product
Purchase of tools   (when sold)
Rent
Repairs
Wages
Salaries
Interest on loans
All other expenditure resulting from production
(Degranges senior, 1801, p.61)

The absence of any reference to stocks in relation to the production account is somewhat surprising, but they are possibly omitted for purposes of simplification since they are included within the 'General Goods' account itself.

According to Edwards, de Cazaux appears to have known "how to adapt double entry to the movement of values *internally* and had no objection to these appearing in the financial books..." (1937c, p.7). Indeed, de Cazaux (1824) suggested that a separate account (*capital partiel,* or partial capital) should be "opened for each item of capital, debited with values received and credited with values imparted" (1937c, p.7). This would enable not only the calculation of total profit, but also the discovery of the sources of that profit, since the difference on any account would represent the profit or loss on that item of capital.[23] The number of such accounts could be adjusted as necessary to follow the movement of capital within the enterprise, from the entry of the raw materials to the production of the finished goods. The form for his 'partial capital' was as follows:

Partial Capital no. x

Debit		Credit
Initial capital value		Sale of finished product
Expenditure		Internal transfers of
(upkeep, repairs)		intermediate products
		Final capital value
+ credit balance (profit)	or	+ debit balance (loss)
(values received)		(values supplied)

We can see that in the absence of regulatory constraints in respect of bookkeeping, French firms in the early nineteenth century saw no need to maintain separate accounts to track external relations and internal flows. Thus, for Payen, industrial accounting simply meant the application of the double entry system for use in industrial enterprises. Unlike the remainder of his contemporaries who wrote on the subject of industrial accounting, however, Payen (1817) advocated distinguishing three kinds of accounting in relation to manufacturing activities: that in the manner of ordinary commercial bookkeeping, i.e. in money (*en argent*); that in kind (*en nature*); and accounting for materials (*en matière*) (Edwards, 1937c, p.1). Accounting in kind had the objectives of recording the employment of all materials and labour, of showing what factors of production had been applied to each product, etc., and thereby finding its cost price, and to arrive at the total cost of goods produced in such a way that it can be agreed with the total expenses of the business. Accounting for materials, however, was designed to show the physical quantities of materials used and the output of the various finished products.[24]

We can therefore see that there occurred a wide ranging debate amongst authors of French accounting texts in the first half of the nineteenth century concerning the classification of accounts, and/or the sub-division of the ledgers, but gradually a single system of accounting was developed which could be adapted to each type of economic activity.

The calculation of cost (price)

A common, central feature of the early texts on industrial accounting was the use of accounting information for the purpose of calculating cost (price). There were, of course, variations in terminology. Payen, for example, wrote about both *prix revenant* and *prix coûtant*; whilst Degranges junior favoured the latter term: "*au débit du compte de marchandises sont notés les achats au prix coûtant*" (1824, p.3) ("purchases are debited to the merchandise account at cost price"). Degranges junior also indicated how the unit cost of coal could be calculated:

> With this account (coal) it is easy to know the exact cost price of a basket of coal; it is only necessary to divide the sum to the debit of this account, which is exactly what the coal costs, by the number of baskets brought to market: it is clear that the quotient of the division will be the unit cost of the basket. (1824, p.23)

One important area where authors differed, was in the exact definition of cost used. This varied from the simplest, i.e. basic material and labour costs, to more complex definitions including overheads of all kinds. Whilst the precise ideas may have been refined over time, the issue of how overheads should be apportioned between products, the calculation of depreciation and the use of transfer prices for the internal movement of goods within an enterprise were discussed within the industrial accounting literature from an early date.[25]

Fixed costs/overheads

One of the main problems faced by industrialists in cost calculation concerns the identification and treatment of overheads or fixed costs. Should they, on the one hand, be kept separate and debited to the overall trading results in the profit and loss account, or should they be included as part of the cost of production? The solution adopted to this problem, in part, depended on the one hand upon whether the overheads were seen as fixed or variable, and on the other whether they were seen as direct or indirect. If they were to be charged to production, this raised the further matter of how they should be apportioned in circumstances where more than one product was manufactured. The nature of such issues was clearly recognised in the nineteenth century by the early French writers on industrial accounting, even if the solutions they proposed may not have been widely followed or are not in total agreement with modern views on these matters.

(i)   *Definition* Payen, in his *Essai sur la tenue des livres d'un manufacturier* (1817), clearly recognised the need to consider overheads which were charged to costs in his *Grand Livre des Comptes en Nature*. In the context of an ironworks, therefore, Payen's definition of costs included not only materials and wages, but also overheads such as the wear and tear on tools, depreciation of the furnaces, interest and rent (Edwards, 1937c, p.5). Both de Cazaux (1824) and Godard-Desmarest (1827) recognised the existence of overheads, though it was not until the second half of the nineteenth century that writers began explicitly to consider the distinction between fixed and variable costs, or whether overheads could be considered as direct or indirect costs.

In 1854, for example, Courcelle-Seneuil (p.199) expressed the idea that, in certain circumstances, some overheads (i.e. indirect costs) could be considered to be special (i.e. direct) costs in relation to a particular group of products, though they may not be traceable to any individual product. He also expressed the view that the majority of overheads were only fixed within the limit of a given structure of production. Guilbault (1865), for whom they were the third component of cost price, after material supplies (*approvisionnements*) and labour costs (*le travail des hommes*), overheads were considered to include the work of machines, fuel, research costs, office costs, the upkeep and provision for depreciation of materials and the interest on money. The following guidance is provided for classifying costs as fixed or variable:

> [Costs] are fixed when they stay the same whatever the level of activity of the industry; conversely they are variable when the expenditure rises or falls in line with production.

Thus fixed costs were seen to comprise "the salary of the head of the firm" (*les honoraires du chef de la maison*), taxes, trade licence, insurance, office costs, rent, etc.

The case of interest, however, is more delicate:

> if an industrialist operates with the funds borrowed at interest from someone else, he only pays interest according to the amount used . . . if he is using his own money he could gain interest outside his own business on the money which he is not using if his own works is stopped. Thus far, the interest follows the work carried out. But the question changes entirely if we consider a company whose members have provided the funds once and for all. In a joint stock limited company, one cannot change the level of capital . . . and the interest on this capital must always be the same whatever the movement in production. A large number of companies, according to their statutes, are required to pay fixed interest charges prior to declaring their dividends; it is thus vital to understand that this interest is a fixed overhead in the cost price. (Guilbault, 1865, p.103)

For Guilbault, overheads, could be divided between fixed and variable elements as follows:

Fixed	Variable
Employee's fees	Property repairs/upkeep
Office costs	Repairs to furnishings
Interest on money	Machine consumption
Depreciation of materials	Indirect operations
Taxes, rent, fixed charges	(mainly machine upkeep)

By means of a detailed numerical example, Guilbault indicated a concern to illustrate the effect of changing levels of production, and hence the capital employed, on the share of fixed costs in total cost price. He concluded that the art of the industrialist lay in his ability to minimise overheads whilst at the same time maximum the productivity of workers.

Barlet (1861) proposed a similar approach to that advocated by Guilbault, namely that cost is partly made up of direct or proportional costs. Amongst these were considered to figure labour costs, materials and equipment, including auxiliary costs such as the depreciation of machines, and partly of fixed or general costs, including the salaries of office staff and management, office costs, the repair and upkeep of buildings, and the depreciation in the value of the main works. In the context of a coal mine, Barlet provides a numerical example detailing these different charges and calculates the amount of coal required to be extracted daily in order to produce a zero level of profit. Following on from this he puts forward the following general formula for establishing the break-even point[26]:

$$x * (a - b) = m$$

where a is the unit selling price, b is the unit cost, x is the amount of coal, and m is the level of fixed costs.

(ii)   *Apportionment of overheads* The apportionment of overheads amongst different products gives rise to a major problem in the calculation of cost, which is usually achieved through the application of some, possibly unsound, accounting concept. Payen (1817), although including overheads within his numerical examples, failed to provide any clear indication of the basis upon which such apportionment was carried out. De Cazaux, in relation to agriculture, suggested that overheads should be apportioned in proportion to throughput:

> of course the costs of reaping, threshing, etc. ... to obtain wheat, and the costs of all kinds to obtain wine, will be divided, proportionally, to each field, to each vineyard, in relation to the number of sheaves and the amount of grapes harvested. (1824, p.75)

Godard-Desmarest (1827, p.51), proposed that overheads should be allocated proportionately to the costs of production of each object. Even a later writer such as Guilbault was non-specific. Noting that overheads cannot be applied to any one specific area of activity rather than another, he concluded that they must be recorded in individual accounts in a proportional manner, though he does not specify in relation to what.

Depreciation

The French accounting literature begins to give serious consideration to the issue of depreciation for the first time during the last quarter of the nineteenth century. The main development occurred in the 1890s as a result of the debate on the normalisation of balance sheets, and hence lies beyond the time period covered by this study. Some of the early French accounting writers, however, did discuss this issue and, as was noted in the preceding section, many considered depreciation in connection with the issue of overhead costs.

Very few of the earliest French writers actually referred to depreciation (*amortissement*) as such, though it is quite clear from their writings that this was the concept that they were describing. The need for depreciation arises, of course, because of the fact that fixed assets tend to lose value as a result of their usage and the passage of time. Thus, the loss in asset values represents a cost to the enterprise and, if the intention is to obtain an accurate figure for the full cost price of producing a good, must be taken into account. Before depreciation can be applied, however, it is necessary to know the value of the asset which is to be depreciated. During much of the nineteenth century, French accounting writers considered that assets should be entered in the books at their market value.[27] Changes in the market value from one period to the next thus resulted in losses or gains, depending as much on the state of the market as reflecting changes in the real worth of the asset. Durand (1879) argues, however, that with assets measured at their market value, there is no sound basis for calculating depreciation, since the charge simply reflects the difference in market value of the asset as between two dates. Furthermore, as pointed out by Godart (1875), there is no guarantee that the market value of an asset will be equal to its liquidation value. Both of these writers therefore advocated depreciation calculated by reference to the perceived life of the asset, its original cost and its estimated residual value.

Several earlier writers on industrial accounting had advocated making provision for depreciation, though their suggestions as to how the issue should be handled technically were somewhat varied. Interestingly de Cazaux (1824) was concerned, not only with the issue of declining asset values due to depreciation, but also those circumstances in which asset values may be increased. In both cases he considered that it was important that variations in asset values should be spread over the accounting periods to which they applied. Thus:

> [land] improvements which will not last more than a year
> do not increase the value at all, since the harvest for which
> the improvements have been made will absorb them.
> (1824, p.77)

Improvements which did last longer than a year, however, should be added to the value of the property, but only for that number of years. Thus, if the improvements were expected to last four years, then the sum total should be debited in the first year, and a quarter of the total to be charged should be credited to each of the four years.

Turning to the loss of value of fixed assets, such as buildings, over time, de Cazaux commented that:

> the valuation of buildings is generally based on price and
> the presumed life-span of each of the parts which make it
> up . . . The annual loss (of each part of capital) is made up
> of (1) the interest on the capital, (2) upkeep, (3) the cost of
> insurance against fire, (4) the imperceptible falling off of
> capital. (1824, pp.87-8)

Both Payen (1817) and Godard-Desmarest (1827) were also concerned with the issue of how such losses should be accounted for. The latter, in discussing the problem of expenses in relation to the acquisition of buildings, talked of 'lost values' (*valeurs perdues*), or what we would today describe as fictitious assets. Noting that "it would not be right to put a serious strain on the first year of management" by treating the cost of acquisition as an expense, he advocated a method of sharing the cost of acquisition over the expected life of the building. Thus, whilst he did not explicitly use the term *amortissement* (depreciation) as such, he clearly had this concept firmly in mind when suggesting that, if the life of the building is declared to be eight years, then one-eighth of its cost should be charged to cost for each of eight years, thereby writing off the acquisition cost over the expected lifetime of the asset. The straight line method of depreciation referred to here was commonly advocated by the early French writers.

Barlet (1861, p.41) suggested a more sophisticated approach towards depreciation when he provided a mathematical formula for calculating the annual repayment, or provision for depreciation. In the context of the initial capital costs of a coal mine, which comprised the cost of carrying out initial research and survey work, sinking the shafts, and constructing buildings and machinery, Barlet showed that the amount of depreciation necessary in order for these to be recovered within a given period of time was:

$$a = [\, A * r * (1 + r)^n \,] / [\, (1 + r)^n - 1 \,]$$

where A is the amount of capital to be recovered, r is the rate of interest and n is the number of years over which the capital is to be recovered. The formula is, of course, that for the constant annual repayment of a loan (capital and interest), or what is known in the context of this discussion as the annuity method of depreciation. Its development by Barlet clearly reflects the close relationship between the industrial and financial provision of depreciation.[28]

        Although some of the early French authors noted the problem of depreciation, there was little consideration of the reasons for its occurrence. In general, of course, depreciation results both from the use of an asset, which therefore will gradually wear out, and through the passage of time, since it will both deteriorate, even if not used, and/or become obsolete. Wearing out due to use can be combated by repair and maintenance, but generally speaking this will not be sufficient to prolong the life of an asset indefinitely. Many of the nineteenth century French writers considered that this could be the case, however, and hence argued that depreciation may not be necessary for some assets. Thus Dugué (1874), for example, noting that in the early nineteenth century many firms had constructed their own fixed assets, argued that these were often so well constructed that, providing adequate maintenance was carried out, they could last a very long time. In such circumstances he considered that it was unnecessary for depreciation to be charged and/or incorporated in cost price. De Valdrôme (1878) concurred in this view.[29]

        However, most assets wear out, even with careful maintenance, and/or become obsolete over time, so that it is necessary for depreciation to be charged if the full cost of a product is to be calculated. Thus, even though he considered that machinery does not wear out if it is not being used, Guilbault (1865) considered that depreciation should be conceived of as being perpetual, and hence as a fixed cost. He argued that this was the only way to reflect adequately the "continual replacements which must be made to keep a machine running smoothly, and the need to change the means of production at certain intervals if firms want to stay ahead of the competition." The methods advocated by the later French writers such as Dugué (1874) and de Valdrôme (1878) were not dissimilar to those of their earlier counterparts. Dugué did, however, note that the method of depreciation varied according to the type of asset:

> It is necessary to place depreciation on accounts representing goods in kind:
>
> - Materials and equipment, one-quarter or one-fifth of their value annually.
> - Horses according to their state and price.
> - Buildings in use according to their state of preservation.
> - The company's own property according to its actual rent or its selling price if there is a fall in value. (1874, p.66)

For Durand (1879), it was important to distinguish between those expenses intended to increase the importance or productive capacity of the factory, which he considered should be charged to a separate establishment account, and maintenance costs. In his view, the 'maintenance and wear and tear' account should register, in addition to maintenance costs, a sum corresponding to the depreciation of materials and furnishings (at five per cent of their acquisition value) and of apparatus (at 12 per cent of its acquisition value). The corresponding entries would be transferred from the 'maintenance and wear and tear' account to the 'materials and furnishings' account at an amount corresponding to the depreciation caused by reason of its usage during the year. In his estimation, the 'materials and furnishings' account would then represent, as closely as possible, the real value of the stock in hand at the moment of taking the inventory, and would not require any reliance on market values.

It is clear that, during the nineteenth century, significant developments did occur in relation to the issue of accounting for depreciation. Most nineteenth century French writers considered that the main, if not sole, motivation behind the calculation of depreciation was to determine accurately the full production cost of a particular good. There was, however, some recognition that, where an asset was used jointly in the production of a number of different goods, the allocation of the depreciation charge might pose a problem. Dugué (1874) suggested that, in such circumstances, the figure for depreciation should be carried directly to the general profit and loss account. Chevandier de Valdrôme (1878) considered that when the articles produced were dissimilar, however, depreciation should be allocated amongst the different products on the basis of labour costs.

Dugué (1874) argued that provision for depreciation was also important in order to have a correct knowledge of the real value of equipment and materials. For de Valdrôme (1878), depreciation served yet another important purpose: it was a means of ensuring a fair calculation of profit for distribution purposes. In his view, the need to provide for depreciation was optional for sole proprietors, but absolutely essential for partnerships and limited companies. Recognising the increasing importance of the latter forms of business organisation, he argued that it was essential to reflect accurately the successive reduction in the value of equipment and property, whether from usage or obsolescence, in order to overcome any difficulties which may arise between partners in the case of liquidation. Similarly, an annual provision for depreciation was essential if shareholders in different time periods were to be treated equitably by those running the company: if depreciation is not calculated regularly, then shareholders in year N may be at an advantage or disadvantage compared with those in the following year since the profit, and hence the dividend, is left to the discretion of those who fix the level of depreciation.

The source of profit and the use of transfer prices
De Cazaux (1824) first considered the issue of the source of profit in the context of a landowner having different parcels of land. His example was that of a landowner whose capital was easily split and who scrutinizes all activities in the search for the most profitable investment for his money. In developing his thoughts on this subject de Cazaux also provided mathematical formulas to explain the difference between simple and compound interest.

Godard-Desmarest (1827), whilst clearly explaining process costing, made no attempt to show profits or losses on intermediate processes, transfers from one process to another being made at cost (Edwards, 1937c, pp.9-10). Indeed, Godard-Desmarest was only concerned to derive profit figures once a year, though he recognised that it would be useful to have figures of cost and product monthly. However, since their main use was to be for the purpose of comparing work done, not to assess relative profitability, he preferred transferring raw materials and intermediate products at a predetermined average price, waiting until the end of the year to calculate the average cost price. He was aware of the fact that this meant that the sum of the estimated profit figures for each month would differ from the total profit for the year, but noted that if it was desired that materials, etc. be charged to the process accounts each month, they would have to be charged at an estimated value, more or less inaccurate, requiring an adjustment at the end of the year (Edwards, 1937c, pp.12-3).

Whilst Godard-Desmarest was wary of monthly transfers at estimated prices, Degranges junior (1824) had been less reticent when it came to the issue of transferring items between departments. In his view, since the method of accounting advocated would not allow the precise calculation of costs each month, a predetermined price (*prix de convention*), based on the actual values of the previous year, should be used. In process industries such as iron manufacture, the cost of the product produced by a department would be the actual costs incurred by the department plus those based on the predetermined prices charged for inputs from departments upstream in the production process. Degranges junior wrote:

> this method of estimated cost pricing, which is then rectified at the end of the year, is advantageous in that it forces the forgemaster to identify and check exactly how much return they get on their raw materials. (1824, pp.21-2)

Degranges junior was aware of the fact that, provided transfers were based on a suitable estimated cost price, the balance of the account before stocktaking should be roughly equal to the value of the remainder ("*la valeur de 'restants'*"). Also, that the difference allowed businessmen us to know the extent of their estimation errors. No other author, in the first half of the nineteenth century, to the best of our knowledge, attempted to consider this issue though companies such as Saint-Gobain and Decazeville were forced, out of practical necessity, to try and solve this problem, with varying degrees of success.

In 1872, Joseph Barré considered a situation in which two distinct centres of operation, within the same enterprise, could sell their products and services at a price determined by *a priori* considerations. The charging of general costs formed the foundation for this consideration:

The second approach, the most rational, is the one we have followed and consists of considering our production account for candles as a client to whom we deliver our main product, stearin, at the average price; that is to say, with the same profit as if we sold the product externally. In this situation, it would not be fair for this production to support the general costs other than those directly necessary for production. And this is just. In effect, instead of delivering our goods to our factories, suppose that we delivered them to Mr. Dumont; our overheads would be identical . . . Mr. Dumont buys our stearin, converts it into candles, selling the finished product and making a profit. In the situation hypothesized above, however, it is we who sell the finished product; the new (extra) profit made on this sale must then be added to that arising from the sale of the stearin. Consequently, the manufacture of the stearin alone must support the other charges which come directly from the manufacture of the candles. (1872, p.68)

Barré's approach is of interest because it justified charging overheads only to the main product line, stearin. In the context of determining whether or not to produce candles, this approach can be justified if capacity, and hence overheads, would remain unchanged if candles were not produced.

Integration of accounts

Under industrial accounting, it was possible to ascertain not only the total output and total expenditure for the whole of the business, but also to calculate the cost price of each object, whilst simultaneously enabling the value of assets and liabilities to be obtained. Many of the early writers clearly saw cost calculation as an inherent and integral component of the accounting system. Whilst Payen (1817) advocated three forms of accounting - *en argent, en nature* and *en matière* - but failed to 'tie in' the cost and financial accounts, Edwards noted that they could easily be agreed (1937c, p.5). In Godard-Desmarest's work (1827), it was suggested that two 'documents of synthesis' should be prepared: a *tableau comparatif des produits de fabrication et des dépenses réelles ou présumées* (a comparative table of output and real or presumed expenses), and a '*Situation en Deniers*' (a 'status of funds' or 'cash position'). For Mézières:

> the object of accounting is to present, in a methodical way, all financial, commercial, industrial and manufacturing operations.
> The manner of presenting the accounts can not be the same for all branches of our industry. Appreciable differences exist between commercial and purely financial operations . . . but this should not cause us to deviate from the fundamental principles of double entry bookkeeping. (1842, p.1)

In France, during the first half of the nineteenth century, in marked contrast to the situation in Britain, the growing needs of large business were increasingly recognised within the accounting literature. A number of writers, amongst the earliest of whom, in part at least, wrote about the techniques they employed in their own businesses, contributed to the development of a branch of general accounting which gradually came to be known by the title, *comptabilité industrielle*. Over time, industrial accounting, which advocated the calculation of cost within the double entry bookkeeping system, became firmly established within the burgeoning French accounting literature. In part, industrial accounting owed its emergence to the virtual absence of any significant statutory constraints relating to bookkeeping, which meant that industrialists were under no compulsion to utilise different methods, or systems of books, to account for external and internal flows. Given the flexibility of double entry bookkeeping over the centuries, it was perhaps natural that writers should advocate variations on merchant accounting which explicitly took account of the particular needs of industrialists. Hence the literature focussed on developing a branch of general accounting which enabled cost calculation and financial accounting were carried out in one single set of books. Given this development, it is easy to see why French texts on industrial accounting prior to 1880 failed to address the issue of the integration of cost and financial information - there was no need since they had never been considered anything other than part and parcel of the same accounting system. Industrial accounting, therefore, was merely a branch of French general accounting, but one which, within the double entry system enabled the calculation not only of the assets and liabilities, production, expenditure and profit/loss of the enterprise as a whole, but also the unit cost and the profit/loss for each process and/or manufactured good.

IV.   Conclusion

It is quite clear from the evidence presented in this chapter that the accounting literature in France, particularly that dealing with the needs of industrialists, was much in advance of that in Britain up until the 1880s. Whilst a number of British writers during the first eighty years of the nineteenth century paid lip-service to the need to address manufacturers' needs, few if any did so, and even then only in a cursory manner, with little illustrative detail. By contrast, in France, several books on the general theme of industrial accounting were published in the first forty years of the century, to which were added many more in the next forty years. By the time of the publication in 1887 of the first classic British text on factory accounting, that of Garcke and Fells, the French industrial accounting literature had been firmly established for many years. In addition, a large part of the French literature dealt with the specific application of industrial accounting concepts to particular industries or sectors, an issue which only began to be addressed in Britain at the end of the nineteenth century.

Within the French accounting texts of the nineteenth century there can also be found a much more advanced discussion of key issues for businessmen, long before the British accounting literature begins to discuss them. Thus, whilst in Britain overheads and their apportionment only became a major issue at the end of the nineteenth century, the earlier French literature was full of discussions of this issue. Likewise, French texts discussed the issue of depreciation, transfer prices, the distinction between fixed and variable costs and the idea of break-even analysis, long before these issues were discussed in the Anglo-Saxon literature. Perhaps of equal importance is that, whilst these ideas were initially developed in France within the accounting literature, in the Anglo-Saxon world many of them were initially discussed within the context of the economics or engineering literature.

Whilst the French accounting literature was undoubtedly well in advance of its British counterpart in discussing issues pertinent to manufacturers, it should not automatically be assumed that the practice of accounting in French industry throughout the eighteenth and nineteenth centuries was necessarily in advance of that in Britain. The next chapter will examine accounting practice in both countries in the light of some of the findings presented above. In particular, we will investigate issues such as the practice of industrial accounting, i.e. cost calculation within double entry bookkeeping systems, the application of methods to deal with the issue of overhead apportionment, the application of methods to account for depreciation, and the use of transfer prices.

Notes

1   Support for this seems to be provided in Britain by the example of the Staveley enterprise in the eighteenth century - see chapter 3 below.

2   As modified by Mepham (1988).

3   The earliest known text devoted entirely to a branch of manufacturing is that by Jacob Kneppel (Amsterdam, c. 1789) with the author observing that "as far as I know no one had yet undertaken to bring out a separate publication concerning a factory or distinct branch of trade".

4   The stock account contains quantity columns to identify any deficiency; transfers and closing stock are each valued at cost.

5   Under the putting out system, although their would be no need for a factory as such, it would be necessary to have a warehouse through which the handling of the raw materials and finished goods could be carried out. Indeed, Edwards (1937b, p.229) remarks that Thompson refers to spinners, weavers, trimmers and dyers bringing in their work weekly, whilst the bleacher does so only once a month. There is no indication, however, of how any warehouse costs are accounted for.

6   Solomons (1952, p. 8) quotes, with approval, Littleton's (1933) categorisation of Cronhelm's illustration as 'deficient'. However, the system would have enabled control to have been exerted over the physical movement of goods, which appears to have been the principal concern: "the manufacturer's goods are controlled throughout their multifarious situations [movements], so that merely the very petty embezzlements can escape discovery" (Cronhelm, 1818, p. 46) and "any deficiency in the number of Manufactured Pieces, would be immediately detected".

7   This implies the need to record internal transfers in order to discover the amounts debited to the finished goods account, but this matter is not elaborated upon.

8   If space was the criterion, then this possibly suggests that the material was considered to be of relatively little practical experience, compared to the material retained, making it either superfluous and/or expendable.

9   We are grateful to Rudi Thoemmes of Thoemmes Antiquarian Books Ltd, Bristol, for allowing access to the collection which was in the process of being catalogued prior to its transfer to Osaka University library.

10   Edward Thomas Jones (1796) is of course the most famous exception.

11   Wood (c.1777) and Tuck (1843) imply a specialisation in manufacturing which is not borne out by the content of these texts.

12   This implies the use of transfer prices at a figure above cost.

13   The Pattern book, the Pattern book outwards, or Petty Pattern book, the Order book, the Day Book, Journal or Invoice book, the Cash book, the Bill Book, Ledger, the Letter Book, the Carriage, or Packing book, the Shipping book, the Direction book, and the Memorandum book.

14   This amount is credited direct to the company's profit and loss account, which also reflects sundry profits of £5,714. 15. 1 (see Journal Entry I) including 'residual income' on pork of £566. 10. 0.

15   It is possible that Degranges senior may have discussed this issue in the first edition of his book, published in 1795, but we have been unable to see a copy of this. Our comments are therefore based on the second edition of the book, published in 1801.

16   There is some evidence here of a similar approach to that adopted in Britain later in the century by Barnes (1872)

17   In the light of this, it seems somewhat odd that Simon recommends the distribution of general expenses over all products, rather than simply treating them as a debit to the global profit and loss account.

18   Barlet was, in fact, not French but Belgian. He taught at Liège and mainly published textbooks adapted to the Belgian

education system. However, since some of his ideas, written in French, were of importance, they have been included in this study.

19   The wide variation in both form and coverage of French accounting literature during the period 1817-1908 is clearly indicated in the bibliography produced by Reymondin (1909).

20   By contrast, similar works, relating to specific sectors did not begin to appear in Britain until the end of the nineteenth century, such as that by Norton (1889).

21   Zan (1994, p. 256), in commenting on the difference between the Continental Europe and Anglo-Saxon accounting models, notes that in the former, accounting is seen as part of a broader business economics discipline, following on from the dominant national philosophical traditions in countries like Italy and Germany which has generated literature of a strong positive/descriptive character. In the Anglo-Saxon world, however, he argues that the tendency has been for a fragmentation within the field of management studies between numerous branches, of which accounting is one, rather than to any cross-fertilisation between them within a broader framework. Under this system, the Anglo-Saxon world has thus developed a prescriptive and problem-solving approach to accounting which is very different from that on the Continent.

22   According to Stevelinck (1977) this division of accounts into three classes can be traced to Abraham de Graaf (1688).

23   In many ways this resembles a voyage or venture account - for a more detailed discussion of the development from the venture account to the factory account in France in the late eighteenth and early nineteenth centuries, see Lemarchand (1996), and of the types of voyage accounts found in England, see Yamey (1962).

24   Payen can be seen as the first to recognise the need for a distinction between accounting *en argent* (financial accounting) and accounting *en nature* (cost/industrial accounting). The modern concept of the *tableau du bord* in France, similarly draws on elements of cost/industrial accounting, financial accounting and physical yield data (Payen's accounting *en matière*).

25   These kinds of matters received significant discussion in the
      British literature only after the period covered by this study
      (Solomons, 1952).

26   In Britain, the first writer to discuss the distinction between
      fixed and variable costs was Babbage (1832), and he was
      followed by the economist Lardner (1850). The matter was
      first recognised in the accounting literature by Garcke and
      Fells (1887), but break-even analysis was developed in the
      early twentieth century, mainly in America rather than Britain,
      and by engineers rather than accountants - see Parker (1969,
      ch. 4).

27   An early view which indicated that there were alternative
      methods was that of De Cazaux (1824, pp.75-6) who
      suggested that there were three alternative methods by which
      an asset such as land could be valued: the going market price;
      the purchase price; or the estimated average revenue. The last
      would be calculated in the following manner: if it is assumed
      that there is an interest rate of 5%, then a piece of land would
      be worth 20 times its average net revenue.

28   It is of interest to note that the annuity method of providing for
      depreciation, through setting up a depreciation fund, was
      advocated in Britain in the second half of the nineteenth
      century by William Armstrong who was brought in to advise a
      number of iron and coal companies on various matters linked
      to their operations, including asset valuations and other
      accounting matters (see chapter 3, especially section relating to
      Staveley).

29   This kind of view was also widespread in Britain in the
      nineteenth century, in both theory and practice (Brief, 1965,
      pp. 14-21; Garcke and Fells, 1893, ch. vi.; Matheson, 1893, ch.
      i; Edwards, 1989a).

Appendix: Potted biographies of some early British and French writers of key accounting texts related to the development of industrial accounting

British writers

Benjamin Booth (? -1807) An English merchant and resident partner in New York of a London merchant house. On his return to England he wrote his book, partly because he felt there was a need for a book which enabled practical accounting in a large scale business. In particular he wanted to provide guidance for the young bookkeeper who wanted to be able to perform their duties correctly. Thus the book is not a theoretical text but a practical one, based on 30 years experience of keeping accounts.

Robert Colinson (?-?) According to material in the book, he was a Captain, and had 25 years experience in commerce as "student and practitioner". Otherwise, little is known about him. It is not absolutely certain but he may be the 'Colinson' who was linked with the accounts of the New Mills Cloth Manufactory, Haddingtonshire.

John Collins (1624-83). Son of a poor non-conformist minister who became a learned mathematical Fellow of the Royal Society. Studies accounts in his leisure time and, after holding a number of jobs, including being s seaman, he began to teach mathematics and accounts. In the course of this he prepared some books of accounts and drew up some questions for his students, which were put together in book form in 1653. The book was published in several editions. His publisher asked him to include material on public accounts but he did not feel he knew enough about this. However, after the 1664 edition he added further material relating to partnerships, including that of the dyer which Edwards (1937b) has referred to as possibly marking Collins out as the first English writer to recognise the different requirements of industrial as opposed to commercial accounting.

James Dodson (1710-57) A mathematician of some distinction, elected to the Royal Society in 1755. Between 1735 and 1747 he probably ran a writing school - writing, bookkeeping and arithmetic being key elements of a commercial education at this time. In 1755 he became

Master of the Royal Mathematical School at Christ's Hospital. In his book, published in 1750, he describes himself as a teacher of mathematics, but indicates that he also provides services as an accountant.

Robert Hamilton (1743-1829) The eighth son of a leading Edinburgh bookseller, a partner in a paper-mill, with his father, and printer to the University of Edinburgh. He had an academic ability in mathematics. In 1769 he became Rector of Perth Academy. By the time that the second edition of his book was published, he had become Professor of Natural Philosophy at Aberdeen University. He taught mathematics and eventually became the Professor of Mathematics there, until his death.

Edward Thomas Jones (1767-1833) Experienced as an accountant, he wrote his book because he was appalled at the poor quality of bookkeeping that he had come across and the ease with which fraud was being carried on. His system was devised to "counteract these alarming evils" (1796, p.11, quoted in Bywater and Yamey, 1982, p.196). A patent was granted for his system on 26 January 1796. Over 4,000 subscribers paid 1 guinea each for a copy of his work and the right to use his method. There were 15 different translations of his book into seven different languages. Degranges senior in France was inspired to publication by Jones' book (Bywater and Yamey, 1982, p.199).

Patrick Kelly (1756-1842) Master of Finsbury Square Academy, a well known private school, for commercial and mathematical learning, in London, open from at least 1792. He was also mathematical examiner at Christ's Hospital School and to Trinity House, and an authority on weights and measures. Twelve editions of his book on bookkeeping, explaining both single and double entry, appeared between 1801 and 1847, chiefly designed for use in schools.

John Mair (1702/3-69) A graduate from St. Andrews University he became assistant master at Ayr Grammar School where he taught arithmetic, bookkeeping, geography and navigation. In 1761 he became Rector of a new academy at Perth where he remained until his death. Eight editions of his book appeared between 1736 and 1765, and then it was thoroughly revised in 1768 (published posthumously in 1773). The 6th edition of his book was the first English book on bookkeeping to be translated into a foreign language (Norwegian) in 1775.

Stephen Monteage (1623?-87) A practitioner rather than, as were most seventeenth century writers of bookkeeping texts, a teacher. The text was written for "my Children and Friends". It appeared in three editions. Note that his book for rent-gatherers was charge and discharge not double entry (Bywater and Yamey, 1982, p.130).

Roger North (1653-1735) Went to Cambridge University and then became a lawyer. Having taken over the family estate he wrote books on a number of subjects. His text on bookkeeping was addressed to 'private gentlemen' and the titles contained in the ledger accounts are appropriate to a landed estate.

French writers

L.F.G. de Cazaux (? - ?) He was a landowner in the south-west of France, and wrote *De la comptabilité dans une entreprise industrielle et spécialement dans une exploitation rurale* in 1824. He also wrote books on economics. Otherwise, little is known about him.

Mathieu de la Porte (c.1660-c.1732) Described on the title page as professor of bookkeeping, arithmetician, scrivener (*écrivain juré*) and expert in the verification of documents, signatures, accounts and reckonings (Bywater and Yamey, 1982, p.142). Published two books, both in several editions. He established a categorisation comprising three types of ledger accounts: accounts of the merchant himself; accounts of material objects; and accounts of debtors and creditors. De Graaf had utilised a similar classificatory system, and English texts followed suit with their classification of nominal or fictitious, real and personal, but it is not clear whether this was derived or not from de la Porte (Bywater and Yamey, 1982, p.143). Fulton, and Cronhelm (1818), later criticised this categorisation. In his book, de la Porte refers to the French Code of Commerce of 1673 and notes that it prescribed certain official procedures for authenticating account books. Later editions of his book (e.g. that of 1753) indicate that this clause of the Code was virtually a dead letter (Bywater and Yamey, 1982, pp.144-5.). De la Porte was Dutch, but became a naturalised Frenchman in 1705, having moved there as a young man. "He is described as 'Keeper of His Majesty's books' (he probably was a clerk in the financial administration) and as sworn writing-master" (Bywater and Yamey, 1982, p.145).

Edmond Degranges senior (? -1818) There were many editions of his book, some published by his son after his death, many imitators and not a few plagiarists. Active in Revolutionary France, he supported the Girondins but managed to avoid their fate. He then left politics to concentrate on teaching and writing on commercial subjects, and became a commercial arbitrator and financial adviser (*arbitre en matière de commerce*) and a member of the *Société Académique des Sciences de Paris*. The first edition of his accounting text, *La tenue des livres rendue facile* (*Book-keeping made easy*), was published in 1795, and a second edition appeared in 1801. In this work he advocated five general accounts: general merchandise; cash; bills (or similar objects) receivable; bills payable; and profit and loss. His combined 'journal-ledger' won him great renown, but eventually became known as the 'American' system of bookkeeping (Bywater and Yamey, 1982, p.215). Up to 1830 about 18 or 19 editions of his book had been published, although there was something of a lull around this time as his son, Edmond junior, a ship-owner, was badly hit by the revolution of 1830. Editions of his work, however, continued to be published until 1897, long after his death.

Edmond Degranges junior (? -1888?) He studied mathematics before becoming an artillery officer. On leaving the army, in turn, he became a merchant, a banker, a shipowner and a professor. Published *Tenue des livres des maîtres de forges et des usines à fer* (*Bookkeeping for ironmasters and ironworks*) in 1824.

Pierre-Antoine Godard-Desmarest (1767-1850) An officer in military administration (accounting) who became the administrator of the Baccarat crystalworks from 1822. Wrote *Traité général et sommaire de la comptabilité commerciale* published in 1827, and a number of other works, including one on accounting for state finances (1821) and another on political economy (1835).

Mce Jeannin (? - ?) An ex attaché to the general accounting section of the Interior Ministry, a professor of mathematics and an expert in commercial matters. Wrote *Traité de la comptabilité commerciale, régulière et frauduleuse*, published in 1828. Since the ideas expressed in his book are similar to those of Godard-Desmarest, and that they worked in the Interior Ministy during the same period, it is possible that the two authors knew each other.

L. Mézières (? - ?) A teacher at the Royal Arts and Crafts School at Châlons-sur-Marne, which was established under the Napoleonic regime as part of its attempt to develop technical training in France. He was also the establishment's accountant. First published in 1842, *Comptabilité commerciale, industrielle et manufacturière*, went through five editions, the last being published in 1862. The book was written for technical schools but with an eye to practical use as well (Edwards, 1937c, p.30)

Jean-Baptiste Payen (1759-1820) The son of a well-off Paris merchant who became a magistrate then moved into the chemical industry. Impressed by Edward Jones' book (1796), which he considered a 'work of genius', he determined to apply his ideas. However, he only did so in 1817, writing his *Essai sur la tenue des livres d'un manufacturier* when a fall confined him to his room for several months.

Count Michel-Frédéric Pillet-Will (1781-1860) From a family of protestant bankers he was involved in the establishment of the Société des houillères et fonderies de l'Aveyron (Decazeville). He was one of the principal managers of the company which was run from Paris. In 1832 he was sent to Decazeville for seven weeks to study operations and his book, *Examen analytique de l'usine de Decazeville*, published that year, is the product of his study. In it he describes in minute detail the different accounts opened for cost calculation. He was also a founder, with Benjamin Delessert, of the Caisse d'épargne and a *régent* (member of the board) of the Banque de France after 1828 (DBF, 1965).

F.N. Simon (? - ?) He published *Méthode complète de tenue des livres* in 1830. This book, c.1000 pages long, is mainly devoted to an exposition of single entry bookkeeping, with only the last 150 pages concerned with double entry techniques. In the book he argues that single entry methods are sufficient to carry out relatively complicated accounting tasks, without the need for any profound knowledge of accounting theory. Simon was the *régisseur* (steward) of Lord Marmont's ironworks (near Dijon) and claimed that he had been using single entry for 'decades in ironworks' (1830, p.6). It seems likely that he received his education in the *ancien régime* and that the book was published towards the end of his career.

Chapter 4 - Developments in industrial accounting practice in Britain and France, c.1700-c.1880

Accounting is a discipline which may be seen, at a particular point in time, to encompass a body of ideas, a number of conventions, a set of available tools/techniques and a variety of actual practices. At any single point in time, therefore, one might expect there to exist a number of sets of actual practices reflecting a variety of ideas and the range of requirements of different end-users. Furthermore, whilst a particular set of practices *may* predominate in a specific time period, changes in either end-user requirements and/or ideas may increase the available set of tools/techniques, thereby possibly increasing accounting's potentialities and altering predominant accounting practice. To understand fully accounting's development, it is necessary to have an understanding of both practical developments and the development of ideas and tools/techniques available. Chapter 3 explored developments in accounting ideas and tools as reflected in the contemporary literature and, in an attempt to gain a further insight into such developments in both Britain and France, this chapter explores developments in practice.

The aim of this chapter is to establish the nature of accounting practices within industrial enterprises in the eighteenth and nineteenth centuries in both Britain and France. For each country individually, commencing with Britain, we will present a general overview of the work of previous historians, and then look at specific evidence, both from our own work and that of others, of the development of accounting in industry. Having established the nature of such developments, the chapter closes with a brief consideration of those factors which have been highlighted by the various writers as explaining this development. We will commence this survey, however, by clearly establishing the particular aspects of accounting with which we are concerned, and then look at the evidence.

I.   Accounting in industrial enterprises

The principal focus of this text is with what came to be known during the nineteenth century, in the French context, by the term *comptabilité industrielle* ('industrial accounting'). In the British context, however, the term 'industrial accounting' has rarely been used, though previous writers on British accounting change have adopted a wide variety of related terms. Sometimes these terms, including cost recording, costing, cost accounting, managerial accounting and management accounting, have been used almost interchangeably, whilst on other occasions they have been used in a specific, discrete manner. The variety of approaches arises partly from the fact that, even today, a key term such as management accounting does not have a generally accepted meaning, and partly from the failure of writers to distinguish between specific tools/techniques, practices and ideas on the one hand, and the label used to encompass the whole potential range of tools/techniques, ideas and practices on the other.

From the point of view of the historian, it is our belief that any term used needs to be clearly defined, whether this should be a broad definition or a narrow one. Once the definition has been established, it should then be possible to concentrate arguments on the historical facts and their interpretation, rather than what is being meant by the terms being used. To illustrate this issue, consider the term 'cost accounting'. Parker (1984) suggests that there are at least two different meanings to this term: "in its original meaning [it means] the accumulation and assignment of historical costs to units of product and departments, primarily for the purpose of stock valuation and profit measurement [whereas] in its modern meaning, it is difficult to distinguish from management accounting" (1984, p.47). But what is meant by the term 'management accounting'? For Parker it is defined as "that part of accounting which is concerned mainly with internal reporting to the manager of an enterprise. It emphasizes the control and decision making rather than the stewardship aspects of accounting" (1984, p.115). Some historians, for example Miller and Napier (1993), argue that accounting terminology should be used only in relation to the period in which it was current. For them, therefore, the term 'management accounting', which entered into the accounting terminology on this side of the Atlantic in the 1950s, is inapplicable in respect of earlier time periods. Whilst we do not totally disagree with this concept, we believe that wholehearted acceptance of such a view can lead erroneously to the view that, in the past, activities which would now be termed management accounting did not take place.

From the historians point of view, we find that the most serviceable definitions of management accounting are those which were first put forward in Britain in the 1950s. Following the visit to the United States by the Management Accounting Team, led by the chartered accountant Ian Morrow, under the auspices of the Anglo-American Council on Productivity (1950), a number of the accountancy bodies issued pamphlets outlining the nature of management accounting (ICAEW, 1954; ACCA, 1954). The definitions contained in these pamphlets were broad-based: the ICAEW indicating that "any form of accounting which enables business to be conducted more efficiently can be regarded as management accounting . . . " (1954, para. 2). Whilst the modern view of management accounting may be that it comprises techniques such as standard costing, budgeting, activity-based costing, broad-based definitions avoid any confusion of specific tools/techniques with the practice itself. Neither do historians have to establish that, for example, standard costing was being operated in order to conclude that management accounting was being practiced. It is merely enough to establish that the accounting systems being operated provided information which was used by management to help them to run the business more efficiently.

Starting from a position which accepts such a broad-based definition of management accounting, we are able to conclude that the searches which we have carried out of the archives of enterprises in both Britain and France have revealed significant evidence of the use of accounting systems and accounting information to guide business decision-making. In those businesses, evidence has been found of the use of total costing, of the use of double entry bookkeeping, and the integration of costing with financial information within the ledgers. Additionally we have also found evidence of *ad hoc* costings and of an understanding, on the part of businessmen, of the difference between fixed and variable costs. In all cases, the information contained in, or drawn from, the accounting system has been utilised in business decision making, with *ad hoc* costings often playing an important role.

In order that our use of terminology, particularly in regard to the British context, should be free from confusion and not be encumbered by the baggage of past usage, we intend to utilise the term 'industrial accounting' to describe the calculation, by industrial organisations, of costs within a double entry framework. Where we use the terms cost and management accounting, these are intended to imply their broad-based meanings. For our purposes, therefore, cost accounting is defined as "the accumulation of relevant costs to be used by managers for the purposes of planning, decision making and control". Where other writers have discussed the use of cost accounting within an industrial context, we will refer to it as *industrial* cost accounting.

II.   British accounting development c.1700-c.1880

The views of other historians

Over the years ideas have changed concerning what dates, and events, have seen significant developments in industrial cost accounting, and this process is likely to continue as more information comes available. Solomons (1952) undertook the first thorough examination of the development of cost accounting[1], and he identified the year 1875 as being of particular importance. From the early fourteenth century to 1875 major cost accounting developments dealt with the following technical matters: bringing records of industrial activity within the double entry framework of bookkeeping, and devising a means of tracking internal transfers of goods from one process to another. After 1875 the broader issue of making accounting records mean something, in terms of the provision of information for decision making, is given greater stress. Solomons refers to this period as seeing a 'costing renaissance' but, while there was undoubtedly a burgeoning of the literature after 1875, it does not necessarily follow that this reflected a corresponding upsurge of interest in costing procedures on the part of businessmen.

The notion that costing procedures developed on a significant scale only after 1875 seems inconsistent with the fairly persuasive demand/response theory of accounting development, which sees it as a social technology continually responding to changes in business requirements. Solomons's explanation for the lack of progress, echoed by Pollard (1968) more specifically in relation to the industrial revolution period, is that, in the absence of keen competition, prices could be set at a level which produced generous profit margins and, therefore, the need for detailed costing data was not strongly felt.

McKendrick (1970) and Fleischman and Parker (1990), however, have provided evidence relating, respectively, to Josiah Wedgwood and the Carron Company which suggest that significant cost accounting was being carried on in certain enterprises as much as a century before Solomon's costing renaissance. Moreover, in McKendrick's view, Wedgwood clearly adopted costing as a response to a downturn in trade in 1772, suggesting that, even in an industry where profit margins were large, trade fluctuations could provide a strong incentive for leading entrepreneurs to develop a cost consciousness (McKendrick, 1970; Hopwood, 1987).

It would appear, therefore, that Solomons' view that there was a costing renaissance may be incorrect, but why should this be so? One problem with Solomons' study is that it was based mainly on a survey of the engineering literature, much of which was American. Thus he scanned articles in *Engineering*, *The Engineer* and *The Engineering Magazine*, but largely ignored other contemporary trade journals and, of course, the accounting journals[2]. Since much of this material commenced only around the 1870s, it is not surprising that his findings should stress the developments of the late nineteenth and early twentieth centuries. A concentration on the non-accounting literature, however, undoubtedly limits the validity of Solomons' findings.

A more persuasive scenario, and one that pushes back the origins into the late eighteenth century, is put forward by Garner (1954, p.3) who argues that the initial impetus for the development of cost accounting was the replacement of the domestic system by capitalist processes of production. In his view, the British industrial revolution (conventionally assigned to the period 1760-1830) accelerated the rate of change, but was not the main stimulus for change, as is claimed by accounting historians such as Littleton who described it as "one of the many consequences of the industrial revolution" (p.321). Nevertheless, Garner's statement that "during the decades 1820-1880 little can be found which is of interest in the development of cost accounting, either in this country [the United States] or abroad" (1955, p.9) is altogether too sweeping.

Pioneering work on the issues of strategy, structure and their relationship to accounting has been carried out by Alfred Chandler jr. (1977, 1990) in the US context. He does not explicitly spell out the nature of the link between these issues, but it is clearly implied in his work that the direction of causation runs from strategy, through structure to accounting. Thus, for Chandler, the emergence of large-scale business in the late nineteenth century, which ultimately led to the development of the multi-divisional business form, created a demand for new management information systems. As managerial structures developed in response to strategic changes, they themselves necessitated changes in the accounting system, developments which ultimately led to a distinction being made between, on the one hand, management accounting and, on the other, financial accounting.

Johnson (1984) has applied the Chandlerian analysis more explicitly to accounting development, and has argued that it was the change in the organisational structure of business activity which provided the principal stimulus for the development of cost accounting. Prior to 1780, much of what might be broadly described as industrial activity was carried on within the domestic system and comprised a fairly simple series of market transactions. The businessmen purchased materials which were then 'put out' to a variety of artisans, each to perform a particular processing function paid for on the piece rate basis. The product, when finished, was sold. At each stage of manufacture, the businessman needed very little by way of accounting information to decide which course of action was preferable, e.g. further processing or sale, as most of the data was provided by readily available market prices. It is therefore within what Johnson describes as the 'single activity organisation' which flourished between 1780-1900, that the internalisation of activities (both employees and manufacturing processes) gave rise to the need for the development of cost and profit finding techniques as the basis for both performance assessment and resource allocation decisions.

If we accept the Chandler/Johnson view that the scope and scale of business activity is likely to have implications for the design and development of the management information system, we might *expect* to find developments in accounting occurring earlier in Britain since factory development had begun at a significantly earlier stage. Proto-industrialization during the seventeenth and early eighteenth centuries had seen the emergence of the proto-factory,[3] involving a significant investment in tools and implements and a labour force which was assembled to perform specialist functions under supervision (Flinn, 1962; Marshall, 1980, chapter 6; Mepham, 1988, pp.57-8).

The pace of industrialization picked up in Britain during the second half of the eighteenth century with the textile, especially cotton but also woollen, and iron industries coming to the fore. By 1812, in the neighbourhood of Birmingham alone, there were 10 iron works, each of which cost over £50,000 to establish and typically engaged between 300-500 workmen apart from the colliers (Ashton, quoted in Edwards, 1937b, p.193). An example of an organization growing rapidly during the first half of the nineteenth century, under the leadership of Sir John Guest, was the Dowlais Iron Company which employed 5,192 people in 1842. In the same year, it was described as "the first [iron works] in the world,"[4] but it is not necessary to go beyond the locality of south Wales for other examples of substantial British companies at this early date.[5]

Given Chandler's (1977, 1990) assessment of the impact of the large-scale business enterprise on cost accounting developments, it would be surprising if progress in this direction had not been made early on by companies at the forefront of Britain's Industrial Revolution. Indeed, research has been undertaken which suggests that important costing developments did in fact occur in Britain both prior to and during the Industrial Revolution (Roll, 1930; Burley, 1958; Rimmer, 1960; McKendrick, 1970; Stone, 1973; Marshall, 1980; Jones, 1985; Fleischman and Parker, 1990, 1991, 1992; Fleischman, Parker and Vamplew, 1991; Edwards and Newell, 1991; Edwards and Boyns, 1992; McLean, 1995). Moreover, refinements of accounting technique, of fundamental importance in terms of departmental profit and performance measurement, occurred in relatively small iron making establishments (Edwards and Boyns, 1992).

Early cost accounting developments in British industry

Two important studies which have examined the nature of costing in two significant British enterprises during the late eighteenth century, namely those of Josiah Wedgwood and the Carron Company, have been published by McKendrick (1970) and Fleischman and Parker (1990). These are illustrative of important aspects of cost accounting in the second half of the eighteenth century, just at the time when the industrial revolution in Britain was beginning to gather momentum, and we paraphrase the main findings below.

Wedgwood

In August and September 1772, Josiah Wedgwood was spurred by economic depression to "attempt to solve the problem of accurate industrial accounting" (McKendrick, 1970, p.48). In periods of normal trade, Wedgwood was able to charge prices for his high quality pottery products which yielded handsome profit margins, and thus, in McKendrick's view, "the incentives towards anything more than routine costing were usually rather slight" (1970, p.48). Wedgwood expressed reservations on occasions concerning the accuracy of his calculations, but nevertheless used them in pricing decisions, lowering prices in depressions and restoring them when trade picked up, and for costing new techniques before they were introduced. In McKendrick's view, Wedgwood's costings also made him "acutely aware of the savings to be achieved through accurate costing, and acutely aware of the permanent role in production costs played by rent and administration" (1970, p.54). As well as aiding business decision-making, Wedgwood's costings identified "a history of embezzlement, blackmail, chicanery, and what Wedgwood called 'extravagance and dissipation'" (McKendrick, 1970, p.63).

Overall, McKendrick's examination of the Wedgwood archive indicates a key role for cost accounting in business management during years of financial crisis but, due to the generally high level of profit generated, McKendrick notes a failure to utilise cost accounting to its full potential. Thus whilst the level of sophistication of Wedgwood's business methods has been considered 'surprisingly high', "the occasions when he was moved to a full-scale investigation of his production costs [were] very few and far between" (McKendrick, 1970, p.47). Indeed, there is little evidence of Wedgwood persisting with any systematic costing operations, and many of his costings are described as rough jottings and of existing "*in vacuo . . .* " (McKendrick, 1970, pp.56-8). Despite this lack of systematic costing analysis, however, Wedgwood clearly understood the distinction between fixed and variable costs, long before the issue was discussed in the British accounting literature. In 1772, for example, he observed that some expenses "move like clockwork and are much the same whether the quantity of goods [produced] be large or small" (McKendrick, 1970, p.55).[6]

McKendrick's study, however, tells us nothing about the technical nature of Wedgwood's accounting system, for example whether or not it was based on double entry bookkeeping, and provides no evidence of integration between the costings and the financial accounts. The references to rough jottings, etc., suggests that costing was done on an *ad hoc* basis, but we cannot be sure. The Wedgwood case is a prime example of the type of *ad hoc* costing which Pollard

(1965) found to be quite widespread in Britain during the industrial revolution period. Unlike many of those other instances, however, we have a reasonable knowledge of why such calculations were made. Applying the different categories of historian put forward in chapter 1, McKendrick would be classified as economic rationalist. Historians from other persuasions have viewed events at Etruria from a different perspective and added value to the explanatory role of the archive. For Hopwood (1987), the Wedgwood case has a further significance, in that it is seen as representing a discontinuity in accounting's development, since it is a prime example of accounting being put where it had not previously been. For Hopwood, the significant point is that a concept of cost had to be constructed, and a way of making it operable had to be devised (1987, p.215). In the view of Miller and Napier, the Wedgwood development should be seen more in terms of its outcomes rather than its origins. They note in particular that it provided "a basis for transforming the functioning of the enterprise" (1993, p.642), since it facilitated control at a distance.

The Carron Company

The Carron Company commenced operations in 1759 as a partnership between two Birmingham men - the medical practitioner and inventor John Roebuck and the prominent merchant and businessman Samuel Garbett - and a Cockenzie merchant, William Cadell. For the period 1759-86, i.e. that to which most of the surviving cost management material relates, Garbett, Cadell and Gascoigne, who took over as general manager in 1769 from Cadell, were at the helm (1990, p.214). Fleischman and Parker have clearly identified widespread evidence of cost management activity at Carron during the early stages of the industrial revolution in Britain. There was bountiful data on departmental costs, reflecting a "system of responsibility accounting and departmental cost management" with costing being "employed extensively in management decision-making, ranging from the development of production standards to departmental and product line evaluations" (1990, p.220).

From an early stage, a basic system of overhead cost allocation was in place which was used for assessing departmental performance and, on occasions, the impact of excessive allocations on department profitability was apparently recognised (Fleischman and Parker, 1990, p.216). Between 1770 and 1772, a detailed system of cost estimates and intracompany charges was in place, with the cost of ironstone to the furnaces, for example, based on the average cost over the previous six months plus royalty and carriage (Fleischman and Parker, 1990, p.216). Fleischman and Parker also found evidence that, during the 1790s, the blast furnace supervisor "was transmitting monthly cost comparisons of his operations to the partners. These reports were calculations of cost per ton of good iron at each blast furnace" (1990, p.216).

In marked contrast to the quality and extent of the costing information available to the Carron management, and perhaps somewhat surprisingly given the merchant background of Garbett and Cadell, Fleischman and Parker confirm Campbell's assessment that there was a "disarray of Carron's financial statements during these early years" (1990, p.214). In particular they note that the firm's founders had great difficulty coping adequately with depreciation, inventory valuation, and the owners' capital accounts, and it was possibly such problems with the financial accounts that explain the high quality of the costing information: the "Cost management processes in Carron appear to have been motivated by the firm's early problems with securing adequate partnership capital, attaining profitability, and maintaining liquidity" (1990, p.220) Furthermore, Fleischman and Parker judge that "Previous to 1786, the Carron records reflected all the correct instincts about cost accounting methodologies but a failure to integrate costing with acceptable financial reporting" (1990, p.214).

After 1786, the surviving evidence suggests an improvement in financial reporting, but a disappearance of the earlier costing sophistication, though the explanation here may lie in the paucity of surviving records during the periods when Stainton and Dawson controlled the affairs of the enterprise. Overall, Fleischman and Parker are unable to confirm whether the financial accounts of Carron were based on a system of double entry bookkeeping, but they do suggest that attempts were made to integrate the accounts which "failed because of the financial reporting shortcomings" (1990, p.220). It was not until 25 April 1854 that the company's General Court appointed a professional accountant (James Brown, of Edinburgh) "to determine if the financial accounting books had been properly kept in the past and to achieve a needed simplification of the system" (Fleischman and Parker, 1990, p.220).

Summary

The above studies demonstrate the fact that, prior to the end of the eighteenth century, sophisticated costing techniques were utilised to enable the entrepreneurs to make important business decisions, such as pricing (Wedgwood) and closure of unremunerative operations (Carron). Unfortunately, neither of these studies is able to confirm or deny that the costing was being carried out within the framework of the general accounting system, or whether these companies employed double entry bookkeeping. In the case of Wedgwood, there is a strong implication, given the largely *ad hoc* nature of the costing, and the fact that it does not seem to have occupied the owner's attention except in times of depression, that any integration of costing within the accounting system is unlikely. At Carron, it is possible that there was an integration but, due to the absence of detailed product costings, Fleischman and Parker (1990) were unable to fully investigate the relationship between the financial and cost accounts. In his study, Campbell gives hints that Carron may have been using double entry, by mentioning trial balances and debits and credits (1961, p.166), but his evidence is also inconclusive. At one point he refers to the "meticulous but fragmented system of book-keeping", noting that, whilst the overall credits and debits were sufficiently accurate, the attribution of costs and revenue between different items was "often largely a matter of guesswork" (1961, p.168).

In their broader study of cost management within 25 'large' enterprises during the industrial revolution period, Fleischman and Parker (1991) do not examine the issue of integration between the cost and financial accounts. Indeed, they appear to believe that costing during the industrial revolution period was carried out independently since, following Solomons, they judge that it was only during the 'costing renaissance' associated with the scientific management movement at the end of the nineteenth century that "integration was achieved with financial reporting" (1991, p.372).

This conclusion is at odds with more recent evidence, which suggests that at a number of British firms in the late eighteenth and early nineteenth centuries, routine costing procedures were carried out firmly within an overall accounting system based on double entry bookkeeping. As the British economy underwent industrialisation in the late eighteenth century and throughout the nineteenth century, those running businesses began to develop accounting systems to cater for their needs. In those industries where large, single items were produced to order, such as shipbuilding, the accounting problems were somewhat less pressing than in vast manufacturing enterprises, but nevertheless examples can be found early in the nineteenth century of the mercantile system of double entry accounting being adapted to enable the costs of each ship to be calculated. Developments in shipbuilding might well provide an important link between mercantile and industrial accounting, and we will examine the results of McLean's study (1995) before proceeding to examine the development of more mainstream industrial accounting.

From mercantile to industrial accounting in the nineteenth century: the case of shipbuilding

McLean's (1995) study of the development of the Sunderland shipbuilding industry between 1818 and 1917, spanning the transition c.1870 from the building of wooden ships to the construction of iron ships, demonstrates the widespread use of contract accounting and costing. Systems designs varied between firms and over time at individual businesses, but there is clear evidence of "an evolution from systems based on integrated accounting, through to the production of memorandum cost data, and systems of contract accounting and costing incorporating financial and cost accounting sub-systems" (1995, p.142). Records examined by McLean for the diverse mercantile partnership of Tanner and Beckwith (1995, pp.121-4), which had interests as timber merchants and coal fitters (exporters) as well as shipowners and shipbuilders, for the period 1819-25, show the use of a "comprehensive mercantile accounting system", within which a 'new ship' account was opened in the double-entry ledgers for every ship built. These accounts contained entries for all cost transactions carried out in connection with construction and outfitting, written-up chronologically within the double-entry accounting system.

At Laings, "a mixed activity firm, engaged in trading, shipowning and shipbuilding" and which remained a partnership until 1898, McLean found a rudimentary double-entry ledger in use between 1818 and 1824, wherein "separate, unique accounts were used to calculate the profit on each ship built, the cost entries being summary transfers from subsidiary accounts" (1995, p.124). By the early 1840s the costs were gathered together in the subsidiary accounts, with only summary amounts of prime cost being transferred to the ship account in the ledger (1995, pp.125-6). The lack of archival material for the 1850s makes precise dating difficult, but there is evidence of a major change in the accounting system c.1864. From that time, until 1903, Laings used a "cost book system, containing an individual record for each ship built. These records were memorandum summaries, outside the double-entry accounting system, and were compiled after the completion of the ship, probably as pricing information" (1995, p.126). McLean is nevertheless of the view that the cost books were probably prepared by the accounting staff from information extracted largely from the main accounting system. He considers the move to cost books "as a positive development of managerial information for pricing decisions as Laings moved from wooden to iron shipbuilding" (1995, p.129).

Doxfords started out essentially as timber merchants, in 1833, but they also owned and rented property and from 1840 William Doxford began to build ships on his own account. From the partnership's commencement in 1833, a complete mercantile accounting system was in place, and this "was readily adapted to the requirements of construction by both putting-out and shipbuilding" (McLean, 1995, p.132), though different sub-systems were employed for two alternative methods of construction. In McLean's judgement, "The system dealt with mercantile activities as a matter of course, adapted readily to account for putting-out and extended to deal with shipbuilding" (1995, p.132). Ultimately this extension involved establishing an individual account for each ship, to enable the calculation of the profit made thereon.

The final concern examined, Shorts, was not established until 1870. In that year, George Short, a former ship's carpenter and foreman shipwright, who had commenced his own yard to build wooden ships in 1850, moved to a larger iron shipbuilding yard. From the outset, the new iron shipbuilding venture used a double-entry bookkeeping system, possibly continuing a practice used at the wooden shipyard, and profit or loss on each individual ship was calculated in a separate ship account (1995, p.136). McLean describes the system in use in the 1870s as follows:

> Hull construction costs were debited on a chronological basis; summarized outfitting cost was debited as a single item; revenue was credited and profit calculated. The

accounting system encompassed a host of external transactions and a series of internal transfers, but it did have its analytical limitations. Within the ship accounts of the early 1870s, there were attempts to prepare sub-analyses of hull construction costs by cost type, but such efforts were soon abandoned, perhaps because they proved too cumbersome. Profits and losses on individual ships were transferred to the firm's half-yearly profit and loss account where summarized 'charges', or overheads, were written off and the balance of profit calculated and apportioned between partners. No statement resembling a trial balance or balance sheet has been traced. (1995, p.136)

Shorts moved over to the use of separate cost books somewhat later than Laings, around 1890, possibly due to the increasingly complex nature of the business organization which ultimately led to the partnership becoming a limited company by the early 1900s.

Industrial accounting: costing within double entry bookkeeping

It is widely acknowledged that the development of the vertically integrated manufacturing business in order to secure sources of supply and outlets for goods manufactured, or simply to organize more efficiently the flow of goods from raw materials to the ultimate consumer, and thereby drive the 'slack' out of market transactions, generated a need for a new form of accounting. What needs further consideration is the circumstances in which these problems arose and the way in which accounting responded to them. There is general agreement that the vertically integrated plant became more firmly established in British and North American industry in the second half of the nineteenth century, and this observation has led to the conclusion that the integration of financial and management accounting systems was a product of this era. According to Chandler (1962, pp.174-85 and 1977, pp.109-20) this, and other cost accounting developments, occurred in order to cope with the uncertainty and risk associated with oligopolistic markets, complex production processes and the problems of the large scale business organization. It might be further pointed out that the adoption of an integrated financial and management accounting system received reinforcement from the literature which stressed the possibility that, otherwise, important costs might be omitted. According to Dicksee, for example, "cost records which are not capable of being reconciled, or agreed, with the actual results shown by the financial books are practically valueless" (1903, p.20).

Johnson's appraisal of the development of management accounting systems led him to conclude (1972) that the study of more business records would show that *many* companies probably integrated their cost and mercantile accounts ("that characterizes modern cost accounting", p.467) at an earlier date than was previously believed, and he uses the accounting records of the Lyman Mills, a cotton textile firm incorporated in Boston in 1854, to illustrate this hypothesis. Johnson's claim (1981) that it was the early nineteenth century textile factories which first applied the principles of double entry bookkeeping to the maintenance of cost accounts, however, is no longer tenable. Indeed, recent evidence indicates the use of such systems in Britain in the late eighteenth and early nineteenth centuries, particularly in the mining and metal industries, in addition to its earlier observed use in textiles. Thus whilst Stone (1973) observed its use at the Charlton Cotton Mills, Manchester, possibly as early as 1800, Jones (1985) has found evidence of its use at the Cyfarthfa Ironworks, Merthyr, from 1791, and at the Mona Mine Company possibly as early as the 1780s. Furthermore, Edwards and his associates (Edwards and Boyns, 1992; Boyns and Edwards, 1995, 1996c,d; Edwards *et al*, 1995) have found evidence of industrial accounting at a number of iron companies spanning the period from the end of the seventeenth century (Staveley) to the middle of the nineteenth century (Dowlais and Consett). We examine, in roughly chronological order, the relevant features of these companies' accounting systems in the sections which follow.

Staveley

The Staveley Forge and Furnace, near Sheffield, are believed to have been erected during the first decade of the seventeenth century. By the end of that century they formed part of the group of furnaces, forges and a slitting mill controlled by the Derbyshire and Nottingham Company. During the eighteenth century the interests of this group became closely integrated with those of another partnership, the Duke of Norfolk's Works. Both partnerships had members in common, but at no time were they under identical control. Nevertheless, the accounting records of both partnerships, the Duke of Norfolk's Works from 1690, and the Derbyshire and Nottingham Company from 1750, reveal the operation of double entry bookkeeping systems which were used to provide management information. Edwards and Boyns have found that the bookkeeping system did not hamper in anyway the development of costing information but rather "seems to have provided a logical and convenient framework for its creation and use" (1992, p.168).

An analysis of the surviving records for 1750-65, which were undoubtedly merely a continuation of earlier records which have not survived, shows that Staveley used the concept of profit centres in relation to its four, vertically integrated production sites. Each 'department' had its own ledger account, the profit or loss on which, together with those from other nominal accounts, was transferred to a general profit and loss account. These ledger accounts recorded all of the direct costs incurred by each 'department' and the amount of output.[7] Although the separate physical location of the 'departments' meant that the bulk of each department's costs could be traced direct, there was still the need for certain apportionments to be made in order to calculate total costs of production. Some shared costs were apportioned between departments in accordance with unidentifiable 'cost drivers', some were split equally, and other items, which bore no clear relation to the departmental activities, were debited directly to the profit and loss account (Edwards and Boyns, 1992, p.163).

The Staveley ledgers also appear to exhibit the use of market prices for transfer of pig iron from the furnace to each of the two forges, and for the bar iron supplied by the forge to the mill (Edwards and Boyns, 1992, pp.161-2, 165). According to Edwards and Boyns (1992, pp.165-6), the disaggregation of profits by activity centre can be explained in terms of the requirements of management for decision-making purposes. Costing/profit information was generated that was relevant for decisions affecting production and closure, and in exercising choice between suppliers of charcoal. Thus examples have been found of detailed calculations, both inside and outside the journal, of the average cost of individual batches of charcoal, enabling both comparison and providing a financial basis for future purchasing decisions. There is evidence of a concern with physical as well as financial measures, with use made of 'yield' calculations which express output of, for example, a ton of bar iron in terms of the quantity of pig iron required for that purpose. This would have enabled experiments to be made of production efficiency between periods and forges.

Overall, Edwards and Boyns have summarised their findings thus:

> The most remarkable feature of the accounting system described in this paper is the integration of the cost and financial records starting in 1690. The operation of the system involved no very complex accounting adjustments, but enabled the identification of departmental profits and, to achieve this objective, a system of transfer pricing based on market rates was employed. (1992, p.167)

Further they were "impressed by the ease with which management at the Duke's works, in 1690, coped with the modification of double-entry bookkeeping procedures in order to provide relevant information for decision making in a vertically integrated plant" (Edwards and Boyns, 1992, p.167).

The development of the accounting system at Staveley during the nineteenth century is examined in a later paper (Edwards *et al*, 1995). Following dissolution of the two partnerships, the Duke of Norfolk's Works and the Derbyshire and Nottingham Company, in 1783, the site at Staveley passed through a number of hands. By 1815 George Barrow had assumed full responsibility for the works and ran it until 1841 when the lease was transferred to his younger brother, Richard. He continued to operate the works until 30 June 1863, when control was passed to the Staveley Coal & Iron Company Ltd., a limited company formed for the purpose of acquiring the assets of Barrow's business. The absence of accounting records between 1783 and 1838 makes it impossible to trace directly any links between the accounting systems of the earlier partnerships and that used in the nineteenth century. However, there are many similarities which led the authors to conclude that the post-1838 series may be seen as the successor to that which ran up to 1783.

By the mid-nineteenth century, Staveley was a fully integrated concern operating collieries, ironstone pits, coke ovens, blast furnaces and a foundry. The accounting system in 1838 revolved around a ledger which "provided a *fully* integrated record of financial and costing information" (Edwards *et al*, 1995, p.12). Each operating department had a separate ledger account, as did limestone, ironstone, pig iron and castings. The system generated "profit or loss measures for each of the operating departments which interfaced either partly (collieries producing coal and furnaces producing pig iron) or wholly (foundry producing castings) with the market" (Edwards *et al*, 1995, pp.8-10). As far as the authors were able to judge, the system of internal transfer prices was designed to recover cost, with any under or over-recovery affecting the valuation of closing stock which was inserted as the balancing figure. The switch of control from George to Richard Barrow seems to have been effected without any change in the accounting system, though over time modifications and improvements were made in the system of record keeping. Thus further profit centres (limestone stock and the ironstone pits) were created in the early 1840s; in 1847 a set of final annual accounts was drawn up for each of the previous six years, in which departmental profits were calculated after taking account of the decline in the value of fixed assets and the opportunity cost of Barrow's investment in the enterprise; and in 1856 a new document, the Foundry Statements and Returns Book was introduced, containing the physical data previously contained in the ledger, together with additional comparative material. Overall,

> "The Foundry Statements and Returns Book, together with
> the analyzed final accounts, ... provide a clear picture of
> both the nature of business operations and the financial
> interpretation of these activities suitable for the purpose of
> identifying waste and inefficiency (by comparing
> performance over time), assessing the comparative
> performance of different departments producing similar
> products, and measuring the contribution of each
> department to overall profit" (Edwards *et al*, 1995, p.20).

In 1856, the previous practice of charging most overheads direct to the general profit and loss account was dropped in favour of one where they were charged to individual cost centres.[8] This was done through the creation of a separate schedule of 'establishment charges', which collected together overhead costs and allocated them to the collieries and foundries, but not the ironstone mines (all of whose output was used within the firm). The basis used for this allocation in the early years is not clear, but by 1870 it was clearly based on tonnage of throughput. The basis was clearly modified from time to time, such modifications being consistent with a desire to measure the profitability of departments which interfaced at least partly with the market (Edwards *et al*, 1995, pp.16-17).

The business of Richard Barrow was acquired by a newly incorporated limited company, the Staveley Iron & Coal Company Ltd. in 1863, but the accounting system developed during the Barrow era continued in use. Thus the Foundry Returns and Statements Book spans the period from 1856 to 1879 and, overall, the "company's cost accounting practices continued to exhibit strong evidence of continuity, with changes periodically made presumably in an endeavour to ensure that the system matched perceived business needs" (Edwards *et al*, 1995, p.22). For most of the nineteenth century, the typical period of analysis in the surviving documentation at Staveley was six-monthly or annually. Shorter period analysis may have been undertaken, but the first surviving evidence of weekly or monthly data relates to 1885.

One other major development which occurred following the setting up of the Staveley Iron & Coal Company Ltd. was the introduction of a systematic provision for depreciation. In the years following the company's formation in 1863 there was an important debate within the company over whether it would be more appropriate to use the physical or real capital maintenance methods of provision. An outside adviser, William Armstrong, and the Manchester accountant, David Chadwick, a director of the company, advocated what might be broadly described in today's parlance as the physical capital maintenance method, whilst the company's general manager Charles Markham favoured real capital maintenance. In 1869, the company decided to use the former method, the essential feature of which is that the enterprise creates a depreciation fund based on the annuity method which is designed to enable the company to recoup the cost of an asset by the time it wears out.

In the event, the view of Armstrong prevailed and the company determined upon the use of his annuity method of depreciation, which involved the calculation of the amount that would need to be charged annually "in order to repay the shareholders at the expiry of the [company's] lease" the full amount standing to the balance of capital. The annuity was to be calculated by taking the book/future value of all assets separately, taking into account their varying expected lives, and calculating the appropriate amount needed, the sum of these individual amounts yielding the value of the annuity or depreciation. This method continued to be used at Staveley up till 1877, but in the accounts for the year ending 1878 it is noted that it had been abandoned in favour of the "broad brush" approach advocated by Markham. This change in due course resulted in a public dispute between Chadwick and his former partner, Collier, who was then Staveley's auditor, concerning the details of the bookkeeping to be employed. For the majority of the board, however, the dispute was largely irrelevant, being simply a matter of dispute between two accountants which, ultimately, had no effect on the financial position of the company.[9]

In their study of the development of accounting at Staveley, Edwards and his associates have therefore discovered that, despite the massive increase in the scale of the enterprise over a century and a half between 1750 and 1900 (annual output of pig iron increased from 500 tons to 132,000 tons and of coal from zero to 1.8 million tons), "the accounting system at Staveley displayed a high degree of continuity and, with little evident difficulty, was adapted to meet perceived management requirements in an evolving organizational structure which produced massive growth in the scale and scope of operations and numbers employed" (Edwards *et al*, 1995, p.36).

The Mona Mine Company

Following the discovery of a large copper deposit at Parys mountain on the island of Anglesey in north Wales in 1768 by Roe and Co., a firm of Macclesfield copper merchants, a lengthy legal dispute arose when workings spread from the Mona property of Sir Nicholas Bayly to the neighbouring Parys farm belonging to the Rev. Edward Hughes. The latter brought in his legal adviser, Thomas Williams of Llanidan who, in 1776, effected an agreement for joint working of the Parys farm minerals, with Williams supervising operations on Hughes's behalf. In 1778, the Parys Mine Company, with Williams as managing partner, took over these operations. In 1785 Williams increased his influence in the Anglesey copper trade when Bayly's son, Lord Uxbridge, offered him a quarter share in the mines following the expiry of the 21 year lease of the Mona mine held by Roe and Co. Control was effected through the formation of the Mona Mine Company in 1785 by Uxbridge and Williams, with the latter in control of operations. The company subsequently established subsidiary enterprises, with interlocking but different partnerships, to operate smelting works in Swansea and Lancashire, and a manufacturing plant in Flintshire.[10]

The precise date at which the Mona Mine Company began to develop a system of industrial accounting is unclear, though it seems almost certain that the company was using a double entry bookkeeping system from its commencement in 1785. For example, Jones (1985, p.244) quotes a memorandum from Pascoe Grenfell, an associate of Williams[11], written c.1786, respecting the Mona Mine records and the book-keeper Hunt. In Jones's opinion, the memorandum gives the impression that double entry book-keeping was well established and that the books were reasonably well kept. It is possible that double entry had been used in relation to the Mona enterprise before this, since some elements of the records indicate continuity over a long period of time. Thus, speaking of the wages records, Jones (1985, p.95) notes that "The system from an accounting point of view changed little in principle as the nineteenth century developed. The records for 1817 and 1818 are not dissimilar to those of the 1770's, except they were for periods of 2 months . . . ".

The clearest evidence provided by Jones as to the integration of costing within the double-entry bookkeeping system at Mona is in his description of the system in operation in 1829-30 (1985, pp.141-5). However, he also indicates that his study of the books for this financial year is governed by the fact that he had chosen 1830 as the end-point for his overall study, not because it is when the industrial accounting system commenced. Indeed Jones (1985, p.141) points out that "The accounts to be described here are little different from those forming the system between the year 1817-1829", suggesting that a system of industrial accounting existed at least as early as 1817, if not before. With the company's activities split between mining, smelting and manufacturing, Jones notes that data relating to each activity was separately recorded and presented.

Cyfarthfa

The Cyfarthfa ironworks was erected in 1765 by Anthony Bacon and his fellow Whitehaven merchant, William Brownrigg. Throughout the 1770s and 1780s the furnace operations on the one hand and the forge/mill operations on the other were controlled at different times by a variety of partnerships, until eventually all parts of the works were brought together under the control of Richard Crawshay in 1791. A London iron merchant, with no direct knowledge of iron manufacture, he had first become connected with Cyfarthfa through a contract which

Bacon secured with the Board of Ordnance in 1774, whereupon Crawshay was to have one-third share in all guns sold. Crawshay's involvement with the works proper commenced in 1786 when, in conjunction with James Cockshutt and William Stevens, he acquired the lease of the Cyfarthfa forge and mill. Whilst Stevens was likewise a London merchant, Cockshutt supplied the technical knowledge, having been under-manager to the former leaseholder David Tanner. On 1 January 1787, Crawshay and his partners also took over the lease of the Cyfarthfa furnace following the death of the founder, Anthony Bacon (Evans, 1990a, pp.xi-xii).

On the formation of the partnership or shortly afterwards, Robert Thompson, the younger brother of William Thompson, a partner in Crawshay's London House iron merchants business, was appointed specifically to keep the books at Cyfarthfa (Evans, 1993, pp.63-4). However, in the late 1780s, under Cockshutt as manager and Robert Thompson as bookkeeper, Cyfarthfa was not particularly successful, in part the result of problems encountered with the introduction of the new puddling process for manufacturing bar iron, and also partly due to poor management. Crawshay soon became concerned with the conduct of operations under Cockshutt and Thompson. For him, order and regularity were a precondition for efficient operation, something which, in his eyes, could only be achieved by the establishment of, and steadfast adherence to, clear rules (see GwRO, D2. 167 fo. 47, R. Crawshay to J. Cockshutt, 30 July 1789, quoted in Evans, 1993, pp.64-5). The problem with Cockshutt, according to Crawshay, was not his ability as a mechanic, but rather his:

> want of System in visiting to effect the Mining branch & the Smelting Furnaces & lastly keeping the other Setts of Workmen to performance of yield & quantity of Labour subject to produce the quantity of well-finish'd Iron for Creation of Profitt adequate to the Sum we have advanced.
> (GwRO, D2. 167 fo. 87, R. Crawshay to W. Stevens, January 1791, quoted in Evans, 1993, p.64)

The problems were not, however, confined to manufacturing operations. Thus, on 17 March 1788, for example, Crawshay wrote to Thompson complaining that "the Sheet containing Ballances very imperfectly stated . . . in future by attention to your accounts we shall find less difficulty in Ballancing the Books" (17 March 1788, quoted in

Jones, 1985, p.121). The following year, on 8 October, Crawshay again complained, this time to Cockshutt, that:

> I am very much disappointed in Mr. Thompson - I know he has some common sense if he would but use it and he was placed for the purpose of keeping our accounts regular, my mind is so distressed by your bad management that I can neither write, read, or think of the Concern with any degree of patience. (Quoted in Jones, 1985, p.121)

Crawshay therefore sent his son, William, to Cyfarthfa with the main object of establishing a system for keeping accounts and executing orders quickly and accurately and ensuring the managers adhered to it (14 Oct. 1789, Memo for William Crawshay into Wales, quoted in Jones, 1985, p.121). By February 1790 Crawshay was still dissatisfied and informed Cockshutt that "We want a man of business in our Concerns - at present there's not one among you" (25 February 1790, quoted in Jones, 1985, p.122).

With Crawshay's concern over the quality of the management increasing, and Stevens' wish to be relieved from his obligations, the partnership was dissolved with effect from 22 January 1791. "Stevens gratefully withdrew; Cockshutt was peremptorily dismissed as manager; [and] Crawshay assumed control at Cyfarthfa" (Evans, 1990a, p.xvi). Despite his complicity in the poor management up to 1791, Robert Thompson was not dismissed by Crawshay, but subsequently left Cyfarthfa in 1792 to take up a post as agent at the neighbouring Dowlais ironworks. These developments, together with the fact that the first surviving ledger for Cyfarthfa commences at the beginning of 1791, suggest that a new set of account books was commenced following Crawshay's assumption of sole control of the business. The possibility that a double entry bookkeeping system was in use before this time cannot be ruled out, either inherited from a previous partnership or introduced by Thompson or William Crawshay following the latter's visit to the works. In view of Richard Crawshay's dissatisfaction with the accounting function, however, the more plausible explanation is that the new system was inaugurated by him or, at least, bore his clear imprint, reflecting his strong merchant background (Jones, 1985, p.127). If this is so, it suggests that practices developed in relation to merchanting could be readily adapted by people with the requisite skills to the circumstances of industrial activity.

Shortly after the commencement of Crawshay's period of sole control of Cyfarthfa, the works employed more than 400 men and boys (Jones, 1985, p.118). The capital of the concern increased rapidly from £14,369 in 1790 to £103,398 in 1798 and by 1813 had risen to £160,000 (Boyns et al, 1980, p.108).[12] Although Crawshay was in overall control of the works, technical operations were supervised by Watkin George, who enjoyed a one-eighth share of the profits, the remainder going to Crawshay. According to Jones (1985, p.127), the Cyfarthfa accounting system in the 1790s represents "our first opportunity to look at eighteenth-century double entry accounts on such a scale for so vast (comparatively) an organisation". The system is considered to have been based on "some kind of logical internal office system of keeping certain types of accounts permanently classified together . . ." (Jones, 1985, p.128), and in Jones' estimation (1985, p.130), "those operating the system were well versed in its mechanics." The system remained in place until at least the middle of the nineteenth century, the ledger for 1817 (they continue through to 1846), for example, showing a 'sameness' as the original ledger of 1791 (Jones, 1985, p.137). Within the accounting system, there was an emphasis on allocating the majority of costs to activity or production centres (Jones, 1985, pp.137-8) and in this and other ways the Cyfarthfa system exhibits elements of similarity with those found at other early British iron smelting businesses (Boyns and Edwards, 1995, 1996c,d; Edwards and Boyns, 1992; Edwards *et al*, 1995; Fleischman and Parker, 1990). Most notably it included cost calculation within a double-entry system and, although the system was subject to modification over time, it exhibited a large element of continuity.

Charlton Mills

The Charlton mills in Manchester probably came into existence sometime between 1764 and 1785, but nothing is known of their operation prior to 1810 when it was engaged solely in the spinning of cotton. By 1817, however, operations were extended to the weaving of cotton cloths and calicos and a number of other changes occurred before the mills finally closed in 1889. The earliest surviving accounting records show that the mills were operating in 1810 "with a fully developed accounting system ..." (Stone, 1973, p.71). Owned at that date by the Birley brothers, Hugh Hornby and Joseph, the "capital of £20,189 indicated a large and well established business in 1810" (Stone, 1973, p.71). The accounting system was based on "double entry with the cost records integrated into the system" (Stone, 1973, p.72): the cost accounts following the flow of the manufacturing process at the mills from the opening and cleaning of bales of cotton in the warehouse, through the carding process to the spinning rooms where the twist or weft, as it was alternatively known, was produced before being transferred back to the warehouse prior to sale.

The system in existence contained the following features of modern cost accounting:

> Prime costs for labor and materials were collected for each of fourteen cost centers and general expenses were allocated to these centers using predetermined rates. Transfers of materials-in-process between cost centers made use of intracompany pricing. A manufacturing gain or loss for each of thirteen of these cost centers and the selling profit or loss from the warehouse room were included in the bi-monthly trial balance. (Stone, 1973, p.71)

Stone's study, unfortunately for our purposes, has a number of limitations. For example, although his title indicates a concern with the company over the period between 1810 and 1889, in reality he only considers the accounting system in existence in 1810 and shortly thereafter. Thus there is no information on, or discussion about, how this system developed over time, if indeed it did. Crucially, however, he clearly indicates a system of industrial accounting in use by 1810, and even suggests that it may have existed prior to 1800.

Dowlais

The iron era in the Merthyr Tydfil district of south Wales, an area destined to become the largest iron manufacturing centre in the world in the early nineteenth century, commenced in 1759 with the establishment of a partnership to build the Dowlais furnace. In the nineteenth century the Dowlais enterprise, by then comprising coal and ironstone mines, limestone quarries, blast furnaces, forges and rolling mills, as well as a London sales agency, came under the control of the Guest family. The Guests had first become involved with Dowlais when John Guest, an ironworker from Shropshire, moved to the works in 1767 to manage it on a subcontract basis for the owners. Gradually the Guest family acquired a share in the works and ultimately sole control, mainly through Sir Josiah John Guest who headed the works from 1814 to 1852. The concern remained under private control until almost the end of the nineteenth century.

Dowlais was overshadowed by its near neighbour, the Cyfarthfa works, in the late eighteenth and early nineteenth century, but by the 1830s it had emerged as the largest iron works in the world. With at least 5,000 workers in the early 1840s, a figure that was to reach 8,500 by 1866, Dowlais was a large, complex, vertically-integrated industrial organization. Under Sir Josiah John Guest, control was effected through a combination of departmental agents and sub-agents whose number did not exceed 200 in the mid-1850s. Little of detail is known of the accounting system prior to Sir Josiah John Guest's death in 1852, though a few cost sheets relating to the late 1840s and early 1850s have survived.[13] From 1856, when G.T. Clark assumed control of Dowlais as managing trustee under Sir Josiah John Guest's will, there is a noticeable change in the use made of the accounting system. Surviving evidence suggests that the system itself was not radically altered by the new accountant, William Jenkins, but the emphasis placed upon the system was significantly increased. This involved upgrading the system for routine use as a means of management control and also the use of accounting information to aid strategic decision-making (Boyns and Edwards, 1997). Part of this upgrading process involved the preparation, by Jenkins, of an annual report for Clark, which extended over 40 pages (in addition to the accounting data) in some years. In addition, ad hoc reports were prepared by Jenkins and his colleagues, again based on accounting information, relating to key decisions such as the purchase of the Penydarren coalfield and the switch from manufacturing iron to producing steel.

The cost sheets which have survived, covering various periods between November 1845 and September 1852, give a clear picture of the flow of work throughout the business and of the extent to which the company supplied each stage from its own operations. Virtually all transfers of materials to processes, and transfers of semi-finished products between processes, were made at the average cost per ton (Boyns and Edwards, 1997, p.33). The Dowlais costing system had to cope with the fact that a number of its operating departments produced joint products, and did so through the use of a series of premia which enabled the calculation of a common cost per ton. The problem of apportioning the cost of the blast engines between various departments was solved on the basis of throughput, while general charges were recovered on the basis of round sum allocations. These sums were multiples of a particular amount and though the basis for the choice of amount or multiples applied is not known, it does suggest that some attempt was made to relate the general charges to the benefits received by a specific cost centre.

Thus the costing system exhibited three fundamental features: the use, as far as possible, of transfer prices which exactly recovered costs; total (absorption) costing; and the delay of profit recognition until products were sold to the customer. In addition to providing data on the cost and quantity of inputs and outputs on a total and per ton basis, the cost sheets also provided yield figures (inputs per ton of output expressed in terms of cost and quantity). The lack of any further surviving cost information, other than contained in Jenkins' annual reports, however, makes it impossible for us to detail what developments, if any, occurred in the costing system in the second half of the nineteenth century. The evidence that we do have, however, indicates a system that was very similar to the process costing system operated at the Consett Iron Company in the 1860s.[14]

Consett

Iron production commenced at Consett in 1840, but was not always successful in the early years. Successive failures of the operating companies in 1857 and 1864, led to a reconstruction of the business as the Consett Iron Company in the latter year. The new company was also beset by early financial problems, a revival of the iron trade in the 1870s, following the appointment of the former Dowlais accountant, William Jenkins, as general manager in 1869, saw the Consett Iron Company emerge as the most profitable iron and steel company in Britain in the late nineteenth and early twentieth centuries (Richardson and Bass, 1965; Baldwin et al, 1992). Like Dowlais and Staveley, Consett was a vertically integrated concern, and hence utilised a process costing system which recorded the flow of production through the various intermediate stages to the end products. The system utilised was

inherited from its forerunner, the Derwent and Consett Iron Company
Ltd. which had operated the works between 1858 and 1864.

The Consett process costing system, in the main, presented
data on the basis of products rather than departments though
occasionally, and usually within a product group, figures were also
presented at a more disaggregated level, e.g. in addition to the average
cost of coal, individual average cost figures were also given for each
colliery (Boyns and Edwards, 1995, pp.36-7). A system of absorption
costing was in operation, though the method of apportioning overheads
is unclear, being based on neither of the indices commonly advocated in
the late nineteenth century, i.e. output or labour costs. While most
elements of the Consett costing system remained unchanged throughout
the period from the 1860s to the beginning of the twentieth century, one
area of experiment concerned the treatment of internal transfers of
inputs and semi-finished products. Between 1864 and 1867, the method
of transferring items at cost, inherited from its predecessor, continued to
be used. In 1867, however, the board took the decision to move towards
a system of charging for coal and coke at a price above cost. The
principle of recognising a profit on coal and coke transfers was adopted
in order that a distinction could be made between the profits generated
by the coal and coke operations on the one hand and the ironworks on
the other. It is not possible to discern a logic underlying the transfer
prices set initially for coal and coke but, by the second half of 1869,
certain transfers began to be effected at figures clearly linked to the
selling price of coke.

According to Boyns and Edwards (1995), the introduction of
these transfer prices was connected to the problems facing Consett's
management in the late 1860s. In particular they were debating the
issue of whether to keep open the ironworks. By adopting transfer
prices, the Consett management was able to gain some idea of the
source of the company's profit and, though the resulting calculations
suggested that the iron works was actually making a loss, it was not
closed. The explanation for this apparently aberrant behaviour is given
by a consultant called in to advise. He pointed out that, whilst cheap
coal generated the company's profits, the market for sale coal was
limited and that a lower overall profit would result if the ironworks was
closed. Using its large output of coal to produce iron, which was a more
marketable commodity at the time, albeit apparently unprofitable, was
the best way forward for the concern. The introduction of transfer
prices into the costing system, however, whilst allowing the division of

profits between coal and iron, was not universally appreciated. Indeed, not long after his arrival, Jenkins, in his first annual report to the directors in August 1870, commented unfavourably on the system and shortly afterwards, in 1871/2, the cost books reverted to showing transfers at cost. The company auditors, as they had done since 1867, however, continued to produce two sets of revenue accounts at the end of each year, one based on transfers at costs, and hence showing all profit allocated to only those goods sold externally, and the other based on the system of transfer prices, allocating profits to their origins (Boyns and Edwards, 1995).[15]

Conclusion

The evidence of the above studies, together with that generated by other historians in last ten to fifteen years, is increasingly suggestive of the fact that, during the eighteenth and nineteenth centuries, cost calculation within double entry bookkeeping systems within Britain was much more commonplace than has hitherto been believed. This evidence is not sufficient to prove that the calculation of costs within double-entry bookkeeping was widespread throughout British iron industry in the late eighteenth and early nineteenth centuries. It does suggest, however, that a number of significant enterprises in sectors of the British economy which were instrumental in its industrial and economic development (iron, coal and textiles) had introduced sophisticated accounting systems capable of providing information for management purposes.

III. Accounting developments in French industry, c.1700-c.1880

General background

Whereas the subject of costing and industrial accounting, either in terms of the literature or practice, has been studied for many years by Anglo-Saxon accounting historians, this is much less true in the case of French historians. Thus recent studies of the costing methods utilised at a small number of French firms have largely appeared in something of a vacuum, since there have been no general studies equivalent to

Edwards, Solomons, Garner and Pollard for the Anglo-Saxon world. Whilst at one level this means that there is no conventional wisdom which may hinder the development of alternative views of the development of accounting, it also means that there is no body of past research upon which to build. Whilst research into industrial accounting in France in the nineteenth and twentieth centuries is beginning to develop, there are few general studies which are of relevance to this study. The main recent works are those of Nikitin (1992) and Lemarchand (1993a,b, 1994).

In his work, *Du dépérissement à l'amortissement* (1993a), Lemarchand has examined the use of alternative accounting methods in France during the eighteenth and nineteenth centuries. He has found that many industrial enterprises during the eighteenth century utilised charge and discharge accounting rather than double entry bookkeeping, despite the widespread use of the latter by merchants engaged in trade. Although some French industrialists did adopt the double entry method, its use only became more widespread during the nineteenth century. Gradually then, in the words of Lemarchand:

> Bookkeepers in industry made the merchant model a tool which enabled value added and performance to be monitored. This instrument was practical, not only for cost assessment, but for monitoring different parties in charge, and likely to deliver more useful information than a simple balance to directors, if not shareholders. (1994, p.140)

The crucial period of change, from an emphasis on charge and discharge to double entry bookkeeping, came in France between 1810 and 1830. During this period most of the large industrial concerns increasingly adopted double entry methods (Lemarchand, 1993a, pp.352-65). As the case studies presented below illustrate, in many instances the accounting system adopted by such concerns included cost calculation as an integral element within the double entry framework, i.e. they represent early examples of *comptabilité industrielle* in operation.

Industrial accounting: costing within double entry bookkeeping

Baccarat Crystalworks

Around 1822/23, Pierre-Antoine Godard-Desmarest, together with two partners, Nicolas-Rémy Lolot and François-Marie Augustin Lescuyer, took control of the Baccarat crystalworks, which was founded in 1764. The works produced high quality crystalware and employed 327 workers in 1823. Through concentration on product quality and the national market, rather than exports, Godard-Desmarest and his two sons, Emile and Hyppolite, succeeded in making Baccarat the foremost French producer of crystalware by the 1850s. This policy was backed up by activities to eliminate or subjugate competition, including takeovers and the operation of a cartel with its main rival Saint-Louis of Münzthal, between 1831 and 1857. By 1860 the works employed a labour force of 1500.

According to Nikitin (1996b), a fundamental influence in Baccarat's rise to dominance of the crystal industry was its advanced accounting system, which gave it a 'competitive' edge over its rivals. Thus, even during the period of operation of the cartel with Saint-Louis and a few other small producers, Baccarat, through a more effective knowledge of its costs, was able to operate more profitably. This together with its reputation for quality, and an inability of Saint-Louis to maintain production in line with its quota of the market under the cartel agreement, led to Baccarat assuming a position of dominance which, at the end of the cartel agreement in 1857, saw it in a far stronger position than its competitor.

Prior to Godard-Desmarest's involvement in the company, the accounting system was of a rudimentary nature and restricted to an account of receipts and payments. From the time Godard-Desmarest took over at Baccarat, however, a double entry bookkeeping system was used, within which cost calculation was undertaken. The system is described in Godard-Desmarest's book, published in 1827, entitled *Traité générale et de la comptabilité commerciale.* Godard-Desmarest's knowledge of accounting dates from his career in military administration between 1792 to 1821. Highly critical of the method of state accounting, Godard-Desmarest published a text on this issue in 1821, entitled *Mémoire et propositions sur la comptabilité générale des finances du Royaume, suivi d'un modèle de compte général,* but his recommendations for improvement were largely ignored. At Baccarat he was able to put some of his accounting ideas into practice within an industrial context. He adapted the double-entry system in a manner which enabled cost calculation to be carried out, making it possible for him to pursue a policy of producing high quality products at low prices. To effect such a policy it was vital to know production costs, and this is what Godard-Desmarest's accounting system made possible.

The essence of the system was a separate account for each intermediate item used in the production process, thus making it possible to identify the cost for each item and also upward or downward movements therein. Such movements would then be subjected to analysis in order to see how increases might be avoided in the future. In his accompanying reports, Godard-Desmarest showed an early understanding of the difference between fixed and variable costs. Because of its concentration on a strategy of producing high quality products, which required highly skilled operatives whose training could take up to twenty years, Baccarat needed to retain workers, even in periods when demand was falling, in order that subsequent upturns in demand could be met. In order to prevent workers moving to rival manufacturers, they were retained on full wages, even when there was little or no work. Thus Godard-Desmarest remarked, in 1826, that personnel costs were a fixed cost, and "the only real variable costs are those concerning primary materials and the distribution of goods" (Nikitin, 1996b, p.105).

Baccarat's accounting system also provided scope for an analysis of the impact of changes in the fixed and variable costs on profits. One of Godard-Desmarest's analyses concludes that "two kilns do not generate two-fifths of the profits which can be obtained from three kilns." His conclusion, therefore, was that every endeavour should be made to keeping open all three kilns, even if sacrifices in favour of the merchants, presumably in the form of lower prices, must be made. Godard-Desmarest also further recognised that exceptional charges should not form part of the cost build up used in determining production decisions, the relevant costs being annual charges and those costs which would not last for more than a few years.

The full nature of the double entry system advocated by Godard-Desmarest and employed by him at Baccarat is fully set out in his 1827 treatise. More clearly than Payen (1817), and in far more detail than Degranges senior (1801), Godard-Desmarest explained in his work what came to be known as industrial accounting, that is, an integrated accounting system making possible cost calculation within a system based on double entry bookkeeping.

Decazeville

During the 1820s, following a period as British ambassador, the Duke de Cazes returned to France intent on introducing the English method of producing iron. Together with a number of bankers, he formed the *Société des Houillères et Fonderies de l'Aveyron* in 1826 to establish an iron works in a remote, mountainous area, part of the Aubin coal basin (Aveyron) in south central France, 70 miles to the north-east of Toulouse, which was later to be called Decazeville. Production of coke-smelted iron began at the La Salle works in 1828, but the iron produced was of mediocre quality due to the sulphurous nature of both the local coal and ironstone.

Problems with the quality of the iron meant that the company experienced a period of mixed fortunes during its first ten years of operation, and there was some concern in the late 1830s that the company would go into liquidation. However, an upturn in the demand for rails, a product for which the Decazeville iron was particularly suited, enabled the company to enjoy a period of prosperity through to the end of the 1850s. At its peak year of operation, in 1856, Decazeville produced 33,458 tons of pig-iron, from which were produced 16,304 tons of rails and 4,175 tons of other goods (Reid, 1983, p.3). The company eventually went into receivership in 1865 as a result of the unsuitability of the local coal and iron for producing steel under the Bessemer system (Reid, 1983, p.3). This deficiency made it impossible for the company to compete with cheap imports from Britain consequent upon the opening up of trade between the two countries following the tariff agreements negotiated under the auspices of the Anglo-French Treaty of 1860.

The managerial structure at Decazeville was more complex than that at Baccarat, mainly because the company was backed by a number of protestant bankers, most of whom were based in Paris. The Board met regularly in Paris, whilst the works were under the control of a local manager. Relations between the board and local management were not always good. Initially, in 1827, François Cabrol, a former military man and friend of the Duke of Cazes, was put in charge, but the board soon expressed dissatisfaction with the way in which he kept them informed of operations. Article 20 of the company's statutes required a copy of the journal to be sent fortnightly to the board, but there were clearly problems with the information flow. It is possible that this merely reflected the fact that communications between the works and Paris in the late 1820s were not particularly rapid, the carriage of letters taking about a week, but in the light of views subsequently expressed, it may reflect a more deliberate policy by Cabrol to withhold information.

Members of the board, including Count Michel-Frédéric Pillet-Will, did not see eye-to-eye with Cabrol over the way in which the company should be run. Cabrol, for his part, considered that the board wanted to interfere too much in matters which were really the province of local management. Thus, in 1832, at the time of his growing unease with the way things were developing, Cabrol argued that the company should be run like a limited monarchy:

> If there is a king in the company it must be the board. The
> company would be the nation and the manager the minister
> of this government which, having only one center of
> activity, would need only one ministry - composed of
> several divisions of which the heads would be accountable
> to the *minister* alone. (Quoted in Reid, 1983, p.7 -
> emphasis added)

The board had a different viewpoint, however, and in mid-1833 Cabrol resigned as works manager. The cause of his resignation is unclear but possibly reflects changes made following the visit to the works in 1832 by Pillet-Will. Although the visit was at his own volition, on returning he published an account of events in a book entitled *Examen analytique de l'usine de Decazeville* (1832). Clearly Pillet-Will considered the management system at Decazeville to be deficient, noting that he "had to carry out an analysis to allow the management to assess the operating costs in as much detail as possible..." (Pillet-Will, p.9, quoted in Nikitin (1996a)). One of the recommendations he made on his return was that the board should receive "mandatory quarterly reports from the departmental heads" (quoted in Reid, 1983, p.6). This and other proposals made by Pillet-Will may have been the final straw for Cabrol, whose departure was followed by a succession of general works managers, most of whom stayed in post only for a short while. A major cause of this rapid turnover seems to have been the desire of the Paris board to exercise close control over local management issues, something which had undoubtedly played a major part in Cabrol's departure. Not surprisingly perhaps, the company's fortunes did not prosper during the 1830s, and towards the end of the decade the board began to ask themselves whether the problem lay with any fundamental weakness associated with the nature of the undertaking or whether the problem was due to inefficient management and control. They presumably decided the latter for, in October 1839, Cabrol was asked to resume control of the works, but this time on his own terms (Reid, 1983, p.8). Being now given virtually complete control over the management of the works, Cabrol acceded to board's request and the period of board interference in local management issues began to draw to a close.

Pillet-Will's report provides us with some insights concerning the nature of earlier interference, and the role played by the accounting system in managerial control. Pillet-Will noted that one advantage of a business starting out on a small scale was that it was possible to establish "the best system of administration from the outset". He emphasised the need to create:

> a clear, simple accounting system which provides details of
> expenses, whatever they represent, their destination, their
> use, the cost of each product; breaking down the separate
> elements clearly into labour, raw materials and
> consumption; carefully ensuring everything is in its place,
> arrives on time, works as it should, ultimately to avoid any
> unnecessary downtime, and any consumption without an
> end product. (Pillet-Will, p.9)

It is clear, however, that practice was somewhat different from theory. Both the accounting and administrative systems of the business underwent a period of evolution in the first ten years or so, before eventually settling down in the late 1830s. Nevertheless, during the period between Cabrol's departure and his reinstatement, and following the detailed discussions and experimentations of the early years, the accounting system at Decazeville evolved into one that was significantly in advance of those in use at most enterprises of the time.

For the period under consideration, the discussions at Decazeville reflected an advanced understanding of a number of significant issues in relation to accounting for industrial enterprises.

Although in practice the calculation and application of the principle of depreciation was somewhat short of that outlined in the company's statutes, the concept was recognised (Article 13). The issue of the allocation of overheads was a matter that was discussed at length by the board during the early years, and shows that they were searching for appropriate methods to deal with the real issues with which they were faced. Whilst exceptional items, such as the costs incurred as the result of a fire at one of the mine workings, were charged to the account for the particular mine, overheads were apportioned on a tonnage rate. In 1829, for example, it was stated that a rate of 5F per ton was to be charged on the cast iron produced, one-third of the sum 'raised' being debited from the Forézie construction account and two-thirds from the La Salle construction account. The rate applied to a particular product, however, was not always identical as between years, and the rate applied to different products could vary. In 1834 it was decided that overheads should not be charged to intermediate products, only to finished goods, since these were the products which interfaced with the market.[16]

Costs were calculated each month at Decazeville, for each stage of production. It was clearly recognised that the average cost of production of any item, whether an intermediate or a finished product, was affected by the level of output, and by the price at which items were transferred between the various stages of production. The issue of whether to transfer intermediate items at cost or at some transfer price above cost occupied the attention of both the board and the local manager during the early years. Initially transfers were carried out at a price reflecting the average cost in the preceding year or, recognising the effect of fluctuations in output upon average cost, the preceding three years. In 1829, at a general assembly on accounts, the board explained that:

> In industrial businesses each marketable product must be allocated its own profits. Thus, in the case of the mass production of iron, the departments which are involved, the furnaces, foundries, forges, sheet-metal workshops, etc., must be treated as individual establishments which buy and sell from one another. (Quoted in Nikitin (1996a))

This principle is relatively simple, but putting it into practice can prove more difficult. If a price above cost is to be used to transfer items from one stage to another, how should this price be established? For goods which are readily marketable, then one might argue that market price should be used, but for many items a ready market may not be available. Thus at Decazeville, although coal could have been sold externally as fuel for heating local homes, there was no substantial market, other than within the works itself, for the large quantities being produced by the company's coal mines.[17] Thus current market price may well have exceeded the price which would have prevailed if the company's entire coal output was placed on the market. For this reason, criticisms of the use of 'artificial' transfer prices, even those based on average production costs in previous years, quickly began to be heard from the management. In 1829, for example, Cabrol complained that the prices used for transferring coal resulted in a profit, when compared with the running costs, but a loss if the costs included the dues owed to the Duke of Cazes as mineral landlord. In 1833, the board finally concurred with Cabrol's request to abandon the use of the 'fictitious' prices. They cited three grounds for doing this: (1) they generate deceptive profits which have not really been attained; (2) it has, in the past, been necessary to lower the price at which cast iron has been transferred, "negating the results which seem to have been achieved"; and (3) that it requires twice the amount of effort to obtain the true cost of the finished iron (original quoted in Nikitin, 1996a).

Following the settling down of the accounting system in the 1830s, there is evidence that the accounting information began to be used to analyse the causes of cost variations. Thus an analysis of the differences in the yearly costs of producing finished iron was carried out for the years 1838 and 1839, during which time production fell by 200 tons. Explanations were then provided for the various increases and decreases in particular items. The increase in labour costs of 0.27F per ton was attributed to the greater amount of production in small batches, whilst that of 5.83F per ton in raw materials was put down to increased wastage. A rise of 1.43F per ton in overheads occurred mainly as a result of a 4000F increase in loan interest, most of the items of overhead expenditure falling.

Precise knowledge of the uses to which the calculation of costs were put at Decazeville is not clear from the work of Nikitin (1996a). There has been a suggestion, by Hoskin and Macve (1988a, p.64), that it was connected to the control and disciplining of the workforce. It is certainly true that Reid's study of Decazeville indicated an increasing attention being paid to matters of labour control, following Cabrol's reinstatement in 1839, but the precise role of the accounting system in this process is less clear (Reid, 1983). Reid describes clearly the process by which local management sought increasingly to distance itself from control by the board, customers and certain elements within the workforce. Decazeville, like many of the other ironworks established in France in the 1820s and 1830s to produce iron from *forges à l'anglaise*, initially utilised many British skilled workers and operated according to the British model. Thus skilled workers, employing their own helpers, were engaged to carry out the key productive functions. They were paid piece rates, set by the manager and monitored by the foremen, and, in turn, paid members of their own team from these earnings, usually on a day rate basis or a percentage of their earnings.

The process by which local management attempted to increase their measure of control over the workforce was initially by changing work loads within a given system of division of labour, rather than through changes in that system. Also, they began to switch from a method which emphasised supervision over the final product to one which involved direct supervision of each stage of the work as it was carried out. To enable them to carry out this more direct form of supervision of the workforce, however, local management had to replace the existing shopfloor supervisors, who had worked their way up from amongst the skilled workers and tended to understand the concerns and demands of those workers better than they understood the interests of the company. Thus local management gradually introduced individuals who were devoted solely to the company's interests (Reid, 1983, pp.14-15). Part of this process inevitably involved the replacement of British workers by others, chiefly French, and it led to the development of an alternative to the British model of work supervision. However, as Reid has pointed out, "Industrial technology did not dictate a single form of labour management. Although dependent on British technology, French ironworks like Decazeville developed their own methods of dealing with labour" (1983, p.17)

Despite his detailed consideration of the change in the method of work supervision at Decazeville, Reid gives little direct evidence that the accounting system played a key role. It is true that it proved possible for work loads to be increased, and Reid details how that for rollers and heaters was achieved (1983, pp.14-15). He describes an iterative procedure whereby changes in piece rates resulted in workers 'stopping' at a level of 64 bars per shift, when Cabrol believed they could do 72. Cabrol thus set the rate according to a level of 68 bars.

There is no indication, however, of accounting information being used to calculate the 'standard' of 68, or that it played a role in changing the balance of each group of workers and the number of furnaces controlled, thereby enabling a subsequent rise in output to 85 bars per shift. Even if accounting information was used, there remains the possibility that it was a one-off exercise, such as that observed at Boulton and Watt by Fleischman, Hoskin and Macve (1995). There is, however, no strong evidence that the accounting system was being used to discipline workers in the Foucauldian sense. Nevertheless, on the basis of Reid's analysis, Hoskin and Macve feel able to cite Decazeville as a French example of the genesis of accountability, in the same way that the Springfield Armory is claimed to have been in the United States (1988a, p.64).

Saint-Gobain

The production of glass in France commenced in 1665, when the Manufacture Royale des Glaces de Miroirs was created in Paris following the granting of special privileges by royal decree. In 1688 a second company, the Manufacture Royale de Grandes Glaces, operating from the castle of Saint-Gobain, was granted a royal monopoly for the manufacture of mirrors measuring over sixty by forty inches (Bhimani, 1994, p.402). In 1695, following disagreements between the two concerns, Louis XIV ordered their amalgamation, and the Manufacture des Glaces de France (MGF) was created, but soon ran into financial difficulties as a result of the economic downturn caused by the Spanish war of succession in 1702. The company's creditors forced a reconstruction of the business in that year, and the shareholders ruled that no future borrowings were to be made (Bhimani, 1994, p.402). Throughout the eighteenth century the company operated a system of charge and discharge accounting, but increasingly this system appears to have found difficulty in coping with the demands placed upon it. These included problems resulting from increasing size, and the need to develop a more profit-orientated outlook towards the end of the eighteenth century and in the early nineteenth century, as the company's monopoly privileges were removed and competitors began to appear.[18] It was only in 1820, however, that charge and discharge accounting was finally abandoned in favour of a system of double entry bookkeeping.

During the earliest phase of the company's operation, up to 1702, little is known of the accounting system in use beyond the fact that the statutes required the production of quarterly statements for the purpose of paying dividends. Following the 1702 financial crisis, a system of internal administration of the business was introduced, based on systematic regulation and co-ordination through a hierarchy of posts and structured responsibilities. According to Scoville (1942, p.686), an "elaborate system of bookkeeping" was installed in 1703, which aided "organizational control [by] providing support to directors charged with overseeing the manufacturing shops' activities" (Bhimani, 1994, p.404). Although described as an 'elaborate system', it was based on charge and discharge and did not require the presence of a skilled accountant.

According to Bhimani, the accounting system in the early eighteenth century comprised the following structure:

> The accountant of each manufacturing site was to maintain, for every aspect of production operations, information on "all that could be financially quantified" (Pris, 1981, p.185). Each week, a detailed statement of receipts and expenditures was submitted to the general accountant and all books were balanced at the end of each month. The general accountant subsequently prepared a summary statement of receipts and expenditures as well as a "balance sheet" (ibid., p.55) for each quarter. This information was presented to the shareholders in addition to monthly summary advice on the cash status. Annually, a reconciliation of the recorded accounting figure for inventory and a physical inventory count was performed for the whole company. (1994, p.405)

The system satisfied two purposes: it computed the wealth (inventory) and enrichment (receipts and payments) of the partners; and, through a comprehensive system of vouchers, it made possible control of the internal movement of goods and cash. According to Bhimani, the administrative controls and internal accounting practices at Saint-Gobain became more extensive and detailed during the second half of the eighteenth century in response to subtle changes in commercial philosophy (1994, p.415). As mercantilist regulation began to be relaxed, the increasing pressure of competition was felt at Saint-Gobain. The system of maintaining accounts on the basis of '*tenus en finance*' utilised between 1702 and 1770 created some problems for the concern in the 1770s. Pris has argued that the system was used to obviate the need for the "complicated accounting entries which double-entry would have necessitated" (1981, p.186). A general ledger for receipts, expenses and deposits, with entries made in succession rather than through debits and credits, was kept, and profit was calculated as the difference between receipts and expenses net of deposits (Bhimani, 1994, p.425).[19] The system had the undoubted advantage that an administrator not trained in accounting could maintain the general ledger *sans confidens*, thereby securing secrecy of the company's affairs.

Bhimani makes no reference to the debate at Saint-Gobain between des Franches and Saladin de Crans on the one hand and Jean-Francois Sellon, all directors of the company. Des Franches wrote a critique of the accounting system in 1769 and advocated the adoption of double entry both because the company was akin to a trading establishment and because the existing system was obscure and suffered from prolixity and irrelevance (Lemarchand, 1994, p.139). Most notably the system failed to provide management information, and des Franches was concerned to make sure that "the associates had easy access to information required to run the business or assess the success of their investment" (Lemarchand, 1994, p.139). Although supported in his view by de Crans, who was also a director of the Compagnie des Indes, des Franches' view was opposed by the banker Sellon. Whilst Sellon agreed that the double entry system was the preferred method for trading concerns, he considered that it would involve too much work for a factory. De Crans considered that double entry would only require the appointment of one extra bookkeeper, but Sellon argued successfully that the charge and discharge system provided sufficiently clear and simple accounts giving directors enough information by which to have an overall knowledge of the business. There is evidence that the directors were also worried that the introduction of double entry would enable a large number of bookkeepers to have an intimate knowledge of the company's affairs (Lemarchand, 1994, p.140).[20]

The charge and discharge system found it difficult to cope, in the 1770s, with the rising level of credit provided by the sale outlets and with the differing time periods over which these items remained in the account. The system was also unsuitable for the purpose of tracking the level of merchandise in stock and at the sales outlets, making it difficult to assess when replenishment was required. The directors attempted to remedy matters by increasing the number and the detail contained in the accounts in the period up to 1789, but difficulties remained (Bhimani, 1994, p.425). In Bhimani's judgement, the changes made in the 1770s and 1780s were partly driven by the political and economic environment within which Saint-Gobain was operating, and partly as a result of the appointment of Deslandes as director of the company. According to Bhimani:

> To Deslandes, "no detail was useless" (Frémy, 1909, p.180) and his penchant for measures, calculations and personal records on output and production arguably contributed to the greater degree of accounting activity witnessed by MGF during the decades preceding the revolution. (1994, p.426)

Further developments occurred in the early nineteenth century, as competitive pressures increasingly affected the company following its loss of monopoly rights. An increase in the scale of operations, including large investments in new plants and the securing of sources of supply of raw materials, created a need for a change in the internal system of accounting. A principal objective appears to have been to develop a system which would enable the calculation of costs, and between 1820 and 1832 a system of double entry bookkeeping was at last introduced.[21] The new system was subjected to numerous changes and development during the first ten years of its operation, in line with the perceived needs of management. In October 1832 the board finally approved the revised system which, in customary manner at Saint-Gobain, was set out in a series of rules.[22]

This new system, an example of process costing in which charges were classified according to their place in the production process rather than by their nature, echoed those found at British firms such as Staveley at this time. It made possible the calculation of unit cost at each stage in the production process. Year on year analyses were carried out, identifying causes of changes in costs and giving explanations therefore. With the businesses comprising a number of works and a Paris headquarters, the manufacturing cost determined the price at which all finished products were 'sold' to the headquarters "which was the only division of the company that could sell to customers" (Nikitin, 1990, p.81). At the headquarters, a further 'cost price' for each product manufactured was calculated, to which was added amounts for depreciation and dividends. Thus, whilst most of the accounting was carried out the works, issues such as depreciation were carried out at headquarters.

The rules by which the accounting system should function were set down in 1832, but the accounting system nevertheless continued to undergo developments designed to achieve greater maturity. Many aspects of the system changed only in a minor fashion, the method of depreciation, for example, hardly altering at all between 1830 and 1872. In the latter year, however, a major change occurred. Now comprising sixteen branches, some overseas, the company determined on the homogenisation of accounting methods to be used at each branch, publishing a new set of accounts and a user's guide. The adoption of a system of branch accounting placed the company in the position of utilising a cost accounting system which is very similar to that used by many French companies today (Nikitin, 1990, p.89).

Nikitin has suggested that changes between 1820 and 1872 occurred "according to the needs of management alone" (1990, p.91) and resulted from finding practical solutions to problems which they faced (1990, p.83). As a result of discussions and alterations effected in the 1820s, Saint-Gobain established an accounting system that was well in advance of most others at that time. This was particularly evident in the case of fixed asset valuation and the calculation of depreciation. Thus, as early as 1830, "the rate of annual depreciation was set for each type of fixed asset, but the value of the asset was only reduced within the limits of the supposed market price" (Nikitin, 1992, p.4). Other issues that were widely discussed include the use of transfer prices for soda moving between processes within the works, and how overheads should be allocated. Whilst the development of the company's new system in the 1820s coincided with the setting up of a new remuneration system for the workforce, Nikitin (1990, p.86) has found little evidence to suggest that the two events were linked in any way, though the English summary of his thesis does suggest that the two came to maturation over the same period, 1820-c.1832, and notes that the new remuneration system led to a substantial drop in costs (Nikitin, 1992,. 4).

Allevard[23]

The Allevard iron-works developed from an ancient industrial activity, but it was only from 1675, under the management of the de Barral family, that it became a large enterprise. During the de Barral's control, which lasted until 1818, the company operated a single entry bookkeeping system, though there is evidence of an attempt from the 1780s to develop within this framework a method of calculating profit for each branch of the business. The economic slump of the revolutionary period badly affected the company's fortunes and it was acquired by Champel who introduced a rudimentary system of double entry bookkeeping, the central element being the merchant's 'General Goods' account (Nikitin, 1992, pp.342-4). This system proved unsuitable for running a large industrial enterprise and, with the business requiring a substantial injection of capital, the company was sold to Giroud, a banker from Grenoble. An industrial accounting system was introduced, similar to those found at Saint-Gobain, Decazeville and Baccarat. In Nikitin's view (1992, p.116), at Allevard, as at Saint-Gobain, the impetus for the new system came from increased competition, though he puts a strong emphasis on the change in ownership, noting that "accounting systems travel in the pockets of those supplying the capital".

Le Creusot

In the late eighteenth century, an attempt was made at Le Creusot to introduce the English method of smelting iron with coke, but early attempts failed. Although a works was established by de Wendel between 1782 and 1785, the Revolution and economic turmoil of the Napoleonic period led to the works changing hands on several occasions. In 1826 the majority of the shares in the works were sold by the sons of the banker François Chagot to two Englishmen, Aaron Manby and David Wilson. They were already operating a mechanical construction business at Charenton, in the suburbs of Paris, and acquired Le Creusot to provide them with necessary inputs. Manby, Wilson et cie. was formed in 1825 as a société en commandite and, during the period from 1 August 1825 to 30 September 1826, the company's accounts showed a movement of funds of almost 9 million francs. The committee established at the 1827 annual general meeting to verify the inventory, accounts and books of the company, however, made it clear in its report (AFB, 1827) that the company was suffering from a shortage of finance.

The committee's report (AFB, 1827, p.3) tells us that all accounts were kept in double-entry format, as prescribed in article 17 of the company's rules. Moreover, the committee was impressed by the regularity and order displayed in the books, and noted that accounts were held both in cash (*en deniers*) and in materials (*en matières*) (AFB, 1827, p.3). The report also provides a clear indication of the nature of the accounting system:

> Each branch of the concern, each workshop, manufacturing or other, has an account opened in the ledger, where it is debited with the supplies it receives in the course of the year and credited with all that it produces. For each of these accounts there corresponds a particular inventory (*inventaire particulier*) which, when combined together, form the total inventory of the whole establishment. The general inventory of Charenton comprises 37 partial inventories, whilst that of Le Creusot comprises 47.
>
> The keeping of subsidiary books is no less satisfying. These books, which follow the course of production, are kept in a manner whereby one can always establish the real cost to the company of each machine, and the profit that it generates. To this end, each machine, or rather the principal in charge of it, has an account opened that is debited with even the minutest expense occasioned by its operation, and credited with production. The difference expresses the profit.
>
> This method also provides the constructor of the machine with an indication of those parts of the manufacture which are very costly, providing a warning, and the means of rectifying the expenditure in the manufacture of future machines to be made. (AFB, 1827, pp.5-6)

The report (AFB, 1827, pp.6-8) also refers to the need for a depreciation account for fixed assets but recognises that this is not an easy matter, due to the different rates at which assets depreciate. To simplify matters, they suggest that the shareholders should determine amounts to be credited each year to a depreciation account, and that after a certain number of years the amount in this account should be offset against the reduction in asset values.

The company's financial problems meant that it was only able to attract purchasers for 344 of its 500 shares of 20,000 francs each. Added to this, the purchase of Le Creusot was slow to yield benefits, and the authors of the report urged the company to change its status to a *société anonyme* in order to increase public confidence and subscription in the enterprise. The economic crisis of 1830, however, brought a halt to the company's plans for developing Le Creusot, and in 1833 the company was declared bankrupt (Devillers and Huet, 1981, p.36). Le Creusot was subsequently sold, in 1836, to the Schneider brothers, Adolphe and Eugène, who, during the 1820s, had operated the Forges de Basaille. There they had operated an accounting system similar to that employed by Manby, Wilson et cie. and, when they took over at Le Creusot, they continued to operate a double entry system, though they did not incorporate within it any provision for depreciation.[24]

Conclusion

The French case studies show clearly that, during the first half of the nineteenth century, a number of significant French companies operated systems of double entry bookkeeping. Whilst there is some evidence of the use of double entry bookkeeping methods before this date, a number of firms established or taken over in the 1820s began to adopt this method. Moreover, the method was often modified over a period of several years in order to make it more useful to owners and managers for purposes of decision-making. Crucial to this process was the development of the practice of *comptabilité industrielle*, i.e. the incorporation of cost calculation within the double entry system.

IV.   Conclusion

The evidence surveyed in this chapter of the practical use of industrial accounting tends to indicate that its use in British industry preceded that in France. Evidence of the attempt to calculate costs, whether inside or outside the framework of double entry bookkeeping, also suggests a more widespread concern with such matters on the part of British rather than French businessmen. In both countries, however, irrespective of the accounting system, there is evidence of attempts to modify accounting systems, apparently in the light of both internal business needs and changes in the external environment facing businesses. In France, the 1820s was clearly an important decade, with a number of leading enterprises adopting the method of *comptabilité industrielle*, though the sophistication of the methods of cost calculation clearly seems to have developed somewhat more slowly than in Britain. Thus prior to 1880, the end-point for our study, there is no evidence of cost sheets being produced in French companies, cost calculation largely being a matter of annual computation. In Britain, by way of contrast, there is evidence of a widespread use of cost sheets for shorter periods, particularly amongst iron companies.

It is our belief that the use of industrial accounting in Britain and France long before the 1870s is of great significance for the understanding of the development of accounting, and especially what are today generally referred to as cost and management accounting. The emergence, in both France and Britain, of cost calculation within double entry bookkeeping methods suggests to us that industrial accounting played a significant role in aiding management decision making at this time. However, the evidence of this chapter and the previous one presents us with something of a paradox: on the one hand British firms were utilising industrial accounting in practice, despite their being virtually no relevant literature upon which British businessmen could draw; on the other hand, the French usage of industrial accounting was somewhat retarded, even though reasonably rapid strides were made in the development of the industrial accounting literature in France. We consider in the final chapter the means by which Britain was able to utilise a technique which was ignored in the literature, whereas in France development of both practice and literature seem to have gone more hand in hand.

Notes

1	Solomons did however draw heavily on earlier work by Edwards (1937a,b,c) for much of the factual content, particularly English and French developments up to the late nineteenth century.
2	This deficiency has been partly rectified by the recent work of Boyns *et al* (1996).

3   The first factory proper is generally considered to be John
     Lombe's silk-throwing mill near Derby in 1717. It was 500 feet
     long and, with five or six stories resembled "a huge barracks . .
     . with its automatic tools, its continuous and unlimited
     production and the narrowly specialised functions of its [300]
     operatives" (Mantoux, 1928, p. 199).
4   Letter from S. W. Roberts of Philadelphia to Thomas Evans,
     the overseas agent of Dowlais. Glamorgan Record Office,
     Dowlais main series letter book 1842 (2) f. 368.
5   The Plymouth Iron Company employed 3,900, Tredegar
     2,757, Rhymney 2,494, Penydarren 2,071 and Blaenavon
     1,971, while Cyfarthfa employed 2,000 at the forges alone
     (Royal Commission on Childrens' Employment in Mines and
     Manufactories, 1842, Report of Rhys William Jones,
     Appendix, Part 2, p. 594). The Report of the Commissioners
     for the State of the Population in the Mining Districts, 1846,
     puts employment at Dowlais at c. 6,000 and at Rhymney c.
     4,000, of which 1,600 were employed in the mines. It is also
     stated that 1,700 were employed at Dowlais in the mines, but it
     is not clear whether this is part of the 6,000.
6   Although Babbage in 1832 was the first to discuss the
     distinction between fixed and variable costs in the British
     literature, other industrialists, in addition to Wedgwood, who
     clearly recognised it were John Taylor (1824) and the
     accountant of the Melincryddan copper works, Neath (1740s) -
     see Edwards (1980, pp. 310-11).
7   This would appear to be a good example of the point made by
     Yamey (1964, pp. 124-5) that double entry ledgers in the
     seventeenth and eighteenth centuries, rather than leading to a
     withering away of the commercial realities actually enabled
     businessmen to keep a close check on them.
8   During the period 1690-1783, business operations were carried
     out at separate geographical locations and it was possible to
     trace almost all costs directly to one or other activity. Changes
     in organisational structure had, by 1856, resulted in a
     significant growth in shared costs which, at that date, were
     debited directly to the profit and loss account.
9   The finance director, Henry Pochin dismissed the
     disagreement between Collier and Chadwick "as a difference

betwixt tweedledum and tweedledee" (*The Sheffield and Rotherham Independent*, 15 Sept. 1883, p.2)

10 Through his control of the Anglesey copper trade and his connections with the Cornish Metal Company, for a time in the late 1780s and early 1790s Williams effectively controlled the country's copper trade. His monopoly position eventually succumbed to pressures from various sources, however, including declining output on Anglesey, the growing influence of Birmingham copper manufacturers such as Matthew Boulton, and the gradual break-up of the Cornish Metal Company. Nevertheless, he was a still a major force in the industry in the late 1790s, it being estimated that the aggregate capital tied up in the mines and other activities he controlled amounted to some £800,000 in 1799. A powerful man, with strong business interests, he died in 1802.

11 According to Harris (1964, pp. 153-4), Grenfell was established as a merchant in London as early as 1783, and became closely involved with Williams no later than 1785. However, it is unclear whether between then and 1791, when Williams and Grenfell ran a joint office in London, Grenfell was an independent merchant or Williams' agent. Elsewhere Harris indicates that as well as being involved with Williams, for a time, though how long is unknown, Grenfell "acted as an independent agent for Lord Uxbridge. It was his duty to examine the accounts submitted by Williams and to assure Uxbridge that he was being fairly dealt with" (1964, p. 149). It is clear that he made suggestions as to how Lord Uxbridge's accounts should be kept, in order to recognise that he was both landlord and a partner in the enterprise, but it is clear that Grenfell's suggestions were not always acted upon.

12 In contrast, the capital at Dowlais in 1796 was only £20,000, though this rose to £61,072 by 1798, whilst that at another Merthyr ironworks, Plymouth, it was £20,000 in 1803. The final Merthyr works, Penydarren, was commenced in 1784 with a capital of £10,000, but this also rose rapidly to c.£100,000 by 1820.

13 Their precise relationship to the financial accounting system, however, is not totally clear though subsequent evidence

would suggest that they were part and parcel of an integrated accounting system, rather than being outside it.

14   Their similar nature is also suggested by the fact that, when he left Dowlais in 1869 to take over as general manager at Consett, William Jenkins does not appear to have instigated any major changes to that company's accounting system during his tenure of office, which lasted until 1893.

15   In this respect it is perhaps worth noting the precise formula used for calculating the transfer prices was changed in 1872 and 1876, though the reasons for these changes are unknown.

16   This is, of course, consistent with the practice observed at Staveley in Britain.

17   A similar problem can be observed at Consett in the 1860s (Boyns and Edwards, 1995).

18   The company's first competitor, in England, appeared in 1770. Twenty years later the company lost its monopoly privileges in France, but it was not until 1804 that the first French competitor, Saint-Quirin, emerged. In 1823 a second domestic competitor, the Company of Commentry, appeared. See Bhimani (1994), Nikitin (1990).

19   According to Lemarchand (1994, p. 138), however, the board minutes for 17 April 1703 indicate that the cashier was instructed to keep the books in charge and discharge form and to open credit and debit accounts for cash and customers.

20   Since double entry bookkeeping could be arranged in such a way that only one individual has access to the key data, such arguments appear to have been spurious.

21   There is no evidence that the charge and discharge system in use between 1702/3 and the early nineteenth century was ever used to calculate production costs (Nikitin, 1990).

22   A similar set of rules had been devised c.1720 for the accounting and management system at that date (see Bhimani, 1994).

23   This section is based on Nikitin (1992, p.358).

24   Lemarchand (1994, p. 129), indicates evidence that, right from the start, some element of double entry bookkeeping was used at Le Creusot. However, during the first half of the 1780s, he notes that the double entry system seems to have co-existed

with charge and discharge accounting at this company, as at a number of others.

Chapter 5 - Similarities and differences in accounting literature and accounting practice: some tentative explanations

The material presented in chapters 3 and 4 demonstrates the development during the late eighteenth and early nineteenth centuries, in both France and Britain, of a new accounting doctrine, industrial accounting. During that period, a body or system of principles was laid down regarding how cost calculation could be carried on within a system of double entry bookkeeping. The method by which this doctrine emerged in the two countries, and its exact timing and pace of development, however, differed. This chapter first summarises the main similarities and differences and then explores explanations for these observations, as well as drawing some implications for our understanding of the process of accounting development.

The emergence of industrial accounting in Britain and France: a summary

Disciplines such as accounting can clearly change with advances in knowledge or with changes in the issues which a particular department of knowledge addresses. It is our view that changes in the nature of economic activity and business organisation in the late eighteenth and nineteenth centuries led to changes in the nature of accounting. Previously, during the seventeenth and eighteenth centuries, in both France and Britain accounting was based on charge and discharge accounting and, increasingly, the ideas underlying the 'Italian method', that is, the system of double entry bookkeeping popularised by Pacioli which made use of three books: the waste book (memorial), the journal and the ledger. By the early nineteenth century there did exist variations of double entry bookkeeping, but the common factor was that they all undertook the recording of the dual effect (debit and credit) of each transaction entered in the books. The main variations were not in the basic techniques employed, but rather in the manner in which entries were posted to various accounts and the location of these accounts within the books making up the accounting system.

Whilst the doctrine of mercantile accounting held sway for much of the seventeenth and eighteenth centuries, and its influence undoubtedly extended into the nineteenth century, in the late eighteenth and early nineteenth centuries there is evidence of a significant transition taking place to allow the adoption of the doctrine of industrial accounting. This change, however, has not been apparent to earlier historians, particularly British accounting historians, who have placed an undue reliance on the accounting literature as their source material for evidence of accounting change. Thus Yamey, on the basis of the observation that British accounting texts prior to the last quarter of the nineteenth century "reveal striking uniformities in accounting technique, in the nature of the examples used in illustration, and in their general tone", and in the knowledge that such texts were written by a mix of businessmen, bookkeepers and teachers, felt able to write that "this uniformity ... gives one some confidence in generalizing from accounting texts to accounting practice" (1949, pp.100-1). His view that "the knowledge of double entry [through texts] was more widespread than its practice" (Yamey, 1981, p.130), however, no longer seems tenable, at least amongst the industrial community. We have seen in chapters 3 and 4 that, with only one or two minor exceptions, British accounting texts continued to concentrate on explaining the Italian system of double entry bookkeeping as applicable to a mercantile or commercial activity, but that a number of British businesses during the eighteenth and nineteenth centuries began to utilise the methods of industrial accounting.

By way of contrast, the evidence put forward for France in chapter 3 shows that the accounting literature published during the first half of the nineteenth century reflects clear evidence of a change in accounting doctrine. In particular, a number of works explicitly began to consider the internal and external accounting problems of industrial enterprises as a whole. Thus the concept of cost calculation within double entry bookkeeping became enshrined as a mainstream accounting doctrine in France in the nineteenth century, with an increasing number of books, many intended as general educational texts, dealing with the subject of industrial accounting. One of the divisions of accounting texts used by Reymondin (1909), in his bibliography of the French literature, is between those on industrial accounting and those on general accounting, and it is noticeable that there are as many in the former category as in the latter. Moreover, those texts on general accounting often comprise a number of separate sections, one of which would be devoted to industrial accounting.

The existence of an accounting doctrine, however, does not rely purely on its being espoused in the literature. Whilst coverage in accounting texts undoubtedly enables new ideas and doctrines to be more rapidly assimilated, accounting existed long before printing was invented. Before the existence of the printed word, accounting concepts must obviously have been passed on, in the main, through practice and on-the-job training. New ideas may have been written down, but the extent to which these would have become known by others was no doubt limited. But, as noted in chapter 2, just because books are written, and the ideas contained in them more widely disseminated, there can be no certainty that such ideas will necessarily be used. The link between literature and practice, therefore, is difficult to assess, and it is a relationship that requires much greater investigation by accounting historians. Before this link can be investigated, however, more needs to be known about accounting practice. It is clear from the results of the studies summarised in chapter 3 that a number of firms, both in France and Britain, clearly operated systems of industrial accounting. In Britain, there seems to have been a marked movement in this direction during the latter decades of the eighteenth century and early decades of the nineteenth century. In France, the key decades seem to have been the 1820s and 1830s. This apparent lag in the French development, although accompanied by a concurrent rise in the literature, may explain why some British firms, such as Dowlais, appear to have developed their accounting systems more fully by the middle of the nineteenth century, for example through the utilisation of cost sheets which enabled short period cost analysis rather than the annual analysis more typical of the French firms investigated.

But why do we observe such differences in the timing and extent of the development of industrial accounting between Britain and France? And how was it possible for practice to be so much more in advance of the literature in Britain in the nineteenth century? In the remainder of this chapter we attempt to answer these questions though, as the reader will observe, our review of possible answers often raises more questions than it solves.

The methodological approach

Providing answers to historical questions, and indeed the choice of the questions themselves, is undoubtedly influenced by the stand-point of the historian or historians concerned. We noted in chapter 1, the fact that there are a number of different schools of historical thought and, in the recent burgeoning of research into accounting history, a variety of different approaches has emerged, most notably the economic determinist, the Marxist, and the Foucauldian. In large measure there is a growing consensus that, in the ultimate analysis, in order to understand the development of accounting it is necessary to take into consideration a wide variety of factors, including the economic, sociological, cultural, though the three main schools of thought differ as to the emphasis placed on each of these factors. Foucauldian writers, for example, place a greater emphasis on the socio-political context as an explanation for the development of accounting than do economic rationalist historians, who see economic factors as the most significant. We also made it clear in the introductory chapter that we write from essentially an economic determinist stand-point, but one that recognises that other factors can play important roles from time to time and should not be ignored. In what follows, therefore, our emphasis is on examining possible economic explanations for the development of industrial accounting in France and Britain, but where there is little evidence of relevant economic causes, or where general socio-cultural factors seem to have played a role, these are also examined.

Economic factors

The essence of the economic determinist view of accounting history is that changes in accounting occur as either a demand-side phenomenon, i.e. a response to economic demands made of accounting, and/or as a supply-side phenomenon, i.e. as the result of technical developments in accounting which are found to be useful to business. In the context of this study, demand-side explanations would stem from the advent of industrialisation in the late eighteenth and nineteenth centuries (see chapter 2), and the consequential impact of this on competition, size of business, etc. The differential timing of industrialisation in Britain and France, the former dating from c.1780 and the latter from c.1830, would explain why some British businesses such as Cyfarthfa, Charlton

Mills, and the Mona mines began to adopt double entry systems and develop industrial accounting at the end of the eighteenth/beginning of the nineteenth century, whilst a similar phenomenon is not observed in France until the 1820s and 1830s. The development and practical usage of industrial accounting systems in Britain before they were seen in France could thus be attributed to the economic consequences of industrialisation, and the increased pressures which this process placed on businessmen. It is consistent with the view that, in order to face up to greater competitive pressures resulting from industrialisation, and the problems posed by the development of larger, sometimes vertically integrated businesses, those managing them had a need for improved accounting systems to enable them to exercise control.

This line of reasoning requires us to consider the needs of managers of businesses, which were increasing both in size and complexity in the first half of the nineteenth century, and the extent to which the rise of industrial accounting be seen as a natural corollary of these requirements. In writing about later developments, most notably the rise of the multi-unit business enterprise in America since the nineteenth century, Chandler (1962, 1977) has acknowledged that an important role was played by accounting in the development of what he describes as the new economic function, namely that of "administrative co-ordination and allocation" (1977, p.484). It seems pertinent to ask, therefore, whether or not it was also the case that accounting played a significant role in buttressing corresponding developments during the industrial revolution period.

The most comprehensive study of the development of management during the industrial revolution in Britain is that by Pollard (1965). Influenced by the views of accounting historians such as Solomons and R.S. Edwards, Pollard noted four developments in accounting: (1) the adoption of regular, periodic returns; (2) its use for practical purposes such as the preservation of liquidity and the detection of error and fraud; (3) in costing and in aiding management decisions; and (4) the determination of total costs and profits of a firm. From the point of view of the advance of management, the last two developments were seen by Pollard as the most significant (1968, pp.256-7), though overall he concluded that costing developments were embryonic and hesitant. Though there was evidence that "the rationalization of management through accountancy and audit was stirring", it was only a faint stirring and accountancy was deemed to be used only minimally to guide businessmen in their decisions, and even then he considers its guidance to have been unreliable (Pollard, 1968, p.271). Pollard, on the basis of the evidence at the time he was writing, thus concluded that developments within cost accounting and the use of accounting for managerial purposes were limited prior to the middle of the nineteenth century. Moreover, he was convinced, as others had been before him, that the practice of using accounts as a direct aid to management is a phenomenon of the twentieth century, not earlier.

The main problem faced in evaluating the role of accounting in any period, however, is deciding upon the judgement criterion or criteria to be invoked. In relation to an issue such as cost calculation during the industrial revolution, as Fleischman and Parker have pointed out, the specific problem "lies in defining what constitutes good cost management" (1991, p.371). In their study of 25 'large' British manufacturing enterprises during the industrial revolution period, taken mainly from the textile and iron sectors, Fleischman and Parker conclude, in contrast to the earlier finding of Pollard, that costing during the industrial revolution did not universally fail to provide good data for decision making. Despite the absence of textbook guidance, they suggest that "it was the entrepreneurs themselves, sometimes motivated by competitive markets and narrow profit margins, who appear to have developed techniques appropriate for their own enterprises" (1991, p.371).

Whilst Fleischman and Parker appear to take as their criterion for judging the role of accounting in the industrial revolution the suitability of cost data for purposes of management decision making, other accounting historians, in relation to this and other periods, have stressed other criteria. Most notably, in their search for crucial accounting discontinuities over the last two centuries, Hoskin and Macve have focused attention on the "dynamic new alignment of managerialism with accounting" which accompanied the growth of the Chandlerian multi-unit business enterprise (1993, p.46). An essential feature of this new alignment, part of a general disciplinary transformation based around the "new power of writing, examination and grading", was a concern with performativity or human accountability (Hoskin and Macve, 1993, p.32). Thus Hoskin and Macve have searched for the genesis of accountability in terms of the development of the use of accounting, not for decision making purposes but for the purpose of labour control. In so doing, they extend Chandler's analysis of the development of the MBE, where he saw the use of accounting as a means to "control and evaluate the work of the many *managers"* (1977, p.120, our italics), particularly in respect of the development of American railroads, to that of monitoring shopfloor labour. For Hoskin and Macve this crucial discontinuity had its genesis at the Springfield Armory in the United States during the middle decades of the nineteenth century.

The analysis of Hoskin and Macve, however, in our view is incomplete.[1] Whilst it is accepted that, at certain points in time and in specific circumstances, the control of labour may be a major concern of the management of any business, we do not accept that this has always been the over-riding concern of managements. Indeed, managers have to fulfil a number of functions, one well-known formulation of management's functions being Gulick and Urwick's POSDCORB: planning, organizing, staffing, directing, coordinating, reporting and budgeting (Gulick and Urwick, 1937). In relation to the period studied in this analysis, it is argued that labour control, although an issue, was largely effected through means outside the accounting system, whether by direct supervision, the use of sub-contracting, payments linked to sliding scales based on the selling price of the product or whatever. With other means at their disposal to control labour, managements were free to utilise the accounting system for other ends, most particularly decision making and planning.[2]

Management has to fulfil a number of functions, whose relative importance undoubtedly varies with the individual circumstances faced by a firm, both internally and externally, particularly as businesses have changed in size. These circumstances render deficient, in our view, any approach to determining crucial discontinuities in accounting based on a preoccupation with one particular function of management. In our opinion, accounting historians, in assessing and analysing the form of accounting adopted in any period must always be aware of possible alternatives to which that accounting could have been put. Furthermore, they need to analyse closely the needs of the period and to search earnestly for positive evidence of the use of accounting for possibly more than one specific end. We have, we hope, kept an open mind as to the possibility that accounting in Britain and France prior to 1880 could have been used principally to control labour, but we have found no positive evidence of this, and are not convinced by the interpretation of Reid's evidence in relation to Decazeville put forward by Hoskin and Macve (1988a, p.64).[3]

In a similar but somewhat broader vein, Miller (1990) has argued that the development of accounting in France in the second half of the seventeenth century was closely linked to the socio-political context of the time. He perceives there to be a close link between the aim of the French state for knowledge and control over its inhabitants and their economic endeavours on the one hand, and mercantilist rules regulating accounting, such as the *Ordonnance* of 1673, on the other. Little evidence has so far been produced, however, to indicate that mercantilist rules had any major practical impact on methods of accounting and, in any case, they were concerned with establishing a system of accounting for cash flows rather than one designed to serve any internal management purpose. By the beginning of the nineteenth century, of course, things had begun to change in France. The Revolution of 1789 and the subsequent rise of Napoleon, together with the breakdown of mercantilism and a gradual move towards *laissez-faire*, a movement which gathered momentum in the nineteenth century, created a somewhat different economic and socio-political context than had existed under Colbert in the second half of the seventeenth century.

From our perspective, the advent of *laissez-faire*, together with the development of industrialisation in France from around 1830, created new demands on accounting. These derived, however, not from the informational requirements of the state for control or any other purpose, but rather from the needs of those running business. In Britain this process had begun somewhat earlier. Our finding in chapter 3 that accounting on both sides of the Channel was increasingly being used for purposes of decision making and planning, leads us to conclude that, in the period prior to 1880, there was a pressing need to develop of a form of accounting which addressed the provision of information for such purposes. Industrial accounting, since it provided the requisite information, especially that relating to costs, by which firms could help to combat increased competition and the growth of business size consequent upon the process of industrialization, thus developed as the natural form of accounting during the one hundred years or so up to 1880.

The development of industrial accounting can therefore be seen as a natural process between c.1780 and c.1880, given the general economic and socio-political climate of that period, namely the development of industrialisation and the switch from mercantilism towards a philosophy of *laissez-faire*, but the timing of its adoption by any individual business would depend upon firm-specific factors. In some cases it might be a response to financial crisis, in others to increasing complexity, a change of ownership or to a change in key managerial personnel. In Table 1 are summarised key points related to the case studies presented in chapter 4. Of those where we can identify with some degree of precision the reason for the introduction of double entry and/or industrial accounting, a change of ownership was clearly important in the French examples of Godard-Desmarest at Baccarat, and Champel (double entry) and Giroud (industrial accounting) at Allevard. In Britain, the clearest example of a change of ownership generating a move to double entry is that of Richard Crawshay taking sole control at Cyfarthfa. It is also apparent from the table that there is no direct causal link between the use of industrial accounting and the ownership structure of business. Examples can be found of business utilising this method of accounting, whether owned by an individual, a partnership or a limited company.

The classic case of the creation of cost data as a response to business problems, as noted earlier, is that of Wedgwood. For McKendrick, "Wedgwood's cost accountancy was the product of financial crisis and acute depression" (1970, p.63). More directly it was the economic depression of 1772 which spurred him, during August and September, to "attempt to solve the problem of accurate industrial accounting". In most other times, "So handsome were the profit margins which he could normally expect, and so high the prices which he could regularly charge, that the incentives towards anything more than routine costing were usually rather slight" (McKendrick, 1970, p.48). Indeed, his concern with costing and other aspects of business management "faded in years when demand was strong" (McKendrick, 1970, p.46).

General economic factors such as industrialisation, or specific ones such as financial crisis, undoubtedly influenced the choice of, or need for, the development of a system of industrial accounting amongst some British and French firms in the late eighteenth and early nineteenth centuries. It is less easy to explain, in terms of economic factors alone, the failure of the British accounting literature to address the issue of industrial accounting prior to 1880. For one thing, if there was a need for this form of accounting, and we have argued that there is clear evidence of such a demand, then it would seem to follow that anyone writing a text dealing with industrial accounting would undoubtedly have been assured of large sales of their work. Possible explanations for the lack of such texts include the following: the

Table 1. Summary of the case studies

Company	the introduction of double entry/industrial accounting		company form
	person responsible (date)[1]	reason for introduction	
FRANCE			
Baccarat	Godard-Desmarest (1822/3)	change of ownership	partnership (Godard & two partners)
Decazeville	not clear (1826)	formation of company	limited company owned chiefly by protestant bankers
Saint-Gobain	by decision of the board (1820)	increased competitive pressures and/or increased number of shareholders	initially formed by Royal decree in 1665 (no. of shareholders: 10 in 1695; 50 in 1770; 204 in 1830)
Allevard	Champel (1818) Giroud (1831)	change of control in both 1818 and 1831, the latter due to the need for an injection of capital	partnership(?) between Giroud (banker) and Penet (manager) from 1831
Le Creusot	Manby, Wilson et cie. (1826)	change of ownership	limited partnership (société en commandite)

Table 1 contd.

Company	the introduction of double entry/industrial accounting person responsible (date[1])	reason for introduction	company form
BRITAIN			
Staveley	not clear (by 1690)	to provide management information and to help facilitate division of profits between partnerships	series of inter-locking, but distinct, partnerships in the 17th and 18th centuries, sole trader 1838-63 then limited company
Mona	not clear (1785?)	probably the company's formation due to need to distribute profits between partnerships	one of a number of inter-locking partnerships
Cyfarthfa	Richard Crawshay? (1791)	to overcome poor management control	sole ownership (Crawshay)
Charlton Mills	not clear (c.1810)	not clear	partnership (Birley brothers)
Dowlais	not clear (by 1843)	not clear	partnership, latterly owned by Guest family
Consett	not clear (by 1860)	inherited from predecessor company	series of companies, some limited; Consett Iron Company Ltd. from 1864

Note

1   The date given is for the introduction of an industrial accounting system except where information exists that double entry was introduced prior to this, in which case two dates are given, the first being that at which double entry was adopted and the second, the date of introduction of industrial accounting.

demand for a literature on industrial accounting was not particularly widespread; no one was in a position, or willing, to write such a text. The former argument is difficult to assess: we know that there was some demand, since certain firms were operating industrial accounting systems, but how widespread was such demand can only be the subject of speculation at this stage. The one book which contained a sizable amount of material on industrial accounting, and which may have sparked a larger literature was, of course, Hamilton's *An introduction to merchandize.* . . (1777-79). Curiously, however, much of the innovatory material on cost calculation contained in Hamilton's original volume was removed when the second edition was published. A possible explanation for this action is the lack of demand for such material, but other factors could also explain its removal. One possibility is that the decision was made on the grounds of space: having decided to reduce the size of the work,[4] the cost material may have been amongst that omitted on the grounds that it was perceived to be peripheral. Another possibility is that Hamilton, realising the potential worth of his ideas and the personal gain that could be derived from selling his services as an accountant to businesses, decided that publication of his ideas and techniques in the second and subsequent editions of his work would undermine this potentially lucrative market. It cannot be ruled out therefore, that Hamilton was motivated by personal gain, and this was the reason for the omission of the cost material.[5]

The second argument, that nobody was in a position, or willing, to write appropriate texts, however, would clearly seem to be invalidated by the case of Hamilton and the other writers examined in chapter 3 who contributed in some small way to the British literature on industrial accounting in the eighteenth and nineteenth centuries. Nevertheless, it seems appropriate to address the issue of why, if there were people capable of writing texts, there were such a small number who actually did so, both in France but more especially in Britain. This takes us beyond the purely economic sphere and into that of socio-cultural influences, since it requires us to consider the type of person who wrote texts generally, and accounting texts in particular.

The writing of texts in the eighteenth and nineteenth centuries

The pre-conditions for producing an accounting text obviously included a knowledge of accounting, an ability to write and the time in which to do so. As seen in chapter 3 and the Appendix thereto, writers of British accounting texts came essentially from three backgrounds, namely, teachers (e.g. John Mair, 1760), bookkeepers/accountants (e.g. Richard Roose, c.1761) and businessmen (e.g. Robert Colinson, 1683). Furthermore, Bywater and Yamey (1982, p.10) have noted that "the worlds of [accounting] practice and teaching were not completely separated" in Britain between the sixteenth and nineteenth centuries. Mepham, on the basis of his study of the rise of accounting in Scotland in the eighteenth century, goes somewhat further, arguing that "the teachers of accounting and the authors of book-keeping texts usually had practical business experience. There was some overlap so that accountants might do some teaching and teachers might write up a local merchant's books" (1988, p.37). In addition, he notes that eighteenth century Scottish textbook writers "considered book-keeping to be a branch of business mathematics" (1988, p.38). However, while some writers exhibited a business background (e.g. Booth, 1789), we are unaware of any evidence that either a businessmen of any import, or an accountant working for any large manufacturing business wrote a cost accounting text in Britain prior to the publication of Battersby's book in 1878.

In France, however, the situation was somewhat different. Of the nine writers of texts on industrial accounting before 1850 examined in chapter 3, we have detailed knowledge on seven of them. Of these seven, at some stage in their careers, four were connected with education (as teachers or professors), three were in business, three had occupied administrative posts in the army and/or state government, and one had experience as a merchant. Perhaps importantly, three early writers of texts on industrial accounting, Payen, Godard-Desmarest and Pillet-Will, were closely connected with the running of important businesses, the first two in the capacity of owner-manager and the last as a director. This suggests that there may have been a greater willingness of those connected with the running of businesses in France, than was the case amongst their counterparts in Britain, to write texts on accounting matters. But why should this have been the case? Explanations may be related to the organization of businesses and the availability of time to undertake this sort of exercise, or to institutional factors such as the system of education, or to more fundamental socio-cultural differences.

Business organization

There is some evidence that business organization in France in the eighteenth and nineteenth century could have played some role. The existence of the limited partnership, the *société en commandite*, in France, which enabled nobles to provide capital without being directly involved with the running of the business, was without direct parallel in Britain, though sleeping partnerships, but with unlimited liability, did exist. Thus it is a possibility that French nobles, removed from the hurly-burly of everyday management, therefore had sufficient knowledge of business affairs and the time to write texts. Whilst this may explain the text of Pillet-Will, there seems to be little evidence that Godard-Desmarest or Payen, who appear to have both been hands-on managers, had any more time to write texts than the likes of Barrow or Guest in Britain. It is perhaps significant, therefore that Payen wrote his book during a period of confinement following a fall, despite having some years earlier expressed the desire to write such a text.

Education

Whilst the availability of time may have played a role in determining the writing of texts, another possible factor is education. It is difficult to ascertain the precise level of education enjoyed by many businessmen during the period with which we are concerned, and particularly whether Wedgwood or Guest, for example, were more or less educated than, say, Payen or Godard-Desmarest. However, it is possible that the emphasis in Britain on practical, on-the-job training, rather than on formal education, may have a part to play in the explanation of the dearth of literature on industrial accounting.

The precise relationship, both in France and Britain, between education, the writing of accounting texts and business in the period between the sixteenth and nineteenth centuries, is still largely unknown. In both countries, the educational system prior to the nineteenth century seems to have emphasised the importance of a classical education, despite some evidence of the development of commercial and vocational training. In Britain, for example, by the end of the eighteenth century there is evidence of an improved provision of commercial training amongst all forms of educational institution, but most notably the dissenting academies, and in this accounting often played an important role (O'Day, 1982; Hans, 1951).[6] Nevertheless, education, whatever its form, was strictly limited in both countries to those from the wealthier classes of society.

In general terms, the British education system is considered to have lagged behind best European practice in the nineteenth century, including not only that of Germany but also that of France. Although the level of literacy in France may have been inferior to that in Britain in the eighteenth century[7], this situation was rectified during the first half of the nineteenth century. Following the Revolution, the state in France began to replace the Church as superintendent of the education system. Whereas education had been ill co-ordinated under the *Ancien Régime*, Napoleon established the 'University', a system through which the state ran its own schools and supervised private ones (Anderson, 1975, p.5). However, secondary education was considered more important than primary education and, indeed, as late as 1848, "in 'centralized' France the state did not run a single primary school" (Anderson, 1975, p.8). Indeed, "until after 1815, legislation on primary education did little more than sanction what communes chose to do . . . [but] the decisive step was the *loi Guizot* of 1833 which for the first time obliged every commune to have a school" (Anderson, 1975, p.7). The system of classical secondary education (*l'enseignement secondaire classique*) thus was gradually buttressed by a system of primary education (*l'enseignement primaire*) during the first half of the nineteenth century. Furthermore, in 1833, an intermediary level of education was also established which, according to Coq, resulted in the opening of the first *Ecole Supérieur de Commerce* in Paris in 1840. By way of contrast, Britain lacked any national system of education, whether primary or secondary, prior to 1870, and then the emphasis, in contrast to that in France, was on primary rather than secondary education.

Despite the apparently advanced nature of the French education system around the middle of the nineteenth century, Paul Coq, a professor at the *Ecole Supérieur de Commerce de Paris*, in his *Cours d'économie industrielle* (1876) (*Lectures on industrial economics)*, criticised the failure of the French educational system to produce individuals equipped for industrial service. In particular, he complained that the French education system produced excellent Latin scholars but only mediocre managers/administrators (Coq, 1876, p.ix). He denounced the absence of any provision of general technical education, and specifically that of management education, including the teaching of law and economics. Industrial economics, for example, only began to be taught at the *Ecole Supérieur de Commerce de Paris* in 1866, a year after legislation permitting the development of commercial and technical education under the guise of 'special secondary education' (*enseignement secondaire spécial*) had been passed. However, Coq's comments seem to be inconsistent with the evidence and certainly do not match up with the modern conventional wisdom which suggests that the French education system was markedly superior to that in Britain in the second half of the nineteenth century. Indeed Kindleberger and others have suggested that the high quality of French technical and scientific education was an important factor in explaining the significant role that France played in the late nineteenth century in the development of new industries, including the motor car.

The importance of the teaching of accounting within the French education system of the nineteenth century, however, is difficult to assess. If Barlet's (1861) assessment of the Belgian experience is valid and has a more general application, we must believe that the education system had little influence on the diffusion of accounting knowledge. He complained that many engineers, fresh from the Belgian School of Mines (*l'école des Mines*), found their careers frustrated through a lack of accounting knowledge. In France, Colasse and Durand (1994, p.41), have also noted that accounting education was originally carried out in private professional schools, of which two *grandes écoles*, the *Ecole supérieur de commerce de Paris* and the *Ecole des hautes études commerciales* (founded in 1881), were important. It was only later that it spread to state-run technical institutions.[8] Nevertheless there is some evidence that, towards the very end of the period of our study, there was some movement towards providing individuals with the skills necessary for business in France, through the development of industrial economics and a greater provision of technical education. Price (1975, p.169), for example, notes that the *grandes écoles* provided specialists who increasingly occupied managerial and engineering roles, whilst the five *écoles d'art et métiers* provided individuals capable of occupying lower levels within large business organizations. Whilst their training was essentially technical, and may have lacked the scientific basis considered by some to be an essential requirement, it did prepare them "to improve machinery and factory organisation rather than make scientific discoveries" (Price, 1975, p.169).

In Britain, however, private academies and tutors seem to have remained the major sources of business education, including commerce and bookkeeping, throughout much of the nineteenth century, but a lack of clear knowledge of the nature and extent of accounting education there, as in France, makes it difficult to judge whether accounting education in either country was in advance of that in the other. Much more research needs to be carried out into the nature of the training and education of accountants in both France and Britain, and a particular focus of such research should be on the extent to which education may have played a part in the different propensities to write texts on industrial accounting in the two countries. *Prima facie*, it seems likely that since many texts were written for educational purposes, there may be a strong link between the education of accountants and the writing of texts. Furthermore, the speed and process of the professionalization of accounting may also have had an effect, both on the provision of education and the writing of texts, since the formation of professional bodies led to the introduction of formal examinations. The interlinkage between education, the writing of texts and the professionalization of accounting would appear to be a key element in any understanding of the development of accounting literature and practice in the nineteenth century.[9]

The emergence of the accounting profession in France and Britain

Lemarchand and Parker (1996, pp.xxxvi-xxxvii) have identified four directions in which research into French accounting history would be highly desirable. These include the question of why professional accountancy bodies did not develop in late nineteenth century France in the same way that they did in Britain, and why the history of professional accountancy in France is so different from that in Britain. It is certainly true that, at this point in time, our knowledge of the rise of the accounting profession in France, by comparison with that in Britain, is somewhat limited. We therefore summarise below some of the salient differences regarding the process of professionalization in the two countries, and then make suggestions as to the impact that these

differences had on the development of accounting doctrines in the two
countries, both prior to 1880 and thereafter.

The accounting profession in Britain emerged and rose to a
position of importance during the nineteenth century, first in Scotland
and later in England and Wales. Mepham (1988) has argued that there
were signs of an emerging Scottish profession as early as the second
half of the eighteenth century. In this respect, he considers that the
profession's growth out of merchant book-keeping "had its roots in the
legal profession" as some Edinburgh lawyers moved towards a
specialisation in accountancy, some one hundred years before the
profession was formally established (Mepham, 1988, p.38). In
Glasgow, however, accountants in the second half of the eighteenth
century were more likely to have had a merchant background than a
legal one (Mepham, 1988, p.38). Despite these early beginnings, it was
not until the second half of the nineteenth century that professional
accounting organisations began to be established in Scotland: those in
Edinburgh and Glasgow being set up in 1853, followed by a third in
Aberdeen in 1867. Whilst the three Scottish organisations did not
finally join together to form the Institute of Chartered Accountants of
Scotland until 1951, the Institute of Chartered Accountants in England
and Wales (ICAEW) was formed in 1880. It came into being as the
result of a merger between the Society of Accountants in England
(formed in 1872) and several provincial societies formed a few years
earlier, namely those of Liverpool (formed in 1870), London (1870),
Manchester (1871) and Sheffield (1877).

The first moves towards the formation of an accounting
profession in France, however, only occurred with the formation, in
1881, of the *Société Académique de Comptabilité*. Brown was of the
view that even by the beginning of the twentieth century that French
accountants were "still far from any regular organisation, although the
need for it appears more and more" (1905, p.291). Part of the
explanation for the slow pace of development of an accounting
profession in France in the nineteenth century was the low esteem in
which accountants were generally held. Indeed, in France, as in Britain,
the growth of new professions was often met initially with a barrage of
jibes indicating the lack of worthiness of those involved to call
themselves professionals. Thus Brown has argued, in the French
context, that:

Till within the last few years, the profession of accountant was considered by the public as something altogether inferior. With a few exceptions it was practised by people of little education, and of a generally mediocre standing, both intellectually and socially - people who tried, without special training, to gain a livelihood by this means after having failed in other careers. (1905, pp.290-1)

A similar view has been expressed more recently by Colasse and Durand who note that, traditionally, accounting in France has been assigned an inferior intellectual status and has often been treated with intellectual disdain (1994, p.42). "Considered above all to be a discipline essentially practical in scope, accounting could only be, at best, a subject linked to technical training for bookkeepers" (Colasse and Durand, 1994, p.41). Such assessments, however, seem at first glance surprising, given that today's *experts comptables* can be seen as the distant heirs of the *maîtres écrivains* (writing masters) who, "organized as a guild up till the 1789 Revolution, practised accounting, within the framework of judicial procedures, as an extension of their tasks as teachers and as bookkeepers" (Lemarchand and Parker, 1996, p.xxxviii). Despite this background, however, there is little evidence that by the end of the nineteenth century the future *experts comptables* had yet become judicial experts and liquidators.

Lemarchand and Parker (1996, p.xxxix) note that amongst the founder members of the *Société Académique de Comptabilité* there was only one *expert comptable liquidateur*, and one teacher, but five company accountants. They attribute the failure of an independent accountancy profession to develop in France as being partly due to the role of the French state in providing finance for the development of the railways and the public utilities. As a consequence, the French state exercised its own accounting control over these companies, limiting the opportunities for independent accountants, in marked contrast to the situation in Britain where the use of private enterprise capital in the railway and utility sectors created a demand for the services of accountants and auditors. A further retarding factor in France was that the audit function, in companies limited by shares, was generally carried out by shareholders chosen from those attending the annual general meeting, rather than by outside specialists. This framework did not alter until after the First World War, when both an increase in the number of financial scandals and the introduction of income provided opportunities for *experts comptables*.[10] According to Lemarchand and Parker (1996, p.xxxix), however, it was only direct action by the Vichy Government which forged the multitude of societies and other local associations of *experts comptables* that had grown up in the intervening period into a single, national organisation of accountants, with disciplinary powers over its members.

The influence of the emerging accounting profession on accounting doctrine

The motivation behind the formation of professions is the subject of differing views:

> The 'altruistic' view regards professions as providing services which make a distinctive contribution to the smooth operation of society, that they possess specialist knowledge and self-discipline, and that the high level of prestige and financial reward enjoyed are a fair price for these services. The 'cynical' assessment is that the professions comprise groups of individuals pursuing self-interest, striving to convince others of their entitlement to professional recognition and reward, and doing a job which is just enough to satisfy clients and maintain their professional status. (Edwards, 1989a, p.276)

A corollary of either interpretation, therefore, is that members of the emerging profession had an incentive to identify themselves with a set of tools and tasks, since these are what help to define them and maintain their distinctiveness from non-members of the profession. Furthermore, they also have an incentive to resist change, and hence maintain the *status quo* in respect of those tools and tasks with which they are identified, which action serves to militate against change and the introduction of new ideas. Following this line of argument, the perception of what comprises accounting will be crucially influenced by which doctrine is dominant at the time of the professionalization of the discipline. Furthermore, the more important the accounting profession within the social and economic structure of a country, the greater the likelihood that new developments, particularly ones outside the profession, will be resisted.

In Britain, the professionalization of accounting began somewhat earlier than in France, i.e. from the late eighteenth century. The process, however, was a slow and long drawn out one, and it was not until the second half of the nineteenth century that professional accounting bodies began to appear. The early nineteenth century, however, did witness a growth in the number of accountants, but in 1882 there were still only 1,486 chartered accountants, representing only 0.01 per cent of the labour force, in Britain, 1,193 of whom were members of the ICAEW and 293 members of the Scottish organizations. Given this earlier development then, it is hardly surprising that what became enshrined as the dominant doctrine in accounting in Britain was somewhat different from that which developed in France. Accounting literature and training was concentrated on traditional double entry bookkeeping in the Italian method in the first half of the nineteenth century, and despite evidence concerning the adoption by business of industrial accounting, it was the Italian method which became firmly entrenched as the true concept of accounting in Britain. Once enshrined, the developing accounting profession had a vested interest in maintaining the *status quo*. The profession therefore championed accounting for external transactions as the essence of 'true' accounting. Cost calculation was not a matter for the accounting profession and hence industrial accounting, i.e. the treatment of costs within a double entry framework, or any other form of cost calculation, was 'frozen out', by the newly emerging profession, even though it was practised within industrial enterprises by 'non-professionals'. The lack of reference to industrial accounting techniques and method in British accounting texts before 1880 can therefore be seen as a reflection of the view that the concepts and methods of industrial accounting were irrelevant to the training of professional accountants, being outside their area of expertise. Since such texts were often written in order to educate those wishing to join the newly emerging profession, it is hardly surprising that they should reflect the mainstream view of what constituted accounting, namely mercantile accounting. The introduction of examinations by the newly formed professional bodies in the late nineteenth century merely reinforced this tendency.

In France, members of the slowly emerging accounting profession, like any other professional group, including their counterparts in Britain, were no less determined to clearly delineate the boundaries of their profession and hence their area of expertise. The main difference, however, is one of timing. Since the profession did not really begin to emerge in France until the 1880s, by which time the dominant accounting doctrine in the country was industrial accounting, it was this that became enshrined as the 'true' nature of accounting in France. Hence cost analysis within a double entry framework was considered natural in France, in contrast to the situation in Britain, where industrial accounting had been excluded in favour of mercantile accounting. Thus professional accountants in France at the end of the nineteenth century and the beginning of the twentieth century considered cost calculation as part and parcel of their normal activities, whereas in Britain it was viewed as something which should be left to others.

It has been suggested here that, since the accounting profession in France was not as well established in the first half of the nineteenth century as its counterpart in Britain, there was a much higher chance of books discussing new accounting ideas both being written and of influencing accounting doctrine in France. This, however, was more of a passive factor: individuals still had to develop new ideas, and the books still had to be written. The following section examines whether different traditions of thought may have played a role in explaining the greater propensity for the French to write texts on industrial accounting.

Traditions of thought and practice

In chapter 2, it was noted that there were different traditions of scientific thought in Britain and France. In Britain, the emphasis has been on the Newtonian approach which relies on practical experimentation, whilst in France the Cartesian approach, with its emphasis on grand theorizing, has dominated. We noted that during the eighteenth century, however, as a result of the influence of individuals like Voltaire, there was some fusing together of these two approaches in France. This fundamental difference in approach, however, suggests two possibilities: a greater emphasis in France on writing texts than in Britain; and a tendency for French writers, in their texts, to concentrate on theoretical principles underlying the issues being discussed. Thus the French could be expected to have written not only more accounting texts than the British, but also that their texts would show a predisposition with the theoretical principles underlying the bookkeeping methods being put forward.

In chapter 2 we noted that French accounting texts generally seem to have been more concerned with the issue of classification than was true of the British literature. It is possible that this concern, which later manifested itself in terms of advocating charts of accounts, the decimalisation of accounts and the *Plan comptable général*, and the personification of accounts, reflects the French Cartesian tradition. It may, however, reflect a much older tradition of codification which can be traced back to Roman law.[11] One further aspect of the scientific tradition which needs to be mentioned is that of sharing knowledge. A possible explanation for writing texts is the desire to share one's ideas with one's fellow human being. It may be merely a coincidence, but Payen was a chemist, and it might have been his scientific background which led him to write his text.

Knowledge and skills, however, are not solely passed on through the writing and reading of texts. Indeed, whatever the exact nature of the links between the education systems and traditions of thought in Britain and France and the writing of texts, it is generally accepted that for the period under consideration in this study Britain developed its industrial skills through on-the-job training, via formal apprenticeships or otherwise, rather than through formal education. Whilst it is difficult to be certain whether such training was more or less prevalent in Britain than in France, if technical information relating to skills and work practices was capable of being disseminated in this way, it is equally possible that the same is true of accounting knowledge and techniques.

Harris's (1976) review of the technical literature relating to mining and metals during the eighteenth century produces conclusions identical to those which result from our examination of the literature on industrial accounting in the nineteenth century, namely that it is more extensive in France than in Britain. He cautions against reading too much into this difference, however, suggesting that there is much need for a close examination of the extent of plagiarism, the extent to which methods described mirrored contemporary practice, and the extent to which ideas were borrowed from works published in other countries (Harris, 1992, pp.19-20). In addition, he warned against drawing the conclusion that, simply because the literature in one country was ahead of that in another, practice must similarly have been more advanced. In respect of industrial accounting, our results confirm the wisdom of this warning: although the British literature was inferior in respect of industrial accounting, its practice was more advanced. Harris further noted that, despite the advanced nature of the coal industry in Britain, remarkably little was written about it by contemporaries in the eighteenth century, there being only two works of value written during the entire century (1992, p.21). One reason he suggests for this was a long-established familiarity with most aspects of coal technology. He further notes that:

> The very able managers with their on-the-job training carried on with their work largely unregarded outside their own coalfields, though sometimes minor deities within them. Interestingly, they were often mathematically able, and had early in the century carried the surveying of coal below ground to considerable lengths - their 'dialling' was the *géométrie souterraine* whose lack in France was so deeply bewailed by her technocrats. (Harris, 1992, p.21)

It is equally possible that the reason that those responsible for accounting in large industrial enterprises saw no need for books on industrial accounting was likewise a familiarity with the underlying concepts and their practical application.

Given the small number of texts on industrial accounting published, even in France, before 1840, therefore, it seems likely that on-the-job training, and the movement of personnel from one firm to another, must have played an important part in the dissemination of the ideas of industrial accounting in both countries in the first half of the nineteenth century, if not beyond.

The dissemination of accounting ideas

Given that industrial accounting developed in both France and Britain at very roughly the same time, i.e. within a 40-50 year period spanning the end of the eighteenth and beginning of the nineteenth centuries, it is conceivable that there may have been some link between these two events, i.e. there may have some transfer of accounting ideas between the two countries. Given the language barrier, however, it seems highly unlikely that accounting texts, in whichever language they were initially written, were likely to have been the main conduit by which any dissemination of ideas between the two countries occurred.[12] It is known, however, that industrial techniques did move across the

Channel in the eighteenth and nineteenth centuries, and if accounting is viewed as a technology, then the mechanism for international technology transfer discussed by Jeremy (1991) may form an appropriate model to explain the dissemination process. An alternative model, discussed further here, is that of 'change agents' and 'recipients' utilised by Parker in relation to the dissemination of accounting ideas.

According to Arthur H. Niehoff (quoted in Parker, 1979, p.125) the most important factors in the dissemination process from the viewpoint of "change agents" are: the methods of communication used; the kind of participation obtained from the recipient; and the manner in which the innovation is used and adapted to the existing cultural patterns. From the standpoint of the "recipients", the most important factors are: whether they feel a need for the new thought or practice; whether they perceive a practical benefit in adopting a change; and whether their traditional leaders are brought into the planning and implementation of the process. Parker's work on "change agents" (Parker, 1979; Carnegie and Parker, 1996) has suggested that the important group at one point in time may be quite different from that which is important at another. Thus, in disseminating the concept of consolidated accounts during the twentieth century, Parker finds that international accounting firms are seen as most important (1979, p.126). In a more recent joint work (Carnegie and Parker, 1996), however, it was found that the only individual to play a role in the process of transferring accounting technology to the British colonies of Australia, New Zealand and South Africa during the late nineteenth and early twentieth centuries, was William Butler Yaldwyn, a peripatetic accountant and author of accounting texts.

If accounting historians are to understand better the development of accounting theory, and the precise relationship between theory and practice, it is clear that they will need to investigate the process by which accounting ideas and practices are disseminated. This will require the identification of, and the role played by, the various "change agents". This, however, will be no easy task since evidence relating to such dissemination may never have been recorded or, where recorded, such record may not have survived the passage of time. To build up a picture of the dissemination process will therefore require painstaking research and will probably have to rely as much on circumstantial evidence as on "hard facts". Recent studies of the dissemination process in Britain between c.1750 and c.1870 (Boyns and Edwards, 1996a,b) have suggested that, whilst much more research needs to be done, on-the-job training and practical experience, coupled with the large movement of key personnel between businesses, possibly explains the development of industrial accounting in Britain, in the absence of any relevant accounting literature.

The movement of personnel may therefore help explain the dissemination process, but there remains the question of who provided the original training and/or introduced the accounting systems in the first place. One possibility is that there were a few individuals (accountants such as Hamilton), or certain groups of specialists in various businesses, who initiated such systems. Another possibility is that there were groups of itinerant individuals with the requisite skill, such as colliery viewers, or surveyors (such as the consulting engineer William Armstrong in Britain in the second half of the nineteenth century), who may have had a knowledge of accounting which could be adapted to the needs of a particular industrial sector and/or specific firms. Such individuals, by moving between firms and sectors, may have helped to establish new accounting systems and/or modify existing ones, thereby acting as a major force for disseminating ideas and techniques. But from where did such individuals get their knowledge: Was it from the formal education system or was it from their own practical experience?

According to Yamey (1981, p.131), "a history of accounting . . . without some knowledge of the actors - those for whom as well as those by which the records were kept - must be rather anaemic and thin." The fact is, however, that we do not yet know enough about these actors, especially those who were responsible for disseminating the ideas associated with industrial accounting, to be able to answer the questions posed in the preceding paragraph. We do know that in Britain, colliery viewers in the north-east of England played an important role in the dissemination of certain accounting ideas within the coal industry during the eighteenth century (Oldroyd, 1996). For France, the work of Lemarchand (1993a,b, 1994) indicates a lack of any similar force; all the mining companies studied were found to be using charge and discharge accounting during the eighteenth century. Among enterprises engaged in other industrial activities, especially metallurgy and textiles, however, he did observe that some had begun to use double entry.

Given our current knowledge, or rather lack of it, it is difficult to ascertain whether there was any significant difference in the dissemination process between France and Britain. In the French context, it has been suggested that accounting ideas and techniques travelled in the pockets of those who supplied the capital (Nikitin, 1992). From the data presented by Lemarchand (1993a,b, 1994), however, there is an indication that shareholders of French companies came from three distinct backgrounds: merchant, financial and specialist. The endeavour to discern any clear pattern between the choice of accounting system, whether charge and discharge or double entry, and the background of those providing the capital, however, remains unrewarded.

The process of internal dissemination of accounting technology remains problematic, and the same is the case with international transfers of accounting knowledge. It is well known that there was an interchange between Britain and France of production technology and personnel at various times in certain industries, especially iron, during the eighteenth and nineteenth centuries. In more general terms, Crouzet believes that France and Britain, despite intense rivalry and personal antipathy, have "never ceased to borrow ideas, institutions, techniques, [or] works of art from each other" (1990, p.7). The socialist, Cabet, writing in 1843 put it thus:

> France and England are marching together in the forefront of humankind; if one looks more closely at the progress of these two peoples in the vanguard one sees that they endlessly react upon one another, each guiding or being guided by the other; sometimes France is at the head of the column, sometimes England takes the lead. (Quoted in Crouzet (1990), pp.6-7)

In relation to the dissemination of accounting ideas, however, there is little evidence as yet of any interchange of ideas, though the potential certainly existed through the activities of individuals such as William Wilkinson in the iron industry in the late eighteenth century (Harris, 1985), and the establishment of firms such as Manby, Wilson et cie. in France. Evidence from the field of business legislation, however, suggests that, at one level at least, whilst knowledge of alternative frameworks may have existed, it rarely if ever resulted in the unadulterated adoption of the other's ideas. Thus c.1830, the British government asked Sir John Bowring to investigate the French and other systems of government accounting.[13] Though he spoke highly of them, and despite his promptings in parliament, no change was made to the

British system. In the area of company law, a committee was also established about the same time to investigate the possibility of introducing the limited partnership on the lines of the French *société en commandite*. The report of this committee, published in 1837, however, whilst influencing subsequent legislation on joint stock companies in 1844, did not result in the introduction of limited partnerships in Britain at this time, though they were eventually legalised in 1907. In this case, as in others, Britain may have consciously spurned innovations elsewhere in Europe and determined its own route (Napier, 1993, p.375).

Conclusion

It has been observed that there is a close correlation between the early examples of industrial accounting in both Britain and France and the timing of the industrial revolution in the two countries. Furthermore, we would argue that there is strong evidence that the rise of the former, from the 1780s in Britain, and from the 1820s in France, resulted from the pressures placed upon businessmen during the industrialisation process. The exact mechanism by which industrial accounting developed to serve the needs of businessmen, however, remains unclear, though we have unearthed what would appear to have been a number of important influences.

In Britain. for example, it is clear that businessmen and/or key individuals employed by them, developed a set of accounting techniques despite the lack of any significant industrial accounting literature to guide them.[14]   Furthermore, they were not inspired themselves to write such texts, possibly due to the preference for practical training over other means of education, whether formal or informal, giving rise to a major gap in the British industrial accounting literature until the end of the nineteenth century. Whilst it seems unlikely that the French were any less reliant upon on-the-job training, some French writers, sometimes businessmen who introduced the accounting systems in their own businesses, did write texts detailing their ideas on industrial accounting. Further investigation is clearly required into the precise extent of the use of industrial accounting[15] and especially of two related areas: the link between accounting practice and literature, and the means by which accounting techniques were disseminated in the eighteenth and nineteenth centuries.

Additional research, it is to be hoped, will provide a better, more clearer understanding of the developments in accounting prior to 1880, and may help to provide historians with an understanding of the process of accounting change, including that which has occurred in the twentieth century. Many of the themes and factors which have been highlighted in this study also seem to have relevance to the study of twentieth century accounting developments in Britain and France. These give rise to the following questions with which we conclude our book: What was the nature and purpose of accounting (was it for financial reporting, for decision making, for labour control)? What were the influences of the underlying economic and socio-political philosophies of the period? What role did the accounting profession play in the development of accounting? Did businesses necessarily carry out accounting as espoused in the literature? Did Britain and France borrow ideas from one another?

Notes

1   For a fuller critique of the Hoskin and Macve approach, see Boyns and Edwards (1996c).
2   The modern perceived role of accounting in relation to management is stated by Arnold and Hope to be of a three-fold and dynamic nature: it should aid decision-making, planning and control (1983, p. 356).
3   A fuller discussion of Decazeville was carried out in chapter 3 above. If there was any use of accounting in setting production standards for labour at Decazeville, there is little evidence that it represented anything more than a one-off occurrence, as found in the joint study of Boulton and Watt by Fleischman, Hoskin and Macve (1995). In Britain, our analysis of Dowlais failed to find any evidence of the use of accounting for labour control even in the second half of the nineteenth century (Boyns and Edwards, 1996c)
4   The first edition was in two volumes and comprised 720 pages; the second edition ran to only 563 pages.
5   Stevelinck (1977) has suggested that Bertrand-François Barrême delayed publication of his major work, *Traité des parties doubles* (1721), though he had published a lesser work, *Livre des comptes faits* in 1680, in order not to harm the

lucrative income he enjoyed from teaching, fearing that early publication would reduce the supply of students to his school.

6   The seventeenth and eighteenth centuries witnessed in Britain the growth of private academies, dissenting academies and of the private tutor, to compete with the private schools, grammar schools and universities.

7   According to Crouzet (1990, p. 72), roughly twice as many people in Britain than in France could sign their names on documents at the beginning of the eighteenth century. Throughout the century, since literacy advanced at the same pace on both sides of the Channel, Britain held on to its lead.

8   It is perhaps worth noting that, even today, training for accountancy is largely carried out outside the university sector.

9   One possible argument is that the reason for few, if any, books on industrial accounting in Britain until the 1880s is due to the view within the emerging accounting profession and the education system that what constituted accounting was the Italian method of double entry bookkeeping, and hence the pre-1880 accounting texts concentrated on this to the exclusion of any reference to industrial accounting.

10   In Britain, the joint stock company audit is also initially thought to have been the province of the amateur/shareholder auditor but, by 1886, 77 per cent of quoted companies, whose audit position can be ascertained, was audited by professionals (Anderson *et al*, forthcoming).

11   If this is the case, it could be conjectured that Colbertian regulations, including the *Ordonnance* of 1673, should be seen not as part of a new socio-political context, as argued by Miller (1990), but rather as part of a much longer tradition which reflected a more general desire for establishing rules and orderliness.

12   There is evidence that some texts published on the Continent in one language would either be simultaneously or subsequently translated into another Continental European language, and although the scale of this seems to have been small in the eighteenth and nineteenth centuries, it was probably greater than that of British books being translated into French or *vice versa*. One well-known text that was translated from English to French at the beginning of the

nineteenth century, for example, was Jones' *English system of bookkeeping, by single or double entry* .... (1796).

13 For a fuller account of Bowring's role, see Parker (1993).

14 Whilst, as we saw in chapter 3, French texts on industrial accounting were clearly more numerous than similar texts in Britain, it should be remembered that the British accounting literature as a whole in the nineteenth century nevertheless exceeded its French counterpart.

15 There are still large numbers of archives in both countries which remain largely untapped by accounting historians and, until these are investigated, our knowledge base will continue to remain small.

References

Primary sources

Académie François Bourdon, *Rapport à l'assemblée générale des actionnaires de la société Manby, Wilson et cie.*, 1827
Gwent Record Office (GwRO), Crawshay Ledger, Crawshay Letterbooks.
Glamorgan Record Office (GRO), Dowlais Collection (D/D G).

Parliamentary Publications

Royal Commission on Children's Employment in Mines and Manufactories, P.P. 1842, XVII.
Report of the Commissioner for the State of the Population in the Mining Districts, 1846, P.P. 1846, XXIV.

Secondary sources

ACCA (1954) *Management accounting*, London: Association of Certified and Corporate Accountants.
Anderson, M., J.R. Edwards and D. Matthews (1995) 'Accountability in a free market economy. The British company audit 1886', paper presented at the annual conference of the European Accounting Association, Birmingham.
Anderson, M., J.R. Edwards and D. Matthews (1996) 'A study of the quoted company audit market in 1886', *Accounting, Business and Financial History*, vol. 6 no. 3, pp.363-87.
Anderson, R.D. (1975) *Education in France, 1848-70*, Oxford: Clarendon Press.
Anglo-American Council on Productivity (1950) *Management accounting*, London: Anglo-American Council on Productivity.
Arnold, J. and T. Hope (1983) *Accounting for management decisions*, Englewood Cliffs, NJ: Prentice Hall International.
Babbage, C. (1832) *On the economy of machinery and manufactures*, London: Charles Knight.

Baldwin, T.J., R.H. Berry, and R.A. Church (1992) 'The accounts of the
    Consett Iron Company, 1864-1914', *Accounting and Business
    Research*, vol. 22 (86), pp.99-109.
Barlet, C.-H. (1861) *Tenue des livres appliquée à la comptabilité des
    mines de houille, des hauts-fourneaux et des usines à fer
    (Book-keeping applied to coal mines, blast furnaces and
    ironworks)*, Malines, Belgium: Van Velsen.
Barnes, R.Y. (1872) *A new and improved universal system of book-
    keeping, suitable to be used in all businesses . . .* , London: the
    author.
Barré, J. (1872) *Comptabilité industrielle (Industrial accounting)*, Paris:
    Masson.
Battersby, T. (1878) *The perfect double entry book-keeper (abridged),
    and the perfect prime cost and profit demonstrator (on the
    departmental system), for iron and brass founders, machinists,
    engineers, ship-builders, manufacturers &c.*, Manchester and
    London: John Heywood.
Baxter, W.T. (1981) 'Accounting history as a worthwhile study',
    Accounting Historians Notebook, Spring, pp.5-8.
Bhimani, A. (1994) 'Accounting enlightenment in the age of reason',
    The European Accounting Review, 3(3), pp.399-442.
Bolton, K.N. (1975) *Historical accounting literature*, London: Mansell.
Booth, B. (1789) *A complete system of book-keeping ... To which are
    added, a new method of stating factorage accounts ...* ,
    London: Welles, Grosvenor, & Chater, and J. Johnson.
Boulard, M.-S. (1791) *Le manuel de l'imprimeur (The printer's
    manual)*, Paris: Boulard.
Boyns, T. and J.R. Edwards (1991) 'Nineteenth century accounting
    practices and the capital market: a study of the Staveley Coal
    & Iron Co. Ltd.', paper presented to the third Accounting,
    Business and Financial History conference, Cardiff.
Boyns, T. and J.R. Edwards (1995) 'Accounting systems and decision-
    making in the mid-Victorian period: the case of the Consett
    Iron Company', *Business History*, vol. 37 no. 3, pp.28-51.
Boyns, T. and J.R. Edwards (1996a) 'The dissemination of accounting
    techniques in Wales' basic industries, c.1750-c.1870',
    L'association Française de comptabilité, cahiers de recherche,
    no.1, pp.23-34.
Boyns, T. and J.R. Edwards (1996b) 'Change agents and the
    dissemination of accounting technology: Wales' basic

industries, c.1750-c.1870', *Accounting History*, NS vol. 1 no. 1, pp.9-34.

Boyns, T. and J.R. Edwards (1996c) 'The development of accounting in mid-nineteenth century Britain: a non-disciplinary view', *Accounting, Audit and Accountability Journal*, vol. 9(3), pp.40-60.

Boyns, T. and J.R. Edwards (1997) 'Cost and management accounting in early-Victorian Britain: a Chandleresque analysis?', *Management Accounting Research*, vol. 8 no. 1, pp.19-46.

Boyns, T., M. Anderson and J.R. Edwards (eds.) (1996) *British cost accounting 1887-1952: contemporary essays from the accounting literature*, New York and London: Garland Publishing.

Bronowski, J. and B. Mazlish (1960) *The western intellectual tradition: from Leonardo to Hegel*, London: Hutchinson.

Brown, R. (ed.) (1905), *A history of accounting and accountants*, Edinburgh: Jack (reprinted by Franklin, New York, 1966).

Burley, K.H. (1958) 'Some accounting records of an eighteenth-century clothier', *Accounting Research*, January, pp.50-60.

Bywater, M.F. and B.S. Yamey (1982) *Historic accounting literature: a companion guide*, London: Scolar Press; Tokyo: Yushodo Press.

Caldecott, J. (1851) *A practical guide for retail tradesmen and others to book-keeping by double entry, or according to the Italian method of debtor and creditor, with preliminary remarks showing its general utility and urging its application to all kinds of accounts....* , London: W. & T. Piper.

Campbell, R.H. (1961) *Carron company*, Edinburgh and London: Oliver and Boyd.

Carnegie, G.D. and R.H. Parker (1996) 'The transfer of accounting technology to the southern hemisphere: the case of William Butler Yaldwyn', *Accounting, Business and Financial History*, vol. 6, no. 1, pp.23-48.

Carpenter, J. (1632) *A most excellent instruction for the exact and perfect keeping merchants bookes of accounts, by way of debitor and creditor after the italian manner: most usefull for all merchants, factors, and tradesman* . . . London: James Boler.

Caron, F. (1979) *An economic history of modern France*, London: Methuen & Co.

Cassis, Y., F. Crouzet and T. Gourvish (1995) *Management and business in Britain and France: the age of the corporate economy*, Oxford: Clarendon Press.

Chandler, A.D. Jr. (1962) *Strategy and structure: chapters in the history of American industrial enterprise*, Harvard University Press, Cambridge MA.

Chandler, A.D. Jr. (1977) *The visible hand: the managerial revolution in American business*, Belknap Press of the Harvard University Press, Cambridge, MA.

Chandler, A.D. Jr. (1990) *Scale and scope: the dynamics of industrial capitalism*, Belknap Press of the Harvard University Press, Cambridge, MA.

Chatfield, M. (1977) *A history of accounting thought*, revised edition, Huntington, New York: R.E. Krieger publishing.

Chevandier de Valdrôme, E. (1878) *Notes sur la comptabilité appliquée à l'industrie* (*Notes on accounting applied to industry*), Paris: Berger-Levrault.

Clousier, D. (1838) *Traité de la comptabilité du menuisier* (*Treatise on accounting for joiners*), Dijon.

Colasse, B. (1995) 'A quoi sert la recherche comptable? Des fonctions du chercheur en comptabilité (What is the purpose of accounting research? Some functions of accounting research)', *Revue Française de Comptabilité*, no. 264, *Fevrier*, pp.67-74.

Colasse, B. and R. Durand (1994) 'French accounting theorists of the twentieth century', in J.R. Edwards (1994), *Twentieth-century accounting thinkers*, London: Routledge, pp.41-59 (reprinted in Lemarchand, Y and R.H. Parker (1996) *Accounting in France/La comptabilité en France: Historical Essays/Etudes historiques*, New York and London: Garland Publishing).

Colinson, R. (1683) *Idea rationaria, or perfect accomptant*, Edinburgh: printed by David Lindsay, James Kniblo, Josua van Solingen and John Colmar.

Collins, J. (1697) *The perfect method of merchants-accompts demonstrated*, London: Thomas Horne.

Comins, P. (1814) *The science of commerce ... To which is added a selection of new systems, plans, and forms of accounts, for anonymous co-partnership, manufacturers ...* , Dublin: Ptd. by J. J. Nolan.

Coq, P. (1876) *Cours d'économie industrielle* (*Lectures in industrial economics*), Paris: Delagrave.

Courcelle-Seneuil, J.G. (1854) *Traité théorique et pratique des entreprises industrielles, commerciales et agricoles ou manuel des affaires (Theoretical and practical treatise for industrial, commercial and agricultural enterprises or business manual)*, Paris: Guillaumin.

Crafts, N.F.R. (1977) 'Industrial revolution in England and France: some thoughts on the question, "Why was England first?"', *The Economic History Review*, XXX, 3, August, pp.429-41.

Cronhelm, F.W. (1818) *Double entry by single, a new method of book-keeping, applicable to all kinds of business* ... , London: the author.

Crouzet, F. (1967) 'England and France in the eighteenth century: a comparative analysis of two economic growths', in R.M. Hartwell (ed.), *The causes of the industrial revolution in England*, London: Methuen (reprinted in F. Crouzet (1990), pp.12-43).

Crouzet, F. (1990) *Britain ascendant: comparative studies in Franco-British economic history*, Cambridge: Cambridge University Press (originally published in French in 1985 by Libraire Académique Perrin under the title *De la supériorité de l'Angleterre sur la France*).

de Barrême, B.-F. (1680) *Livres des comptes faits (Keeping accounts)*, Paris.

de Barrême, B.-F. (1721) *Traité des parties doubles (Treatise on double entry bookkeeping)*, Paris: Nyon.

de Cazaux, L.F.G. (1824) *De la comptabilité dans une entreprise industrielle et spécialement dans une exploitation rurale (Accountancy in an industrial firm and especially in a rural undertaking)*, Toulouse.

de la Porte, M. (1685, 1712) *Le guide des négociants et teneurs de livres (Merchant and Bookkeeper's Guide)*, Paris (various editions).

de Graaf, A. (1688) *Instructie van het Italiaans boekhoeden* ..., Amsterdam: Harderwyk.

de Roover, R. (1974) *Business, banking and economic thought in late medieval and early modern Europe, selected studies of Raymond de Roover*, edited by J. Kirshner, Chicago: University of Chicago Press.

Davis, R. (1973) *The rise of the Atlantic economies*, London: Macmillan.

DBF (1965) *Dictionnaire de biographie française (Dictionary of French biography)*, Paris: Libraire Letouzey et Ané.

Degranges Sr., E. (1795, 1801) *La tenue des livres rendue facile (Book-keeping made easy)*, Paris.

Degranges Jr., E. (1824) *Tenue des livres des maîtres de forges et des usines à fer (Bookkeeping for ironmasters and ironworks)*, Paris: Langlois et Leclercq.

Devillers, C. and B. Huet (1981) *Le Creusot: naissance et développement d'une ville industrielle 1782-1914*, Champ Vallon: Presses Universitaires de France.

Dicksee, L.R. (1903) *Advanced accounting*, London: Gee (reprinted by Arno Press, New York, 1976).

Dodson, J. (1750) *The accountant, or, the method of book-keeping, deduced from clear principles, and illustrated by a variety of examples*, London: J. Mourse

Dugué (1874) *Traité de comptabilité et d'administration à l'usage des entrepreneurs de BTP (A treatise on accounting and administration for the use of entrepreneurs of BTP)*, Paris: Dejey.

Durand, E. (1879) *Tablettes du directeur d'usine à gaz (Notes from the manager of a gas works)*, Paris: Journal Le gaz.

Edwards, I. (1980) 'Gilbert Gilpin: clerk to the Wilkinsons at Bersham furnace', *Transactions of the Denbighshire Historical Society*, vol. 29, pp.79-94.

Edwards, J.R. (1989a) *A history of financial accounting*, London: Routledge.

Edwards, J.R. (1989b) 'Ignore history at your peril', *Accountancy*, May, pp.184-5.

Edwards, J.R. (1989c) 'Industrial cost accounting developments in Britain to 1830: a review article', *Accounting and Business Research*, vol. 19, no. 76, Autumn, pp.305-17.

Edwards, J.R. and T. Boyns (1992) 'Industrial organization and accounting innovation: charcoal ironmaking in England 1690-1783', *Management Accounting Research*, 3, pp.151-69.

Edwards, J.R. and T. Boyns (1994) 'Accounting practice and business finance: some case studies from the iron and coal industry, 1865-1914', *Journal of Business Finance and Accounting*, vol. 21 no. 8, December, pp.1151-78.

Edwards, J.R., T. Boyns and M. Anderson (1995) 'British cost accounting development: continuity and change', *The Accounting Historians Journal*, December, pp.1-41.

Edwards, J.R. and E. Newell (1991) 'The development of industrial cost and management accounting before 1850: a survey of the evidence', *Business History*, Spring, pp.35-57.

Edwards, R.S. (1937a) 'The rationale of cost accounting', *The Accountant*, 13 March, pp.389-90.

Edwards, R.S. (1937b) 'Some notes on the early literature and development of cost accounting in Great Britain' (a series of articles in *The Accountant*, August-September 1937) (reprinted in Boyns, T., M. Anderson and J.R. Edwards (eds.) (1996) *British cost accounting 1887-1952: contemporary essays from the accounting literature*, New York and London: Garland Publishing).

Edwards, R.S. (1937c) *A survey of French contributions to the study of cost accounting during the 19th century*, London: The Accounting Research Association (reprinted in Lemarchand, Y and R.H. Parker (1996) *Accounting in France/La comptabilité en France: Historical Essays/Etudes historiques*, New York and London: Garland Publishing).

Evans, C. (1993) *"The labyrinth of flames": work and social conflict in early industrial Merthyr Tydfil*, Cardiff: University of Wales Press.

Fleischman, R.K., K.W. Hoskin, and R.H. Macve (1995) 'The Boulton and Watt Case: The crux of alternative approaches to accounting history?', *Accounting and Business Research*, vol. 25 (99), Summer, pp.162-76.

Fleischman, R.K. and L.D. Parker (1990) 'Managerial accounting early in the British industrial revolution: the Carron company, a case study', *Accounting & Business Research*, vol. 20, no.79, pp.211-21.

Fleischman, R.K. and L.D. Parker (1991) 'British entrepreneurs and pre-industrial revolution evidence of cost management' *The Accounting Review*, April, pp.361-75.

Fleischman, R.K. and Parker, L.D. (1992), 'The cost-accounting environment in the British industrial revolution iron industry', *Accounting, Business and Financial History*, vol. 2 no.2, pp.141-60.

Fleischman, R.K., L.D. Parker and W. Vamplew (1991), 'New cost
    accounting perspectives on technological change in the British
    industrial revolution' in O. F. Graves (ed.), *The costing
    heritage: studies in honor of S. Paul Garner*, Harrisonberg,
    Virginia: The Academy of Accounting Historians, pp.1-24.
Flinn, M.W. (1962), *Men of iron: the Crowleys in the early iron
    industry*, Edinburgh: Edinburgh University Press.
Frémy, E. (1909) *Histoire de la Manufacture Royale des Glaces de
    France au XVIIe et au XVIIIe siècle*, Paris: Libraire Plon.
Funnell, W. (1996) 'Preserving history *in* accounting: seeking common
    ground between "new" and "old" accounting history',
    Accounting, Audit and Accountability Journal, 9(4), pp.38-64.
Garcke, E. and J.M. Fells (1887, 1893) *Factory accounts*, London:
    Crosby Lockwood (various editions).
Garner, S.P. (1954) *Evolution of cost accounting to 1925*, Alabama:
    University of Alabama Press.
Garnier, P. (1947) *La comptabilité, algèbre du droit et méthode
    d'observation des sciences économiques*, Paris: Dunod.
Godard-Desmarest, P-A. (1821) *Memoire et propositions sur la
    comptabilité générale des finances du Royaume, suivi d'un
    modèle de compte général (Memorandum and propositions on
    general State accounting, followed by a model of general
    accounts)*, Paris.
Godard-Desmarest, P-A. (1827) *Traité général et sommaire de la
    comptabilité commerciale (General treatise and summary of
    commercial accounting)*, Paris.
Godard-Desmarest, P-A. (1835) *De l'économie politique en matière
    commerciale et de l'enquête de 1834 (On political economy
    and commercial matters and the enquiry of 1834)*, Paris.
Godart, H. (1875) *Note sur le système d'amortissement de la valeur de
    l'usine établi par la délibération du 7 novembre 1868 (A note
    on the system of depreciating the value of a factory established
    by the decision of 7 November 1868)*.
Gordon, W. (1770) *The general counting-house, and man of business ...
    calculated to promote facility and accuracy in accounts of
    business, relative to the merchant, the banker, underwriter,
    broker, factor, employer, drawer, remitter, partner, trustee,
    manufacturer, warehousekeeper, shopkeeper, storekeeper,
    landed gentleman, chamberlain, farmer &c ...* , 2nd ed.,
    Edinburgh: A. Donaldson.

Henderson, A. (1841) *Book-keeping by single and double entry: the theory and practice familiarly explained and illustrated by examples of modern business*, London: Simpkin, Marshall & Co.

Heudicourt, F.S. (1862) *Etudes sur la comptabilité industrielle* (*Studies in industrial accounting*), Paris: Cosse-Dumaine.

Highmore, B.A. (1821) *An arrangement of the accounts necessary to be kept by executors of wills and codicils, and administrators of intestates' estates.... ,* London: Joseph Butterworth and Son.

Hopwood, A.G. (1987), 'The archaeology of accounting systems', *Accounting, Organizations and Society*, Vol. 12, pp.207-34.

Hoskin, K.W. and R.H. Macve (1986) 'Accounting and the examination: a genealogy of disciplinary power', *Accounting, Organizations and Society*, Vol. 11 No. 2, pp.105-36.

Hoskin, K.W. and R.H. Macve (1988a) 'The genesis of accountability: the West Point connections', *Accounting. Organizations and Society*, Vol. 13 No. 2, pp.37-73.

Hoskin, K.W. and R.H. Macve (1988b) 'Cost accounting and the genesis of managerialism: the Springfield Armory episode', paper presented at the Second Interdisciplinary Perspectives on Accounting Conference, Manchester.

Hoskin, K.W. and R.H. Macve (1992) 'The genesis of modern cost management: a reappraisal of the significance of European initiatives', paper presented at the 15th European Accounting Association Congress, Madrid.

Hoskin, K.W. and R.H. Macve (1993) 'The industrial revolution versus the managerial revolution: distinguishing difference in accounting practice', paper presented to Fifth ABFH conference, Cardiff, September 1993.

Hoskin, K.W. and R.H. Macve (1994) 'Reappraising the genesis of managerialism: a re-examination of the role of accounting at the Springfield Armory, 1815-1845', *Accounting, Auditing and Accountability Journal*, Vol. 7 No. 2, pp.4-29.

Hunt, B.C. (1936) *The development of the business corporation in England, 1800-1867*, Cambridge, MA.: Harvard University Press.

ICAEW (1954) *Management accounting*, London: Institute of Chartered Accountants in England and Wales.

Irson, C. (1678) *Méthode pour bien dresser toutes sortes de comptes à partie doubles, par débit et crédit, et par recette, dépense et reprise (A method for better drawing up all sorts of accounts in double entry, by debit and credit, and by receipts, expenses and carrying back)*, Paris.

Jackson, G. (1836) *A new check journal ...* , 5th ed., London: Effingham Wilson.

Jeannin, M. (1828) *Traité de la comptabilité commerciale, régulière et frauduleuse (Treatise on commercial accounting, regular and fraudulent)*, Paris.

Jeremy, D.J. (ed.) (1991) *International technology transfer: Europe, Japan and the USA*, Aldershot: Edward Elgar.

Johnson, H.T. (1972), 'Early cost accounting for internal management control: Lyman Mills in the 1850s', *Business History Review*, Winter, pp.466-74.

Johnson, H.T. (1981), 'Towards a new understanding of nineteenth-century cost accounting', *The Accounting Review*, July, pp.510-18.

Johnson, H.T. (1984), *The role of accounting history in the education of prospective accountants*, Glasgow: Department of Accountancy, University of Glasgow.

Johnson, H.T. and R.S. Kaplan (1987) *Relevance lost: the rise and fall of management accounting*, Boston: Harvard Business School Press.

Jones E.T. (1796) *Jones's English system of book-keeping by single and double entry, in which it is impossible for an error of the most trifling amount to be passed unnoticed; calculated effectively to prevent the evils attendant on the methods so long established; and adapted to every species of trade*, Bristol.

Jones, H. (1985) *Accounting, costing and cost estimation: Welsh industry: 1700-1830*, Cardiff: University of Wales Press.

Kelly, P. (1801) *The elements of book-keeping, both by single and double entry: comprising a system of merchants accounts, founded on real business, arranged according to modern practice, and adapted to the use of schools*, London: the author.

Kitchener W. (c. 1830) *The housekeeper's ledger: a plain and easy plan for keeping accurate accounts of the expenses of housekeeping, &c.*, London: Geo. B. Whittaker.

Krepp, F.C. (1858) *Statistical book-keeping; being a simplification and abbreviation of the common system by double entry, for the use of merchants, bankers, tradesmen manufactures* ... , London: Longman, Brown, Green, Longmans, and Roberts.

Lardner, D. (1850) *Railway economy*, London: Taylor, Walton and Maberly (reprinted by David & Charles, Newton Abbot, 1968).

Lemarchand, Y. (1993a) *Du dépérissement à l'amortissement: enquête sur l'histoire d'un concept et de sa traduction comptable (From* 'wear & tear' to depreciation: *an enquiry into the history of a concept and its accounting translation)*, Nantes: Ouest éditions.

Lemarchand, Y. (1993b) 'The dark side of the result: self-financing and accounting choices within nineteenth century French industry', *Accounting, Business & Financial History*, 3(3), pp.303-25 (reprinted in Lemarchand, Y and R.H. Parker (1996) *Accounting in France/La comptabilité en France: Historical Essays/Etudes historiques*, New York and London: Garland Publishing).

Lemarchand, Y. (1994) 'Double entry versus charge and discharge in eighteenth-century France', *Accounting, Business and Financial History*, vol. 4, no. 1, pp.119-45.

Lemarchand, Y. (1996) 'Operating costs in merchant bookkeeping systems around 1800', paper presented to 'Merchants' archives in Europe, 1750-1850' conference, Dortmund, 9-11 May.

Lemarchand, Y and R.H. Parker (1996) *Accounting in France/La comptabilité en France: Historical Essays/Etudes historiques*, New York and London: Garland Publishing.

Lewis, G. (1993) *The advent of modern capitalism in France, 1770-1840: the contribution of Pierre-François Tubeuf*, Oxford: Clarendon Press.

Liddel, R. (1803) *The seaman's new vade mecum; containing a practical essay on Naval book-keeping, with the method of keeping the captain's books, ...*, London: G. & J. Robinson.

Littleton, A.C. (1933) *Accounting evolution to 1900*, New York: American Institute Publishing Co., 1933 (reprinted by The University of Alabama Press, Alabama, 1981).

Littleton, A.C. and B.S. Yamey (1956) *Studies in the history of accounting*, London: Sweet & Maxwell.

Loft, A. (1986) 'Towards a critical understanding of accounting: the case of cost accounting in the U.K., 1914-1925', *Accounting, Organizations and Society*, vol. 11, no. 2, pp.137-69.

Loft, A. (1990) *Coming into the light: a study of the development of a professional association for cost accountants in Britain in the wake of the First World War*, London: Chartered Institute of Management Accountants.

Loft, A. (1995) 'The history of management accounting: relevance found' in Ashton, D., Hopper, T. and Scapens, R.W. (eds) *Issues in Management Accounting*. London: Prentice Hall: pp.21-44.

Lowrie, W. (1809) *The principles of keeping accounts with bankers in the country and in London...* , London: Longman, Hurst Reece and Orme.

Maddison, A. (1991) *Dynamic forces in capitalist development: a long-run comparative view*, Oxford: Oxford University Press.

Mair, J. (1760) *Book-keeping methodiz'd; or, a methodical treatise of merchant-accompts, according to the Italian form*, Edinburgh: W. Sands, A. Kincaid & J. Bell, and A. Donaldson.

Mantoux, P. (1928) *The industrial revolution in the eighteenth century*, London: Cape.

Marrou, H.-I. (1954) *De la connaissance historique (Historical knowledge)*, 6th ed., Paris: Seuil.

Marshall, G. (1980) *Presbyteries and profits. Calvinism and the development of capitalism in Scotland, 1560-1707*, Oxford: Clarendon Press.

Matheson, E. (1893) *The depreciation of factories*, 2nd ed., London: E & F N Spon.

McKendrick, N. (1970) 'Josiah Wedgwood and cost accounting in the industrial revolution', *Economic History Review*, 2nd.ser., XXIII, pp.45-67.

McLean, T. (1995) 'Contract accounting and costing in the Sunderland shipbuilding industry 1818-1917', *Accounting, Business and Financial History*, vol. 5 no. 1, pp.109-45.

Mepham, M.J. (1988) *Accounting in eighteenth century Scotland*, New York and London: Garland Publishing.

Metcalfe, H. (1885) *The cost of manufactures*, New York: John Wiley & Sons.

Mézières, L. (1842) *Comptabilité commerciale, industrielle et manufacturière (Commercial, industrial and manufacturing accounting)*, Paris: Librairie scientifique et industrielle.

Mikol, A. (1993) 'France', *The European Accounting Review* , 2, pp.329-34

Miller, P. (1990) 'On the interrelationships between accounting and the state', *Accounting, Organizations and Society*, vol. 15 (4), pp.315-38.

Miller, P. and C. Napier (1993) 'Genealogies of calculation', *Accounting, Organizations and Society*, vol. 18 (7/8), pp.631-47.

Miller, P. and T. O'Leary (1987) 'Accounting and the construction of the governable person', *Accounting, Organizations and Society*, vol. 12 (3), pp.235-65.

Monteage, S. (1675) *Debtor and creditor made easie: or, a short instruction for the attaining right use of accounts . . .* , London: Ben Billingsley.

Monteage, S. (1683) *Instructions for rent-gathers accompts, and the &c. made easie*, London: Ben Billingsley.

Morrison, J. (1810) *The elements of book-keeping by single and double entry. Comprising several sets of books. Arranged according to present practice & designed for the use of schools*, London: Richard Phillips.

Napier, C.J. (1993) 'UK', *The European Accounting Review*, vol. 2, pp.370-5.

Nikitin, M. (1990) 'Setting up an industrial accounting system at Saint-Gobain (1820-1880)', *The Accounting Historians Journal*, vol. 17 no. 2, pp.73-93 (reprinted in Lemarchand, Y and R.H. Parker (1996) *Accounting in France/La comptabilité en France: Historical Essays/Etudes historiques*, New York and London: Garland Publishing).

Nikitin, M. (1992) '*La naissance de la comptabilité industrielle en France*' (*The birth of industrial accounting in France*), thesis, doctorat es sciences de gestion, Paris-Dauphine.

Nikitin, M. (1996a) 'Comptabilité et analyse financière à Decazeville dans les années 1830', *Entreprises et Histoire*, no. 13, pp.53-65.

Nikitin, M. (1996b) 'Pierre-Antoine Godard-Desmarest (1767-1850), strategist, industrialist and accountant, or the birth of the world renowned Baccarat Crystalworks', *Accounting, Business and Financial History*, vol. 6 no. 1, pp.93-110.

North, D.C. and R.P. Thomas (1973) *The rise of the western world. A new economic history*, London: Cambridge University Press.

North, R. (1714) *The gentleman accomptant; or, an essay to unfold the mystery of accompts; by way of debtor and creditor, commonly called merchants accompts, and applying the same to the concerns of the nobility and gentry of England*, London.

Norton, G.P. (1889) *Textile manufacturers' book-keeping for the counting house, mill and warehouse . . .* , Huddersfield: Alfred Jubb.

O'Brien, P.K. and C. Keyder (1978) *Economic growth in Britain and France, 1780-1914: two paths to the twentieth century*, London: Allen & Unwin.

O'Day, R. (1982) *Education and society, 1500-1800: the social foundations of education in early modern Britain*, London: Longmans.

Oldroyd, D. (1996) 'The costing records of George Bowes and the Grand Allies in the north-east coal trade in the eighteenth century: their type and significance', *Accounting, Business & Financial History*, vol. 6 no. 1, pp.1-22.

Parker, R.H. (1969) *Management accounting: an historical perspective* London: Macmillan.

Parker, R.H. (1979) 'Explaining national differences in consolidated accounts', in T. A. Lee and R. H. Parker (eds), *The evolution of corporate reporting*, Sunbury-on-Thames: Nelson.

Parker, R.H. (1984) *Macmillan dictionary of accounting*, London: Macmillan Press.

Parker, R.H. (1993) 'Bowring and financial reform: government accountancy and decimalisation, in Youings, J. (ed), *Sir John Bowring 1792-1872*, Exeter: Devonshire Association.

Parker, R.H. and B.S. Yamey (eds) (1994) *Accounting history: some British contributions*, Oxford: Clarendon Press.

Payen, J.-B. (1817) *Essai sur la tenue des livres d'un manufacturier (Essay on a manufacturers' bookkeeping)*, Paris: Johanneau.

Peele J. (1553) *The manner and fourme how to kepe a perfecte reconyng ... and also profitable, not onely unto suche, the trade in the facte of marchaundise, but also unto any other estate, that will learne the same*, London: Richard Grafton.

Pillet-Will, M.-F. (1832) *Examen analytique de l'usine de Decazeville (An analytical examination of the Decazeville factory)*, Paris: Dufart.

Pollard, S. (1965) *The genesis of modern management, a study of the industrial revolution in Great Britain*, London: Arnold.

Pollard, S. (1968) *The genesis of modern management, a study of the industrial revolution in Great Britain*, London: Penguin.

Price, R. (1975) *The economic modernisation of France, 1730-1880*, London: Croom Helm.

Price, R. (1981) *An economic history of modern France, 1730-1914*, London: Macmillan.

Pris, C. (1981) *Une grandes entreprise française sous l'ancien régime: la manufacture Royale des Glaces de Saint-Gobain (1665-1830)*, New York : Arno Press.

Reid, D. (1983) 'The origins of industrial labour management in France: the case of Decazeville ironworks during the July Monarchy', *Business History Review*, vol. 57, pp.1-19.

Reymondin, G. (1909) *Bibliographie méthodique des ouvrages en langue française parus de 1543 à 1908 sur la science des comptes (Bibliography of French language works on accounting from 1543 to 1908)*, Paris: Giard-Brière.

Reymondin, G. (1928) *La vérité comptable en marche*, Paris: Experta.

Richardson, H.W. and J.M. Bass (1965), 'The profitability of the Consett Iron Company before 1914', *Business History*, pp.71-93.

Rimmer, W.G. (1960) *Marshalls of Leeds, flax spinners, 1788-1886*, Cambridge: Cambridge University Press.

Roll, E. (1930) *An early experiment in industrial organization: being a history of the firm of Boulton and Watt, 1775-1805*, London: Longmans.

Rostow, W.W. (1975) *How it all began, origins of the modern economy*, London: Methuen.

Savary, Jacques (1675) *Le parfait négociant*, Paris: Billaine.

Sawyer, J. (1862) *A system of book-keeping, drawn up for and expressly adapted to the tanning trade ...* , 2nd ed., London: the author.

Scapens, R., S. Turley, J. Burns, N. Joseph, L. Lewis, and A. Southworth (1996) 'External reporting and management decisions', presented to the European Accounting Association Congress, Bergen, May.

Scoville, W.C. (1942) 'Large-scale production in the French plate-glass industry 1665-1789', *Journal of Political Economy*, October, pp.669-98.

Shannon, H.A. (1932) 'The first five thousand limited companies and their duration', *Economic History*, vol. II (1930-33), pp.396-424.

Shaw, C. (1995) 'Engineers in the boardroom: Britain and France compared', in Y. Cassis, F. Crouzet and T. Gourvish (eds.) (1995) *Management and business in Britain and France: the age of the corporate economy*, Oxford: Clarendon Press.

Simon, F.N. (1830) *Méthode complète de tenue des livres (Complete method of bookkeeping)*, Châtillon sur Seine: Cornillac.

Smith, T. (1840) *Double entry book-keeping, practically explained and simplified... . . peculiarly adapted to general business, and especially for the use of commercial schools*, second edition, Birmingham: the author.

Solomons, D. (1952) 'The historical development of costing', in D. Solomons (ed.), *Studies in costing*, London: Sweet & Maxwell, pp.1-52.

Stacey, N. (1954) *English accountancy: a study in social and economic history, 1800-1954*, London: Gee.

Stevelinck, E. (1977) *La comptabilité à travers les âges (Accounting through the ages)* Vesoul, France: Pragnos.

Stone, W.E. (1973) 'An early English cotton mill cost accounting system: Charlton mills, 1810-89', *Accounting and Business Research*, Winter, pp.71-8.

Thompson, W. (1777) *The accomptant's oracle: or, key to science, being a compleat practical system of book-keeping*, York.

Tuck, H. (1843) *The manual of book-keeping; or, practical instructions to the manufacturer*, ? edition, London: Bell & Co.

Tuck, H. (1856) *The manual of book-keeping; or, practical instructions to the manufacturer*, Eighth edition, London: George Bell.

Vannier, H. (1840) *Premières notions du commerce et de la comptabilité (First ideas on commerce and accounting)*, Paris.

Vlaemminck, J.-H. (1956) *Histoire et doctrines de la comptabilité*, Brussels: Editions Pragnos.

Walton, P. (1993) 'Company law and accounting in nineteenth-century Europe: Introduction', *The European Accounting Review*, 2, pp.287-91.

Wells, M.C. (1977) 'Some influences on the development of cost accounting', *The Accounting Historians Journal*, Fall, pp.47-61.

Wilson, J.F. (1995) *British business history, 1720-1994*, Manchester: Manchester University Press.

Wood, W. (1777) *Book keeping familiarised: or, the young clerk's, manufacturer's and shop-keeper's directory*, Birmingham.

Yamey, B.S. (1949) 'Scientific bookkeeping and the rise of capitalism', *Economic History Review*, 2nd.ser., I, nos. 2&3, pp.99-113.

Yamey, B.S. (1956) 'Edward Jones and the reform of book-keeping, 1795-1810', in A.C. Littleton and B.S. Yamey (eds) *Studies in the history of accounting*, London: Sweet & Maxwell.

Yamey, B.S. (1962) 'Some topics in the history of financial accounting in England, 1500-1900', in W.T. Baxter and S. Davidson (eds.) *Studies in accounting theory*, London: Sweet & Maxwell, pp.14-43.

Yamey, B.S. (1964) 'Accounting and the rise of capitalism: further notes on a theme by Sombart', *Journal of Accounting Research*, vol.2 no.2, Autumn, pp.117-36.

Yamey, B.S. (1980) 'Some reflections on the writing of a general history of accounting', *Accounting and Business Research*, vol. 11 no.42, Spring, pp.127-35.

Yamey, B. S. (1981) 'Some reflections on the writing of a general history of accounting', *Accounting & Business Research*, Spring, vol. 11, no. 42, pp.127-35.

Zan, L. (1994) 'Toward a history of accounting histories: perspectives from the Italian tradition', *The European Accounting Review*, vol. 3 no. 2, pp.255-307.

Index

Abbeville cloth mill, Picardy, 31
Accounting development, Britain
    and France, 14-16
Accounting history
    methodologies
    general, 5-6
        Foucauldian, 5-6, 178
        Marxist/labour process,
        6, 178
        Traditional, 6
        Neoclassical revisionist/
        economic determinist 6,
        178
    usefulness of, 3-5
Accounting historiography,
    Britain and France, 8-11
Accounting ideas, dissemination
    of, 198-202
Accounting literature, Britain
    development of general, 68-
    83
        conventional wisdom,
        68-73
        revised interpretation,
        73-82
Accounting literature, France
    development of, 83-86
    single entry bookkeeping,
    86-88
    double entry bookkeeping
    idiosyncratic pre-1860,
    88-89
        mainstream pre-1860,
        89-91
    post-1860, 91-95

industrial accounting
    classification of
    accounts, 95-100
        calculation of cost price,
        100-110
        integration of accounts,
        110-112
Accounting models
    Anglo-Saxon, 11, 17, $19n_1$,
    $115n_{21}$
    British, 11, 17, $19n_1$
    Continental European, 12,
    $115n_{21}$
    French, 11-12
Accounting profession,
    emergence of
    in Scotland, 192
    in England & Wales,
    192
    in France, 192-194
    influence on accounting
    doctrine, 194-196
Accounting regulation, Britain
    and France, 54-57
Accounting texts, biographies of
    early writers, 117-122
Allevard ironworks, accounting
    system, 166
Ancien régime, 30, 45, 189
Anglo-French Treaty (1860), 155
Archival research, importance of,
    13
Armstrong, William, $116n_{28}$, 141,
    200